Deleuze and the Schizoanalysis of Religion

Schizoanalytic Applications

Schizoanalysis has the potential to be to Deleuze and Guattari's work what deconstruction is to Derrida's – the standard rubric by which their work is known and, more importantly, applied. Many within the field of Deleuze and Guattari studies would resist this idea, but the goal of this series is to broaden the base of scholars interested in their work. Deleuze and Guattari's ideas are widely known and used, but not in a systematic way, and this is both a strength and weakness. It is a strength because it enables people to pick up their work from a wide variety of perspectives, but it is also a weakness because it makes it difficult to say with any clarity what exactly a 'Deleuzo-Guattarian' approach is. This has inhibited the uptake of Deleuze and Guattari's thinking in the more wilful disciplines such as history, politics, and even philosophy. Without this methodological core, Deleuze and Guattari studies risk becoming simply another intellectual fashion that will soon be superseded by newer figures. The goal of the Schizoanalytic Applications series is to create a methodological core and build a sustainable model of schizoanalysis that will attract new scholars to the field. With this purpose, the series also aims to be at the forefront of the field by starting a discussion about the nature of Deleuze and Guattari's methodology.

Series editors: Ian Buchanan, David Savat, and Marcelo Svirsky

Other titles in the series:

Deleuze and the Schizoanalysis of Cinema, edited by Ian Buchanan and Patricia MacCormack

Deleuze and the Schizoanalysis of Literature, edited by Ian Buchanan, Tim Matts, and Aidan Tynan

Deleuze and the Schizoanalysis of Visual Art, edited by Ian Buchanan and Lorna Collins

Deleuze and the Schizoanalysis of Religion

Lindsay Powell-Jones and F. LeRon Shults

Bloomsbury Academic
An imprint of Bloomsbury Publishing Plc

B L O O M S B U R Y
LONDON • OXFORD • NEW YORK • NEW DELHI • SYDNEY

Bloomsbury Academic
An imprint of Bloomsbury Publishing Plc

50 Bedford Square
London
WC1B 3DP
UK

1385 Broadway
New York
NY 10018
USA

www.bloomsbury.com

BLOOMSBURY and the Diana logo are trademarks of Bloomsbury Publishing Plc

First published 2016

British Library Cataloguing-in-Publication Data
A catalogue record for this book is available from the British Library.

ISBN: HB: 978-1-4742-6689-5
ePDF: 978-1-4742-6690-1
ePub: 978-1-4742-6691-8

Library of Congress Cataloging-in-Publication Data
A catalogue record for this book is available from the Library of Congress.

Series: **Schizoanalytic Applications**

Typeset by Integra Software Services Pvt. Ltd.
Printed and bound in Great Britain

Contents

Notes on Contributors

Brent Adkins is Professor of Philosophy at Roanoke College, the United States. He is co-author of *Rethinking Philosophy and Theology with Deleuze: A New Cartography* (Bloomsbury Press, 2014) and *Deleuze and Guattari's 'A Thousand Plateaus': A Critical Introduction and Guide* (Edinburgh University Press, 2015).

Kristien Justaert is a postdoctoral fellow of the Research Foundation – Flanders (FWO) at the Faculty of Theology and Religious Studies, KU Leuven, where she is a coordinator of the Centre for Liberation Theologies. She is the author of *Theology after Deleuze* (Continuum, 2012).

Lindsay Powell-Jones recently finished her PhD on Deleuze and the films of Andrei Tarkovsky. She is currently preparing her thesis for publication.

Joshua Ramey is an assistant professor at Grinnell College, the United States. His first book was *The Hermetic Deleuze: Philosophy and Spiritual Ordeal* (Duke University Press, 2012), and his recent book is *Politics of Divination: Neoliberal Endgame and the Religion of Contingency* (Rowman and Littlefield, 2016).

Austin Roberts is a PhD student in theology and philosophy at Drew University, the United States.

Inna Semetsky (PhD, Columbia University, New York) serves as a chief consultant to the new Institute for Edusemiotic Studies (IES) registered in Melbourne, Australia. She is the author/editor of nine books including *Deleuze, Education and Becoming* (Sense Publishers, 2006) and *Deleuze and Education* (Edinburgh University Press, 2013). Her latest volume *Edusemiotics – A Handbook* is currently in production with Springer Science.

F. LeRon Shults is Professor of Theology and Philosophy in the Institute for Religion, Philosophy and History at the University of Agder in Kristiansand, Norway. His latest two books are *Iconoclastic Theology: Gilles Deleuze and the*

Secretion of Atheism (Edinburgh University Press, 2014) and *Theology after the Birth of God: Atheist Conceptions in Cognition and Culture* (Palgrave-Macmillan, 2014).

Christopher Ben Simpson is Professor of Philosophical Theology at Lincoln Christian University, the United States. He is the author of *Deleuze and Theology* (Bloomsbury Press, 2012) and *Modern Christian Theology* (Bloomsbury Press, 2016).

Aidan Tynan is a lecturer in English Literature at Cardiff University, the United Kingdom. He is the author of *Deleuze's Literary Clinic: Criticism and the Politics of Symptoms* (Edinburgh University Press, 2012) and co-editor of *Deleuze and the Schizoanalysis of Literature* (Bloomsbury, 2015). He is currently editing a volume of essays on capitalism and religion titled *Credo Credit Crisis: Speculations on Faith and Money*, which will appear from Rowman and Littlefield in 2017.

Introduction

Lindsay Powell-Jones

1. The schizoanalysis of religion

In 1972 the philosopher Gilles Deleuze and the psychoanalyst Félix Guattari collaborated to produce *Anti-Oedipus* (*L'anti-Oedipe*), which they followed up in 1980 with *A Thousand Plateaus* (*Mille Plateaux*). Together, these texts form the *Capitalism and Schizophrenia* project, which they developed in response to what they saw as the pervasive force of the Oedipus construct in French psychiatry during the late 1960s and early 1970s. Challenging the reduction of the psyche to family relations and the elevation of the unified self, which dominated the theory and practice of psychiatry, Deleuze and Guattari instead posited a theory in which desire is understood in terms of a schizophrenic id rather than a neurotic ego. In this system there is no sense of what is 'normal', or what is individual in the human psyche. Deleuze and Guattari described this as a revolutionary 'materialist psychiatry' called 'schizoanalysis'. In a system of schizoanalysis, 'schizo flux' and multiplicity are paramount.

Since the publication of *Anti-Oedipus* and *A Thousand Plateaus*, and their subsequent translation into English, Japanese, Mandarin Chinese, and Korean, the principles of schizoanalysis have been applied in contexts far removed from Deleuze and Guattari's initial study of French psychiatry. There is a wealth of literature that connects Deleuze to subjects as varied as literature (Marks and Buchanan 2000; Buchanan et al. 2015), visual culture (Roberts and Rushton 2011; Buchanan and Collins 2014), as well as technology (Poster and Savat 1999), geo-philosophy (Bonta and Protevi 2004), queer theory (Nigianni and Storr 2009), performance (Cull 2009), space (Buchanan and Lambert 2005), architecture (Frichot 2013), race (Saldanha and Adams 2013), music (Buchanan and Swiboda 2004), the body (Guillaume and Hughes 2011), the postcolonial (Bignall and Patton 2010), sex (Beckman 2011), the schizoanalysis of cinema (Buchanan and MacCormack 2008), film music (Redner 2011), contemporary art (Zepke and O'Sullivan 2010), and more. While significant research has been done on the relation that Deleuze's theory has to religion (notably Bryden 2001), this present volume offers a unique perspective through its focus on the schizoanalysis project. Gathering together some of the best writers on the topic of Deleuze and religion, this book is concerned with the following question: How and why should we practise a schizoanalysis of religion?

Historically, the psychoanalysis of religion has seldom been carried out without an impulse towards reinterpretation and reform. Strictly conceived, it comprises the application of psychological theories to religious traditions, and the related experiences and actions of individuals. With rare exceptions, it has been called upon to question the entirety of religious life. The differences between psychoanalytic methods and their approach to religion make up the background to our present schizoanalytic approach. In this Introduction I shall attempt to sketch something of this background, before giving an overview of the pieces gathered in this volume.

2. Psychoanalysis and religion: The physician of the soul

In 1950, Erich Fromm attempted to explain the purpose and goals of psychoanalysis in relation to ethics and religion in his seminal text *Psychoanalysis and Religion*. In this text he wrote, 'Ours is a life not of brotherliness, happiness, contentment but of spiritual chaos and bewilderment dangerously close to a state of madness – not the hysterical kind of madness which existed in the Middle Ages but a madness akin to schizophrenia in which contact with inner reality is lost and thought is split from affect' (Fromm 1971: 1). For Fromm, psychology as the study of the soul of humans was the theoretical basis for the art of living, by which he meant achieving happiness. He explored the relationship between the psychoanalyst and the priest asking, what is their mutual relationship? Are they adversaries or allies who work for the same ends and who should supplement and interpenetrate each other's field both theoretically and practically?

The former viewpoint was taken up by Sigmund Freud in *The Future of an Illusion* (2008, first published 1927), in which Freud urged his readers, in the name of scientific rationalism, to advance beyond an infantile and neurotic system of ritual and belief. As he summarized in his 1910 text, *Leonardo Da Vinci and a Memory of His Childhood*, the roots of the need for religion can be found in the parental complex:

> The almighty and just God, and kindly nature, appear to us as grand sublimations of father and mother, or rather as revivals and restorations of the young child's ideas of them. Biologically speaking, religiousness is to be traced to the small human child's long-drawn out helplessness and need of help; and when at a later date he perceives how truly forlorn and weak he is when confronted with the great forces of life, he feels his condition as he did in childhood, and attempts to deny his own despondency by a regressive revival of the forces which protected his infancy. (Freud 2013: 80)

Religion fascinated Freud because it is, as he stated, 'an immense power which has the strongest emotions of human beings at it's service' (Freud et al. 2001: 161). In studies like *Totem and Taboo* (2001, first published 1913) and *Moses and Monotheism* (Freud et al. 2001, first published 1939), he explored a psychological understanding of religion as an obsessional neurosis. Statements made by Freud about theology and the Christian church stressed the judgement of intellect and science over the *Weltanschauung* of religion. He treated ritual as an obsessional neurosis, and God as the longing for a father figure (and the associated resentment, fear, and guilt). A similar approach was taken up by Freud's first student, Theodor Reik, who supplemented the arguments contained in *Totem and Taboo* by writing about religion in terms of the obsessive-compulsive actions of neurosis in *Ritual: Psycho-Analytic Studies* (1958, first published 1946). Freud's biographer Ernest Jones, also a principal player in the development of psychoanalysis in England and the United States, touched on religion frequently in correspondence with his mentor. In a letter dated 31 August 1911, Jones expressed delight that Freud had turned to the topic in work that would later form *The Future of Illusion*:

> The most exciting news in your letter, however, was that you had determined to devote yourself to religious problems. Obviously that is the last and firmest stronghold of what may be called the anti-scientific, anti-rational, or anti-objective Weltanschauung, and no doubt it is there we may expect the most intense resistance, and the thick of the fight. (quoted in Paskauskas 1993: 115)

In one of his most direct involvements with religion, 'The Madonna's Conception through the Ear', Jones linked pyschosexual impulses and fantasies to the myth of the virgin's conception.

An early proponent of psychoanalysis, the president of Clark University, G. Stanley Hall, was instrumental in the founding of the American school of the psychology of religion. Struck by the religiosity of many young people,

Hall theorized that religious awakening and sexual awakening were closely connected. In order to explore this, he focused on empirical studies of religious conversion (particularly during adolescence). Hall's major religious contribution, *Jesus, the Christ, in the Light of Psychology* (1917), was an ambitious and controversial text that demonstrated his specific interest in the psychology of Christianity. His work was followed by a brilliant succession of writers including James H. Leuba (*Psychology of Religious Mysticism* (2007, first published 1925)), Edwin Starbuck (*The Psychology of Religion* (1899)), Edward Scribner Ames (*The Psychology of Religious Experience* (1910)), George A. Coe (*The Psychology of Religion* (1916)), William James (*The Varieties of Religious Experience: A Study in Human Nature* (2008, first published 1902)), and James Bissett Pratt (*The Religious Consciousness* (2005, first published 1920)). The 'salient characteristic of this American school', Hall wrote, 'is the careful study of the phenomena of religious experience derived mainly from biographies, introspection, and a systematic use of the questionnaire' (quoted in Taves 1999: 261).

While the dominant trend in the early psychology of religion was focused on Freud's approach, there were other approaches. Unlike Freud's focus on the individual's experience, the Swiss psychoanalyst Carl Jung approached religion in terms of universal underlying features of human life. Drawing on the history of religion and anthropological studies of primitive religion, he developed a theory of religious experiences as symbols of his archetypes. For example, God is a symbol not of some father-figure, but of a more generalized power that can be symbolized in many different ways. The Eucharist, Christ, the Trinity, the spiritual journey – these archetypes occur universally in all cultures and historical periods. Jung's system of psychotherapy argued that neurosis often results from the modern person's inability to find the fresh connections to these old religious instincts.

Other humanist psychologists have likewise offered visions of a religious outlook that has implications for personal growth. Rabbi Joshua Liebman, a contributor to the history of psychology and religion, advocated a broad, non-reductionist psychoanalysis of religious experience. In his popular book *Peace of Mind* (1946), Rabbi Liebman addressed himself to 'the individual whose personal grief and anxiety, unassuageable by social betterment alone, required an inner peace that psychology and religion, working together, could provide' (1946: 45). For Liebman, psychoanalysis is in a position to explore the hidden desires and anxieties behind religion, but not in the name of an atheist scientific rationalism. Rather than seeking to reinterpret religion, he set about establishing its positive values in the human psyche.

Most psychoanalytic investigation of religion has taken place in either a Jungian or a Freudian context, but these two psychological frameworks are not the only background to our present study. In *The Triumph of Religion* (2013, first published in 2005), the French psychoanalyst and philosopher Jacques Lacan, in a fit of pessimism for his field of research, claimed that religion will triumph over psychoanalysis. 'Psychoanalysis will not triumph', Lacan states, 'it will survive or not' (2013–2064). This statement was not a celebration of religion, but a weary acknowledgement of its power to endure. Religion held an abiding fascination for Lacan. His discussion of the 'symbolic order' (or the discours de l' Autre) is scattered with metaphors drawn from Christian theology. Some of Lacan's most important insights have their roots in St Augustine, and he made reference to Abraham's sacrifice of Isaac to theorize his concept of jouissance in *On the Name of the Father* (2013a). In *The Other Side of Psychoanalysis* (2006)[1] he uses the term 'God' as a metaphor for the big Other. Famously, he stated that the true formula for atheism is not 'God is dead' but 'God is unconscious' (1977: 59).

Taking these allusions as his inspiration, the Slovenian Marxist philosopher Slavoj Žižek has since explored religion by way of an engagement with Lacan. Throughout his oeuvre, but notably in his work with John Milbank in *The Monstrosity of Christ* (2011) and in *The Fragile Absolute Or, Why Is the Christian Legacy Worth Fighting For?* (2000), Lacan's work has offered Žižek a means of reflecting on political-philosophical-theological currents in modern life as well as the symbolic core of the Christian legacy: 'The Passion of Christ, this fascinating image which cancels all other images, this fantasy-scenario which condenses all of the libidinal economy of the Christian religion, acquires its meaning only against the background of the unbearable enigma of the desire of the Other (God)' (Žižek 1989: 116). In addition to Žižek's work, two collections have expressly treated the work of Lacan and theology in tandem: *Lacan and Theological Discourse* (Wyschogrod et al. 1989) and *Theology after Lacan* (Davis et al. 2014). In the eyes of these authors, theological discourse is a form of speech, and it therefore operates through a lack that can be theorized.

The psychoanalysis of religion is not only limited to the Judeo-Christian tradition. The dialogue between psychoanalysis and Buddhism was first explored by Fromm in collaboration with D.T. Suzuki and Richard De Martino in the classic *Zen Buddhism and Psychoanalysis* (1960). Eastern religions also had a strong impact on Jung through both his discussion with the Zen philosopher Shin'ichi Hisamatsu and his exchanges with the missionary and sinologist Richard Wilhelm concerning *I Ching* or *Book of Changes* (i.e. of life transformations)[2] and *The Secret of the Golden Flower*,[3] the former being a book on divination, the later on alchemy. This dialogue afforded the field of psychoanalysis the opportunity to develop new ways of thinking about the psyche that was not limited by the Western religious context.

3. Schizoanalysis and religion

Discussions about the relation between Deleuze and religion have tended to emphasize their mutual antagonism. As Mary Bryden writes in *Deleuze and Religion*, the topic might even appear to be a perverse one (2001: 1). Is it not then even stranger to bring a Guattarized Deleuze into proximity with the discourse of God and religion? Certainly, one of the pillars of the schizoanalysis project is the rejection of the all powerful father-figure, which, according to the Oedipal model, is the focus of resentment and supplication. In *A Thousand Plateaus* they gleefully label God 'a lobster, or a double pincer, a double bind' (2005: 4). On the history of religion and psychology, they have this to say:

> Freud held to his atheism in heroic fashion. But all around him, more and more, they respectfully allowed him to speak, they let the old man speak, ready to prepare behind his back the reconciliation of the churches and psychoanalysis, the moment when the Church would train its own psychoanalysts, and when it would become possible to write in the history of the movement: so even we are still pious! (2005: 65)

The chapters in this book argue that, despite their combative relationship with the theoretical and institutional traditions of French psychoanalysis and psychiatry (particular Freud and Lacan), Deleuze and Guattari's do not escape this institution's fascination with religion. Our contributors also argue that the analysis of psychoanalysis and religion can be taken a step further through the practice of schizoanalysis. In order to frame this argument, I will conclude with a brief overview of the schizoanalysis project, before outlining the contents of each chapter.

The first volume of *Capitalism and Schizophrenia, Anti-Oedipus* was both a reaction to theoretical and institutional struggles taking place in French psychoanalysis and psychiatry and an attempt to formulate a coherent response to the events of May '68 (see Buchanan 2008: 7–12). The second volume, *A Thousand Plateaus*, is less engaged with these sociopolitical events. Composed in a non-linear fashion, where the reader is invited to move among plateaus in any order, it offers a broader scope and far more accessible 'bite-size' arguments. Drawing on Freud and especially Lacan, their primary aim in both books is to replace Freudian (and Lacanian) psychoanalysis with a 'revolutionary materialist psychiatry' called schizoanalysis.

Deleuze and Guattari's main problem with psychoanalysis was Freud's conception of the 'Oedipus complex'. They argue that the moment Freud began to 'maintain sexuality under the morbid yoke of the little secret' (Deleuze and Guattari 2004: 385) marked a downward spiral in the operations of psychoanalysis and psychiatry, leading to a humiliating and degrading conception of sexuality: 'What a perverse operation psychoanalysis is, where this neoidealism, this rehabilitated cult of castration, this ideology of lack culminates: the anthropomorphic representation of sex' (2004: 339). To offer a rough summary: the schizoanalytic approach hinges on this re-evaluation of the psychoanalytic concept of the unconscious as being composed of a reservoir of thoughts or ideas that the conscious represses. Rather than finding ways to make latent thoughts or ideas manifest in order to find a cure to a patient's neurosis, a schizoanalysis changes the dynamics of Freud's model of unconscious by affirming the faults and glitches that are taken to be abnormal in psychiatry (but, as they are quick to remind us, never to the point of a schizophrenic breakdown).

A schizoanalysis also opens up the sociopolitical and economic content of desire, challenging the centrality of the Oedipal complex. Drawing on Marx, Deleuze and Guattari argue that the system of Capitalism plays an important part in the reduction of the libido or sexuality to the private sphere of the family. Turning the Oedipal structure on its head, the schizophrenic family commands an entirely different determination: 'a family gasping for breath and stretched out over the dimensions of a social field that does not reclose or withdraw: a family-as-matrix' (2004: 307). They also go so far as to say that psychoanalysis depends on capitalist consumption: 'Psychoanalysis, no less than the bureaucratic or military apparatus, is a mechanism for the absorption of excess value' (344). In this sense, *Capitalism and Schizophrenia* is intimately connected to the events of May 68', but not in the ordinary sense of revolutionary thought. Revolution for Deleuze and Guattari, as Ian Buchanan puts it, means 'schizophrenizing' the existing power structure:

> Making it vibrate to a new rhythm, making it change from within, without at the same time becoming a schizophrenic. But they don't offer a model for a new society, save that it won't replicate the old repressions. Their argument is that

> we'll never get to that new society the militants of every persuasion claim their doctrine is leading us towards if we don't first of all shed off old habits, our old love of power, our manifold addictions to the exercise of force, our customary obsequiousness in the face of power. (2008: 10)

Deleuze and Guattari insist that the schizoanalysis of capitalism must acquire at least as much force as Capitalism in order to produce breaks in this power structure, and to mobilize (and determine the conditions of) the free play of desire. In their assessment, no activity is too malevolent for the schizoanalytic practice. The schizoanalyst will practise desecration, destruction, and perversion, destroying beliefs and representations, and 'watching for the signs of indices that operate like machines and that will cause him to go further' (2004: 350). Deleuze and Guattari speak of the schizoanalytic voyage, conceiving it as a process, or rather an interruption, that undoes all the lands that it traverses for the benefit of the one it is creating. The schizoanalyst is also a mechanic, who examines the formation and functions of desiring-machines, in which the subject is caught as a cog. He asks who drives these machines? What are the circuits that they enter into and operate? What use do you make of them?

4. Preview

The purpose of this Introduction has been to set out the context for the project and to begin to outline what a schizoanalysis of religion might look like. Each of the other chapters deals with ways in which schizoanalysis has encountered and might continue to encounter religion; all are interested in provoking sustained debate over the future of this field.

The first chapter, by Brent Adkins, draws on references to God and religion scattered throughout Deleuze's texts in order to construct a Deleuzian theory of religion, but it also introduces the primary aspiration of this volume taken up in more detail by the other contributors. At the very least, this aspiration is to show that Deleuze and Guattari's work is not necessarily anti-thetical to religious debate and to discuss the ways in which it can contribute to those debates. Adkins reminds us that while certainly there is a tendency towards order in religion, this is not its sole tendency. In developing his Deleuzian general theory of religion, he argues that a schizoanalysis of religious thought and practice must respond to its correlative movement towards escape, breaks, and lines of flight.

The next two chapters deal with two essential components (or mysteries) of Christian theology: the practice of Eucharist, and the idea of the holy Trinity. Kristien Justaert approaches the psychoanalysis project from the perspective of Catholic liberation theology. Traditionally, liberation theology has resisted the mechanisms of oppression created by the logic of Capitalism, so there is already a clear link here with the political purpose of the schizoanalysis project. Recently, the field has expanded to encompass other structures of oppression by way of dialogue with postcolonialist, queer, feminist, and other postmodern critical theories (see Justaert 2012: 119–123). Justaert explores the power dynamics evident in the history and practice of the Eucharist (e.g. its movement from the context of the family home in early Christianity into the space of church, thereby placing the sacrament in the hands of the priest). Using Deleuze and Guattari's schizoanalysis project, she tries to show how the Eucharist both captures and controls desire in a patriarchal Oedipal system, and how it might be restructured in order to escape this ecclesiastical control.

In Chapter 3, Christopher Ben Simpson takes as his focus the mystery of the Trinity in Christian doctrine. Here the focus is on connecting Deleuze's ontology of difference to the notion of a Trinitarian God ('the one is many'/'the many are one'). Simpson posits the existence of a Deleuzian divine that is dynamic and multiple: 'a fecund Chaos that "stands in pace of the one."' Simpson's approach to the dynamic divine life of the Trinity is attentive to the nature and scope of Deleuze and Guattari's work and grounded in the Christian traditions that underpin the peculiarities of 'trinitarian thought'. Like Justaert's chapter, his contribution offers an innovative, theologically situated outlook on what a schizoanalysis has to offer to the rites and intellectual outlook of the Christian tradition.

The next three chapters focus in more detail on specific aspects of Deleuze and Guattari's understanding of the unconscious and desire in relation to religion and spirituality more generally. In Chapter 4, Joshua Ramey explores their 'machinic animism', which can be described as a kind of 'haptic' religion. His focus is on discovering a religiosity *intrinsic to* thinking in Deleuze, that is, a spirituality *immanent* to his own philosophical practice. For Ramey, Deleuze's spiritual project of machinic animism can be conceived as the 'religion' of a society against the state and reclaimed as the battle cry of a decolonized self: *we are not rational animals, but animist rationales*. By beginning to tease out the political implications of the 'hermetic' elements of Deleuze's thought, Ramey's chapter provides a helpful transition to the two contributions that follow.

Aidan Tynan's chapter explores what he calls Deleuze's 'apocalypticism', and its relation to a 'schizoanalytic political theology'. Taking references to apocalypse in the preface to *Difference and Repetition* (2001, first published 1968) and Deleuze's introduction to D.H. Lawrence's *Apocalypse* (1974, first published 1980) as a starting point, Tynan traces apocalyptic and eschatological themes throughout Deleuze's work. At the same time he explores Deleuze and Guattari's most urgent political question, which is 'how can we continue to be pious?', in the context of an endlessly deferred eschaton, the last period of history.

In Chapter 6, Inna Semetsky draws on her empirical research with Tarot and her knowledge of Jungian psychology to explore the connections between tarot hermeneutics and schizoanalysis, elucidating the potential of Tarot well beyond its popular usage. The interpretation of the multiple potential combinations of the tarot layout is framed as a creative, schizoanalytic practice. Semetsky's chapter also explores some of the esoteric references (deliberate, or otherwise) in Deleuze and Guattari's work. Deleuze's 1946 publication called 'Mathesis, Science, and Philosophy' (Deleuze 2007) is of particular relevance to her project as the political impulse of Deleuze's thoughts on mathesis are related to the interpreter of signs as belonging to the 'people to come'.

The final two chapters of the book deal more broadly with the general relation between religion and theology, on the one hand, and Deleuze and Guattari, on the other. In Chapter 7, Austin Roberts provides a typology of ways in which scholars have explored the connections between Deleuze, Guattari, and theology. Roberts divides this literature into three approaches, starting with the orthodox Christian 'confessional' theologians; then the 'progressives', who take a more confrontational approach to Deleuze and religion; and finally, the 'radicals'. The latter approach is illustrated by way of an analysis of Clayton Crocket's radical materialist interpretation of Deleuze's ontology, as well as the appropriation of Deleuze in the work of Catherine Keller and Roland Faber. Building on this literature, Roberts suggests a 'theopoetic' approach to theology, which reads Deleuze alongside Whitehead and Spinoza, outlining the idea of God and theology in relation to the concepts of univocity and immanence.

Like the first chapter by Brent Adkins, the last chapter by LeRon Shults is concerned with Deleuze's general theory of religion. More so than the other authors in this volume, however, Shults focuses on the critical aspects of Deleuze's treatment of religion. He argues that the *Capitalism and Schizophrenia* project as a whole, as well as Deleuze's single-authored corpus, can be considered an 'atheist machine'. Using insights derived from the cognitive and cultural sciences of religion, Shults explores Deleuze and

Guattari's analysis of the territorial, despotic, capitalist, and war machines and demonstrates the special relation between the latter and 'atheism'. For Shults, schizoanalysis cannot be separated from the destructive and creative tasks of *becoming-atheist*.

As a whole, this volume is intended to provide readers with insight into the variety of ways in which philosophers of religion and theologians are currently attempting to appropriate the work of Deleuze and Guattari in the ongoing task of schizoanalysing religion in its various forms.

Notes

1 Jacques Lacan's Seminar XVII. Originally delivered just after the Paris uprisings of May 1968.

2 For an English translation, see Hellmut (1977).

3 For an English translation, see Wilhelm (2001).

Bibliography

Ames, E. (1899) *The Psychology of Religious Experience*. New York: Scribner.

Ames, E. (1910) *The Psychology of Religious Experience*. Boston, MA: Houghton Mifflin Co.

Beckman, F. (2011) *Deleuze and Sex*. Edinburgh: Edinburgh University Press.

Bignall, S. and P. Patton (2010) *Deleuze and the Postcolonial*. Edinburgh: Edinburgh University Press.

Black, D. (2006) *Psychoanalysis and Religion in the 21st Century*. London: Routledge.

Bonta, M. and J. Protevi (2004) *Deleuze and Geophilosophy*. Edinburgh: Edinburgh University Press.

Bryden, M. (2001) *Deleuze and Religion*. London: Routledge.

Buchanan, I. (2008) *Deleuze and Guattari's Anti-Oedipus*. London: Continuum.

Buchanan, I. and L. Collins (2014) *Deleuze and the Schizoanalysis of Visual Art*. London and New York: Bloomsbury.

Buchanan, I. and G. Lambert (2005) *Deleuze and Space*. Edinburgh: Edinburgh University Press.

Buchanan, I. and P. MacCormack (2008) *Deleuze and the Schizoanalysis of Cinema*. London: Continuum.

Buchanan, I. and M. Swiboda (2004) *Deleuze and Music*. Edinburgh: Edinburgh University Press.

Buchanan, I., T. Matts and A. Tynan (2015) *Deleuze and the Schizoanalysis of Literature*. London and New York: Bloomsbury.

Coe, G. (1916) *The Psychology of Religion*. Chicago, IL: The University of Chicago Press.
Cull, L. (2009) *Deleuze and Performance*. Edinburgh: Edinburgh University Press.
Davis, C., M. Pound and C. Crockett (2014) *Theology after Lacan*. Oregon: Cascade Books.
Deleuze, G. and F. Guattari (1986) *Nomadology: The War Machine*. New York: Columbia University Press.
Deleuze, G. and P. Patton (2001) *Difference and Repetition*. London: Continuum.
Deleuze, G. and F. Guattari (2004) *Anti-Oedipus*. London and New York: Continuum.
Deleuze, G. and F. Guattari (2005) *A Thousand Plateaus: Capitalism and Schizophrenia*. Minneapolis: University of Minnesota Press.
Deleuze, G. (2007) 'Mathesis, Science and Philosophy', in R. Mackay (ed.), *Collapse III*, 1st ed., Falmouth: Urbanomic, pp. 141–155.
DiCenso, J. (2005) *The Other Freud*. London and New York: Routledge.
Faber, H. (1976) *Psychology of Religion*. London and Bristol: SCM Press Ltd.
Freud, S. (2001) *Totem and Taboo*. London: Routledge Classics.
Freud, S. (2008) *The Future of an Illusion*. London and New York: Penguin Books.
Freud, S. (2013) *Leonardo Da Vinci*. Oxon: Routledge Classics.
Freud, S., J. Strachey, A. Freud and A. Strachey (2001) *The Standard Edition of the Complete Psychological Works of Sigmund Freud*. London: Vintage.
Frichot, H. (2013) *Deleuze and Architecture*. Edinburgh: Edinburgh University Press.
Fromm, E. (1971) *Psychoanalysis and Religion*. New Haven, CT and London: Yale University Press.
Fromm, E. and D. Suzuki (1960) *Zen Buddhism & Psychoanalysis*. New York: Harper.
Guattari, F. (2012) *Schizoanalytic Cartographies*. New York: Bloomsbury.
Guillaume, L. and J. Hughes (2011) *Deleuze and the Body*. Edinburgh: Edinburgh University Press.
Hall, G. (1917) *Jesus, the Christ, in the Light of Psychology*. Garden City, NY: Doubleday, Page & Company.
Hellmut, R. (1977) *The I Ching*. Princeton, NJ: Princeton University Press.
James, W. (2008) *The Varieties of Religious Experience*. Rockville: Arc Manor.
Jones, J. (1991) *Contemporary Psychoanalysis and Religion*. New Haven, CT: Yale University Press.
Jonte-Pace, D. and W. Parsons (2001) *Religion and Psychology*. London: Routledge.
Justaert, K. (2001) *Theology after Deleuze*. London and Oxford: Continuum.
Lacan, J. (1977) *The Seminar of Jacques Lacan, Book XI: The Four Fundamental Concepts of Psychoanalysis*. New York: W.W. Norton and Company.
Lacan, J. (2006) *The Other Side of Psychoanalysis*. New York: Norton.
Lacan, J. (2013a) *On the Name of the Father*. Cambridge, MA and Malden, MA: Polity Press.
Lacan, J. (2013b) *The Triumph of Religion*. Cambridge, MA and Malden, MA: Polity Press.
Lawrence, D.H. (1974) *Apocalypse*. New York: Viking Press.

Lee, Y. (2013) 'Translating Deleuze: On the Uses of Deleuze in a Non-Western Context', *Deleuze Studies* 7:3, pp. 319–329.

Leuba, J. (2007) *The Psychology of Religious Mysticism*. Oxon: Routledge.

Liebman, J.J. (1946) *Peace of Mind*. New York: Simon and Schuster.

Mackay, R. (2007) *Collapse III*. Falmout: Urbanomic.

Marks, J. and I. Buchanan (2000) *Deleuze and Literature*. Edinburgh: Edinburgh University Press.

Nigianni, C. and M. Storr (2009) *Deleuze and Queer Theory*. Edinburgh: Edinburgh University Press.

Paskauskas, R. (1993) *The Complete Correspondence of Sigmund Freud and Ernest Jones*. Cambridge, MA: The Belknap Press of Harvard University Press.

Poster, M. and D. Savat (2009) *Deleuze and New Technology*. Edinburgh: Edinburgh University Press.

Pratt, J. (2005) *The Religious Consciousness*. New York: Cosimo Books.

Redner, G. (2011) *Deleuze and Film Music*. Bristol, UK: Intellect.

Reik, T. (1958) *Ritual*. New York: International Universities Press.

Roberts, P. and R. Rushton (2011) *Schizoanalysis and Visual Culture*. Edinburgh: Edinburgh University Press.

Saldanha, A. and J. Adams (2013) *Deleuze and Race*. Edinburgh: Edinburgh University Press.

Sigmund, F. (2001) 'Moses and Monotheism', in J. Strachey (ed.), *The Standard Edition of the Complete: Volume XXIII (1937–1939) Psychological Works of Sigmund Freud*, London: Vintag, pp. 3–132.

Starbuck, E. (1901) *The Psychology of Religion*. London: W. Scott.

Taves, A. (1999) *Fits, Trances, & Visions*. Princeton, NJ: Princeton University Press.

Ulanov, A. (1999) *Religion and the Spiritual in Carl Jung*. New York: Paulist Press.

Wilhelm, R. (2001) *The Secret of the Golden Flower*. Oxon: Routledge.

Wyschogrod, E., D. Crownfield and C. Raschke (1989) *Lacan and Theological Discourse*. Albany: State University of New York Press.

Zepke, S. and S. O'Sullivan (2010) *Deleuze and Contemporary Art*. Edinburgh: Edinburgh University Press.

Žižek, S. (1989) *The Sublime Object of Ideology*. London: Verso.

Žižek, S. (2000) *The Fragile Absolute, or, Why Is the Christian Legacy Worth Fighting For?*. London: Verso.

Žižek, S., J. Milbank and C. Davis (2011) *The Monstrosity of Christ*. Cambridge: MIT Press.

1

Deleuze's Theory of Religion

Brent Adkins

Deleuze's texts are littered with references to religion. Deleuze's interest in univocity brings him into contact with scholastic Christian theology. His work on Spinoza and Artaud allows him to countenance a theology that is no longer animated by the judgement of God. This reading of Spinoza and Artaud culminates in the perverse theology of *A Thousand Plateaus* (1980), in which the judgement of God is naturalized into the double articulation of stratification. God is a lobster. Deleuze is not only interested in Christian theology, though. He is also interested in religion in general. He is forced in *What Is Philosophy?* (1994) to distinguish religion in general from philosophy in general. Here the distinction takes the form of a distinction in products. Philosophy produces concepts, while religion produces figures.

What Deleuze does not do, however, in spite of the many references to religion, is provide a general theory of religion in the way that he provides a general theory of philosophy, science, and art. I think it is possible, though, to construct a general theory of religion from the clues in Deleuze's texts. From *What Is Philosophy?* we learn that the distinction between religion and philosophy lies not only in what each creates but in the relation to transcendence. Philosophy tends towards immanence, while religion tends to transcendence. The tendency towards transcendence that characterizes religion means that it organizes territories in a particular way. Posed in this way, though, Deleuze seems to presuppose a schema that has hampered the development of Religious Studies until very recently.

The discipline of Religious Studies has come a long way since Schleiermacher attempted to define religion as 'the feeling of absolute dependence', a feeling on which all other dogma and ritual rested. Hegel rightly lampooned this definition of religion but at the same time reduced religion to the unfolding thought of the absolute. 'Religion' as a concept in academic discourse arises fundamentally as a comparative exercise by which Christianity (particularly Protestant Christianity) could be compared to and found superior to the 'other' religions of the world. Recent critical movements in Religious Studies, particularly those associated with postcolonial studies, sharply question the degree to which this view is still operative in Religious Studies. At the same time, as Religious Studies began to expand and deepen as a discipline there were attempts to reduce all religions to the same level in order to criticize or valorize religion as such. The effect of this reduction was a tacit assumption about the nature of religion that has gone largely unquestioned until recently. That tacit assumption is that religion reflects a belief in and participates in the ordered and harmonious universe established by the gods. Michael Puett states the assumption this way,

> Humans before the modern period believed themselves to be living in a world created and controlled by gods; according to the framework, in which the cosmos was therefore structured, humanity had a predefined place and purpose for existence, and human societies were given order through religious beliefs and institutions. Such a world was cohesive, harmonious, and unified, and religion was the glue that held it together. The dramatic shift in human history, according to this narrative, thus occurred in the modern world, when a loss of belief in the religious sphere led to fragmentation and alienation. Humans no longer had a defined place and purpose in the cosmos and human society no longer had a force leading to harmony and cohesion. (Puett 2012: 109–110)[1]

Puett goes on to argue that different classical theorists of religion have responded to this dichotomy between religious order and modern chaos in different ways. Max Weber, for example, is ambivalent about the shift away from order. Émile Durkheim, though, thinks the shift away from traditional religious order to chaotic modernity represents an important and altogether positive development in human history. Mircea Eliade, in contrast to Durkheim, sees the loss of the ordered universe as a metaphysical loss, a diminution of humanity. Importantly, though, what none of these classical theorists question is the connection between order and religion, on the one hand, and the abandonment of religion with chaos, on the other (Puett 2012: 109–113).

The unquestioned nature of this assumption has made it quite resilient, despite the fact that it is belied by recent empirical research in religion. According to Puett, it still seems to be operative in more recent major theorists, even though the evolutionary frameworks of their predecessors have been abandoned. The association of religion with order is found in both Clifford Geertz and Maurice Bloch, despite their strongly opposed programmes and conclusions (Puett 2012: 116–120). Within the context of the history of Religious Studies, it is initially tempting to include Deleuze and Guattari's scattered references to religion as reproducing this same structure. *What Is Philosophy?* in particular seems to traffic in the facile dualism that would place religion on the side of order and philosophy, art, and science on the side of chaos (and by extension modernity). A closer reading of two key passages in *A Thousand Plateaus*, however, shows that religion is a complex phenomenon with tendencies towards both order and chaos. Furthermore, Deleuze and Guattari are explicit that in opposition to the dominant trend in the history of Religious Studies (and despite quoting Eliade approvingly) religion is not the source of order but the effect of an ordering process they call 'territorialization'.

Finally, a general theory of religion must not only explicate its tendency towards transcendence and the way that it organizes territories, but also its lines of flight. A schizoanalysis is ultimately more interested in what escapes than in what is constrained by religion, because it is precisely on the edge of deterritorialization that the new is created. In short, religion is an assemblage dominated by a tendency towards transcendence but without eliminating all lines of flight. Furthermore, it is precisely these lines of flight that distinguish one religion from another. The fuller explication of this view is to be found in *A Thousand Plateaus* and a rereading of *What Is Philosophy?* in this context. A careful reading shows that, though these texts seem initially to reproduce the traditional framework, ultimately a more complex view of religion is at play, one in which religion can transform from a component of the state into a war machine, and even turn against the state in an international social formation. This position strikes me as quite amenable to what I take to be the current state of empirical research in religion. Furthermore, I think the breadth of religion propounded here has the ability to lead Religious Studies in new directions by, as we'll see below, positing that animals and humans have religion in common.

1. Kant and territory

It is impossible to understand Deleuze's account of religion without understanding his conception of territory. In order to illustrate what is at stake here, I'd like to contrast Deleuze's view of territory with Kant's.[2] Kant's understanding of territory begins with the breakthrough he makes in his Inaugural Dissertation, *On the Form and Principles of the Sensible and the Intelligible World* (1770). In this work that Kant himself considered the beginning of his critical period, Kant seeks to return to the ancient distinction between phenomena and noumena, which he finds best exemplified in Plato. What is at stake in this distinction is the fundamental but easily confused difference between that which is sensed and the form given to that which is sensed. For Kant it is clear that the form of sensation cannot be abstracted from the sensible and must thus be thought of as not merely different in degree but different in kind. Arguing for the qualitative difference of the sensible and its form ran counter to the dominant view, which held that the difference was merely one of degree. Kant singles out Wolff and states flatly that the sensitive is not simply confused cognition.[3] We can also see, though, that the empiricist tradition holds the converse view whereby cognitions are less vivid sensations. In the Inaugural Dissertation Kant thus rejects the continuity of the sensible and intelligible held by both rationalists and empiricists (albeit with different emphases) and replaces this continuity with the radical discontinuity of form and content. Both are necessary but irreducible to one another. Kant thus begins his critical period by establishing a boundary between the sensible and the intelligible. The method he employs throughout his critical works, particularly his works on religion, is the continual re-establishment and defence of this same boundary. The terms by which he establishes and defends this boundary are legal and geographical.

In the *Critique of Pure Reason* (1781), for example, Kant uses both a legal and geographical vocabulary to establish the proper place of reason. The legal vocabulary is explicit in Kant's concern in the 'Preface' to the first edition with whether or not metaphysics deserves to be restored to its title as queen of the sciences. Questions of royalty, however, are ultimately questions of genealogy. The right to rule must be confirmed by descent from a royal ancestor. Locke famously calls the queen's bloodline into question by arguing that heritage is merely common experience. Kant takes up the cause of the queen by attempting to show that her claim to the throne is indeed just. However, Kant is determined that the queen's rule will not be despotic. Thus, he must show that queen's claim is sound but not boundless (Kant 1998: Aviii–x).

The attempt to rehabilitate and at the same time delimit metaphysics lies at the heart of Kant's critical project. For the rehabilitation of metaphysics Kant continues to use legal vocabulary. Recent scholarship has shown that the notoriously difficult 'Transcendental Deduction' is in fact modelled on a legal document that provides precisely the kind of genealogical support required by someone trying to establish her claims to rule (Henrich 1989: 20–46). Thus, the question the deduction seeks to answer in Kant is not a logical question but a legal question: Not, what are the necessary and sufficient conditions that entail the pure concepts of the understanding? But, by what right are we justified in using the pure concepts of the understanding? Do the pure concepts of the understanding have a right to rule experience, or does experience lie outside their jurisdiction?

For Kant the deduction is a success insofar as it establishes that the pure concepts of the understanding have a right to rule. However, what he has not established at this point is the limit of that rule. Over what land does the queen rule? Where are its boundaries? How will she know where her power begins and where it ends? To answer these questions Kant turns to geography. In the first instance he speaks about this negatively, as 'denying knowledge in order to make room for faith' (Kant 1998: Bxxx). Here the claims of the queen are checked by competing claims. For Kant the unlimited rule of the queen is identical to dogmatism. Dogmatism must be reined in by critique. It is only by embracing these limits that the conflicts between unbelief and morality can be resolved and that metaphysics can be set on the sure path of science.

Kant gives a positive account of the queen's land in his discussion of the phenomena/noumena distinction. For Kant the preceding analysis was not merely a tour of the queen's land but a survey, a survey that not only locates but orients everything in the country. The great discovery of this survey is that the queen lives on an island 'enclosed in unalterable boundaries (*Grenzen*) by nature itself' (A235/B294). Thus, the queen rightly rules on this island, but insofar as the boundaries are natural she cannot hope to extend her realm any more than she could hope to turn the ocean into land.

The island is, of course, sensible experience and the ocean is the supersensible that lies beyond experience. The theoretical deployment of reason must be restricted to objects of possible experience. Otherwise, it risks being lost on the stormy sea of the supersensible, forever chasing illusions and chimera created by the use of the categories of the understanding beyond the objects of possible experience. What lies beyond the objects of possible experience for Kant is most importantly morality, reason in its practical deployment. The delimitation of knowledge in order to make room for faith is the restriction of the queen to the island of truth. In order to leave this island, Kant will argue that we must orient ourselves differently.

Kant's longest discussion of the relation between religion and territory occurs in *Religion within the Boundaries of Mere Reason* (1793). Not surprisingly, he relies heavily on images drawn from geography and law. The very title indicates both a geographic and a legal distinction. In order to set a boundary, one must know the spatial limits of a territory as well as having the juridical authority to enforce the boundary. If, for example, I decide to expand the limits of my yard by reasoning that the boundary extends to some natural feature, say a stream, and rebuild my fence accordingly, then I will soon find myself in trouble with local authorities (not to mention my neighbour whose property I steal), since I do not have the authority to move the boundaries of my property.

Kant's contention in the religion book is similar. Religion oversteps its proper bounds whenever it seeks to make theoretical claims about what lies beyond sensible experience. We might extend Kant's thinking here through two additional legal doctrines related to property rights: adverse possession and eminent domain. The doctrine of adverse possession has its roots in English common law and states that if someone occupies a property openly and in opposition to the owner's rights, the occupier may after a certain period of time petition for ownership of the property without remuneration to the original owner. Thus, for example, if I did move my fence and occupied the additional land for twenty years I could petition to assert my rights over the new land. From Kant's perspective, religion has moved the fence and occupied land that it does not possess the right to. However, religion has occupied this land for so long that it has in a sense acquired the right to this new land. Thus, if you were to ask the average person, which discipline has a right to noumenal knowledge – religion or philosophy? The likely answer is religion. The purpose of Kant's critical project, however, is to show that the question is poorly formed. Strictly speaking, there is no noumenal (theoretical) knowledge. There is no (theoretical) knowledge beyond the sensible. Kant is not willing to grant the noumenal to religion, even if according to long-standing tradition, religion has taken it as its domain.

Kant could respond to religion's adverse possession of the noumenal by denying that the criteria of adverse possession have been met. Thus, if I install an invisible, electronic fence to keep my dog in the yard, my neighbour might argue that my possession of his property is not sufficiently open and opposed to his rights to rise to the level of adverse possession. Kant does not use this strategy. Rather, Kant's argument is to show that there are rights of possession that supersede religion's, no matter how ancient religion's claims. Kant's argument, then, does not take place, as it were, between two citizens submitting their case before the state's judgment. Kant's argument takes the form of eminent domain, which says that for the purposes of public utility, private property may be appropriated by the state. While the state has an interest in seeing that the dispute between my neighbour and me gets resolved justly, it is ultimately indifferent to the outcome. The state's indifference lies in the fact that if needed the state has the power to take some or all of my neighbour's and my land for the public good. It can redraw boundaries as it sees fit. This is precisely what Kant is proposing in the religion book. Religion will now be stripped of whatever right it has acquired to the noumenal for the public good. The public good is an end to the interminable bickering caused by religious disputes, and a turning away from the inessential externals of religion to its essential moral core. Religion's new boundaries now lie within reason. Reason, of course, has already undergone its critique, which laid out its legal and geographical dimensions.

In contrast to Kant's account of territory that is both legal and geographic, *A Thousand Plateaus* proposes a profoundly different account of territory. Deleuze and Guattari begin their discussion of this territory with a suggestive image, a child singing in the dark. They write,

> A child in the dark, gripped with fear, comforts himself by singing under his breath. He walks and halts to his song. Lost, he takes shelter, or orients himself with his little song as best he can. The song is like a rough sketch of a calming and stabilizing, calm and stable, center in the heart of chaos. Perhaps the child skips as he sings, hastens or slows his pace. But the song itself is already a skip: it jumps from chaos to the beginnings of order in chaos and is in danger of breaking apart at any moment. (Deleuze and Guattari 1987: 311)

The concern with orientation remains, but four points differentiate this orientation from the kind of orientation that Kant proposes: (1) *The orientation is affective*; (2) *Affects combine to form territories*; (3) *Territories are distinguished from chaos not other territories*; (4) *Boundaries between chaos and territory differ from boundaries between territories*. The first difference is that while Kant proposes an orientation in thinking, the kind of orientation proposed here does not fit neatly into a space of reasons. The process that leads a scared child to sing in the dark seems more intuitive and bodily than it does reasonable. At the same time, however, thought is not thereby excluded either. Perhaps we can draw on Spinoza here and suggest that the child is oriented as a whole and that this orientation can be understood as a series of affective interactions. On this reading, the child is beset by forces set to overwhelm him through fear, and he resists through song. The child doesn't so much overcome the fear as keep it at bay through his singing. Something similar is at work when a scared child pulls the covers over her head. In each case there is an orientation going on here but it is an orientation neither in thought nor by thought.

The second difference from Kant that we find here is the very notion of territory. The stability that the child creates through his song is neither legal nor geographical. It is affective (or 'intensive' in Deleuze's language). In order to make more sense of this notion of an affective territory, let's turn again to Spinoza. To begin with affectivity is a larger category than the emotions. All emotions are affects, but not all affects are emotions. For Spinoza the universe is constituted as an infinitely complex series of interactions among the various parts of the universe. These parts Spinoza labels modes, while the universe he calls substance, nature, or God. The interactions among modes, the way they affect and are affected by one another, are what Spinoza names 'affects'. Many of the interactions that involve the interaction of humans with other parts of the world have taken on distinct names, which we refer to as emotions. Thus, when I stub my toe I describe that interaction as painful. When I lash out at what I stub my toe on, I label my reaction as anger. These interactions that I name with emotions, though, are nothing other than some of the ways that I affect and am affected by the world around me. No doubt, Spinoza's primary concern in the *Ethics* is this subset of affects that have emotional names. Indeed, Part 3 is a taxonomy of these possibilities.

However, Deleuze is concerned with two novel extensions of this notion of affect. The first extension is to pursue at greater length these non-human affects, the ones that don't have a ready emotional label. Deleuze is thus interested in the way that non-human things affect and are affected by one another. Additionally, though, he recognizes that the kind of analysis that Spinoza provides is scalable. One can pursue this on the micro-, meso-, and macrolevels. One can speak about biochemical reactions at a cellular level as affects. One could speak about the migration of caribou being driven by black flies and mosquitoes in terms of a complex set of affects. Finally, one can analyse international politics in affective terms. I do not think this extension of Spinoza is unwarranted, though. He authorizes it in the Preface to Part 3, where he argues that everything is to be understood according to the same set of laws. There are no 'kingdoms within kingdoms' in Spinoza's universe. There is only one universe with one set of laws. The task of understanding is the task of teasing out the ways that these laws combine to create increasingly complex affects on multiple levels.

Deleuze's second extension of Spinoza is an account of the way in which affects combine into more or less stable entities, that is, assemblages. The extension is also warranted by this same commitment to a single universe with a single set of laws. Here both Deleuze and Spinoza run up against a long-standing problem in the history of philosophy, accounting for a universe that seems to have both stable and mutable elements. While Spinoza's solution to this problem is subject to some dispute, on Deleuze's reading and in Deleuze's own thought, he argues for a hylozoic solution to this problem, that is, that matter is self-organizing. Deleuze's hylozoism is correlated with his commitment to a single universe with a single set of laws. With no extra-mundane or intelligible realm to guarantee stability within the world, Deleuze must give an account of the way in which stability is generated out of mutability. Hylozoism is opposed to hylomorphism in all of its forms, whether they be Platonic, Aristotelian, or Kantian. What Deleuze's hylozoism allows him to do is think of stable objects as the result of underlying processes. Stabilities are then temporary coagulations of ongoing and intersecting intensive processes. This is the case not only for geological and biological processes, such as mountains or humans, but it is also the case for cultural products, such as technology, political systems, and religion. In Deleuze's work with Guattari the process by which momentary stabilities arise is 'territorialization'. The result of territorialization is a territory. Territorialization recognizes that affective interactions organize themselves. A flowing river does not distribute sediment equally but in fact sorts it according to size. The result is striated sedimentation that territorializes the material found in the riverbed and in suspension in the flowing water.

The third difference that we see between Kant's notion of orientation and the one proposed by Deleuze is that while Kant is very keen to properly draw the boundaries between territories, for Deleuze the boundary is between the territory and chaos. As we saw, Kant comes close to distinguishing between territory and chaos when he speaks of the island of the sensible and the stormy sea of the supersensible in the first *Critique*, but even here one can orient oneself in the supersensible, just not by the categories of the understanding. The question of orientation and proper boundaries is so important to Kant precisely because a different territory requires a different kind of orientation. For Deleuze the issue is quite different. 'We require just a little order to protect us from chaos' (Deleuze and Guattari 1994: 201). Territories are forged out of chaos in an attempt to guard against it. 'The forces of chaos are kept outside as much as possible, and the interior space protects the germinal forces of a task to fulfill or a deed to do' (Deleuze and Guattari 1987: 311). The child feels overwhelmed by the dark, beset by noises that become sinister because their source cannot be identified, terrified by shapes that loom uncannily all around. What can he do? What possible power does he have in response to the chaos? He can sing, slowly, tremulously at first, but it is enough. The darkness that threatened to engulf him and paralyse him with fear is now coded through song. The song creates a milieu, an orientation, but only the size of the song. But, it is enough. Enough to keep the chaos at bay, so long as he sings. He can no longer hear the strange noises. They are swallowed up in his song. The uncanny shapes do not react to his song but remain motionless and mute. His song goes wherever he goes, and his song, however, tenuously defines the space between order and chaos. It orients him.

The final difference between Kant's notion of orientation and the one we're pursuing here is that boundary itself must be conceived of differently. For Kant boundary is conceived in legal and geographic terms. The result of this conception in Kant's case is a rigid division that may only be crossed at the risk of becoming disoriented. What remains constant in Kant is a transcendental methodology that not only separates conditions and the conditioned but argues for their discontinuity. In contrast to this, Deleuze's hylozoism suggests the continuity of conditions and the conditioned and as a result conceives of boundary differently. We get an inkling of this difference when we return to the child's song. Deleuze writes, '[the song] jumps from chaos to the beginnings of order in chaos and is in danger of breaking apart at any moment' (Deleuze and Guattari 1987: 311). Any territory, religion included, is initially an ordering of chaos, but the distinction between order and chaos is not a transcendental distinction. As we saw above, territory is nothing but the temporary organization of affects that for a time is able to resist the forces of chaos. This is not to say that the territory is ontologically distinct from chaos. The difference is one of degree rather than kind. Territory is formed out of chaos but remains in chaos. It is stable but only temporarily so. The boundary between territory and chaos is both fragile and continually evolving. There is nothing like the discontinuity thesis to guarantee the boundary's existence either legally or geographically.

2. Religion

We are now in a position to begin constructing Deleuze's theory of religion. Not surprisingly the first key passage arises in the context of discussing the nature of territory and territorialization in *A Thousand Plateaus*. The first passage occurs in the same plateau as the discussion of the child's song and begins in this way:

> The situation is the same if we consider the other effect of territorialization. That other effect, which relates not to occupations but to rites and religions,

> consists in this: the territory groups all the forces of the different milieus together in a single sheaf constituted by the forces of the earth. (Deleuze and Guattari 1987: 321)

There is a great deal that needs to be unpacked in this very dense passage before we can begin to understand what is meant by 'religion' here. We've already discussed 'territory', particularly insofar as it's distinct from geographical and political conceptions of territory, but we gain additional insights here as they relate to religion. Additionally, 'milieu' and 'earth' require further explication.

Let's return to the child's song. With this simple story we find ourselves already face to face with the origins of religion. The battle between order and chaos is at the very root of our religious impulses, though as we'll see not as a simple dualism. The starting point for many of our ancient cosmogonies begins with the subduing of chaos. The founding tradition here seems to arise out of Sumer, though, it is, no doubt, much older. In the Sumerian tradition, the storm god Marduk battles the water goddess Tiamat. Tiamat, whose infinite changeability as the infinite ocean, prevented the establishment of anything stable. Marduk establishes order by slaying Tiamat and dividing her carcass to form heaven and earth. The establishment of order by the defeat of chaos resonates throughout the Fertile Crescent and finds its way into Greek and Roman mythology, as well as the Hebrew Bible. In Genesis 1:2, most scholars think that the reference to God hovering over the waters of 'the deep' (*tehom*) is a remnant of this more ancient cosmogony. Furthermore, the description of Leviathan in Job 41 may also be indicative of the older Sumerian tradition. In the Greek tradition, Hesiod names Chaos as the first primordial deity. Beyond that, however, there may be other points of overlap, such as Apollo defeating the python at Delphi. The motif of a hero defeating a giant serpent gets repeated in different forms all across Europe and into India and is the basis for our fascination with dragon slaying. Thus, we can say (at least initially) that religion for Deleuze and Guattari has something to do with fending off chaos. However, they present a demythologized account of this battle with chaos. It begins simply with something like a child singing in the dark.

The child singing in the dark creates what Deleuze and Guattari would call a 'milieu', which is distinct from a 'territory'. In order to illustrate the difference at stake here, let's take a look at the difference between territorial and non-territorial animals. The white-tailed deer does not have a territory but it does have a milieu. This deer gets its name from that fact that it displays the white underside of its tail when fleeing danger. The deer's milieu is constituted by the direction given by the periodic repetition of this component (the white tail).

Deleuze and Guattari call this periodic repetition 'rhythm'. The rhythm 'codes' or gives shape to variables of the deer's life. 'Thus the living thing has an exterior milieu of materials, an interior milieu of composing elements and composed substances, and intermediary milieu of membranes and limits, and an annexed milieu of energy sources and action-perceptions' (Deleuze and Guattari 1987: 313). It is crucial to distinguish at this point between rhythm and metre. Rhythm differs from metre by virtue of the fact that rhythm continually produces difference. In the case of the fleeing deer, the periodic display transports the deer from one milieu to another from an external milieu of danger to one of safety. Rhythm not only codes but at the same time transcodes, whereas metre only codes. We can see the same transcoding at work in the wasp and the orchid example that Deleuze and Guattari use throughout *A Thousand Plateaus*. In the terms they've introduced here, the wasp's milieu and the orchid's milieu are both transcoded by the other's.

Milieus are not territories; they are sub-territorial. That is, milieus when territorialized become components of a territory. 'There is a territory precisely when milieu components cease to be directional, becoming dimensional instead, when they cease to be functional to become expressive' (Deleuze and Guattari 1987: 315). The shift from milieu to territory is thus marked by two shifts from direction to dimension and from function to expression. We've already discussed the way in which milieus are directional in the case of the white-tailed deer. What would it mean, though, for that directionality to become dimensional? In the case of the white-tailed deer, it would mean that the display of the tail no longer simply defines a direction (away from danger), but defines a space. Furthermore, the tail becomes expressive (and not merely functional) when it is no longer tied to a type of action (flight), but 'acquires a temporal constancy and a spatial range that make it a territorial, or rather territorializing, mark: a signature' (Deleuze and Guattari 1987: 315). In the case of the white-tailed deer, then, it would become territorial if it showed its white tail all the time, not just in times of danger.

With the example of the deer and mind we can return to the vignettes at the beginning of 'Of the Refrain'. The second vignette finds us at home. 'But home does not preexist: it was necessary draw a circle around that uncertain and fragile center, to organize a limited space' (Deleuze and Guattari 1987: 311). While the child's song in the dark defined a directionality (away from danger), when that directionality is given dimension it becomes a territory, in this case, a home. Marduk's battle with Tiamat is a milieu, but establishing the division between heaven and earth by drawing the circle of the horizon with Tiamat's body is a territory. Marduk's founding gesture creates dimension. In a much less dramatic way, it is the same with a home. Certainly, physical walls help to create dimensionality, but there is so much more to it than that. A home channels and supports all kinds of flows, flows of sound, flows of smell, flows of food, flows of waste, flows of people. These flows are organized by the territory into kitchens, bathrooms, living rooms, bedrooms, and so on. These flows are coded milieus (directional elements) that are all gathered together into a single territory (dimensional space).

The gathering together and organization of milieus into a stable relation is one of the effects of territorialization, and the one that concerns religion directly. (The other effect of territorialization is a reorganization of functions, which concerns occupations.) Religion concerns the regrouping of forces and at the same time the 'attribution of all the diffuse forces to the earth as receptacle or base' (Deleuze and Guattari 1987: 321). 'Earth' in this context then is the source of forces insofar as they are coded. That is, the process of territorialization establishes a territory, which is the consistent grouping of coded forces, and, at the same time, posits an earth, that is, the primal well-spring of these coded forces.

Importantly, though, coded forces are not the only kind of forces for Deleuze and Guattari. There are also decoded (and decoding) forces. The forces that lie outside of coding milieus and territories, in short, the forces that are neither dimensional nor directional, are the forces of chaos. The process of territorialization selects some of these forces and groups them as a consistent stability, but necessarily discriminates against some of the forces and necessarily keeps them outside. This process is clearly illustrated in the first two vignettes. The child codes his milieu through song and as a result creates a sufficiently stable orientation to keep the chaos of darkness away. The home territorializes multiple milieus and thus draws a circle around a space. Here at the level of extension the distinction between home and chaos reproduces the spatial distinction of inside and outside. Order reigns inside the home, while chaos reigns outside of it. Deleuze and Guattari, however, note a further complexity,

> Moreover, although in extension the territory separates the interior forces of the earth from the exterior forces of chaos, the same does not occur 'intension,' in the dimension of depth, where the two types of force clasp and are wed in a battle whose only criterion and stakes is the earth. There is always a place, a tree or grove, in the territory where all the forces come together in a hand-to-hand combat of energies. The earth is the close embrace. (Deleuze and Guattari 1987: 321)

The operative distinction here is between intensive and extensive. The establishment of a territory entails that on the extensive level order and chaos are discrete, but on the intensive level order and chaos remain locked in battle. In terms of ancient mythology we could say that for Deleuze and Guattari the battle between order and chaos is simultaneously completed (extensively) and ongoing (intensively). Extensively, Marduk has defeated Tiamat. Order reigns; territory is established. Chaos is banished to an outside. In the case of mythology the outside is a promised future when chaos will return, as in the Norse Ragnarök when after a great battle and the death of many gods the earth will be submerged in water, thus chaos re-emerges. Intensively, though, this battle is continuous and ongoing. It is the place where codes are decoded and territories are deterritorialized. It is the place of becoming, of creation and destruction. The sacred grove that lies at the centre of a territory is simultaneously the centre of the territory and its edge, the place of passage to an outside, another world. 'This intense centre is simultaneously inside the territory, and outside several territories that converge on it at the end of an immense pilgrimage' (Deleuze and Guattari 1987: 321). While the journey to the sacred place may happen extensively in migration or pilgrimage, the passage outside the territory happens intensively (Deleuze and Guattari 1987: 482). This intensive journey is an affective journey that occurs without moving. This is why religious ritual is so often bound up with drugs, chants, and trances. This makes the passage from order to chaos, from extensive to intensive easier. It is precisely for the same reason that the time, place, and people participating in these rituals are strictly regulated according to the coded milieus that are gathered to form the territory in the first place.

Deleuze and Guattari make the connection to religion explicit again precisely at this point. 'So, we must once again acknowledge that religion, which is common to both humans beings and animals, occupies territory only because it depends on the raw aesthetic and territorialising factor as its necessary condition' (Deleuze and Guattari 1987: 321). Religion is a function of territory. All religions are predicated on territory. Though it is clear that there cannot be religion without territory, the question that Deleuze and Guattari do not address here (or anywhere that I'm aware of) is whether there can be a territory without a religion. There are a couple of clues here that suggest that this is not the case.

Reorganization of functions and regrouping of forces are the two effects of a territory. Rites and religion are related to the regrouping of forces. On the one hand, relation is not identity. Additionally, Deleuze and Guattari give the example of home as an instance of territory, and we do not tend to think of our homes as religious sites. At the same time, however, there is a long tradition of thinking of the home as a sacred space harbouring the Penates, the gods of the hearth. In this context we can also think about the long-standing rituals surrounding hospitality as an expression of the same sacredness. This becomes especially clear when the promise of hospitality is broken. Readers of George R.R. Martin's *Song of Ice and Fire* series and watchers of the HBO series based on it have difficulty coming to terms with the brutal slaying of a wedding party that was promised hospitality by the host. In a series filled with murder and mayhem this scene stands out as beyond the pale, and for most the offensiveness lies in breaking the promise of hospitality. The home that was supposed to be a safe haven becomes an abattoir. Rite and religion are thus ubiquitous for Deleuze and Guattari, even if they are not institutionalized, and follow from territorialization.

The ubiquity of rite and religion is further supported by Deleuze and Guattari's casual aside that religion 'is common to both human beings and animals'. It's unfortunate that they did not explore further the implications of animal religion, but it is clear that they think of religion as a phenomenon not relegated solely to humans. Why? Again, the answer to this question lies in their conception of territorialization. Humans and some animals are territorial. Religion is predicated on territory. Thus, both humans and some animals have religion. What also becomes clear from this provocative aside is that Deleuze and Guattari think of religion much more broadly than most and without resorting to a facile dichotomy between order and chaos. All that they need for religion is territory, the constitution of which posits a centre that is both the heart of the territory and its limit. The male Stagemaker bird creates a stage of upturned leaves and displays itself on the 'stage' when a female approaches. The stage is the centre of the Stagemaker's territory. It is the place where a transformation occurs, where a single male bird becomes a courtship couple. Here external forces of chaos are coded and regrouped, but at the same time these coded and regrouped forces undergo transformation in the shift from solitary bird to couple. A nest is built. A new territory is established and with it a new religion.

The difficulty, of course, with Deleuze and Guattari's account of religion is that any account broad enough to include animals risks losing sight of the religious phenomena we are most familiar with, such as institutionalized religious traditions. Despite this broadness there are several factors that recommend this general theory of religion. First, this broadness is a virtue insofar as it allows heterogeneous materials to be thought together. That is, if one of the results of territorialization is religion, then religion itself can be thought of in transversal rather than essentialist terms. Deleuze and Guattari are not attempting to list a set of criteria that must obtain in order for religion to exist. Rather, religion on their reading becomes completely naturalized: so naturalized, in fact, that it is not simply a human product but an effect of regrouping forces. Second, on this reading, it is no longer possible to impose an evolutionary schema on religion. Religion no longer has a teleology that culminates in Protestant Christianity. Rather, any given religion will be the expression of the territory that it's associated with. Finally, and this follows from the first two points, the project of comparative religion, while useful for illustrative purposes in some cases, is replaced with a much more fine-grained analysis of the forces being grouped in each case. The result of such a fine-grained analysis may be the recognition of certain homologies and convergences, but as in biology these homologies and convergences need not entail a singular lineage. In this case the focus would remain on contingency and particularity rather than necessity and universality, and as a result would be more in keeping with current empirical studies of religions.

3. Religions

If the concepts that Deleuze and Guattari develop in 'Of the Refrain' help us situate religion in general with regard to territorialization, we might think of the 'Nomadology' and 'Apparatus of Capture' plateaus as providing the beginnings of a more fine-grained analysis of specific religions, in this case monotheistic religions. Analysing specific religions is, of course, not the goal of these plateaus, any more than it's the goal of *A Thousand Plateaus* as a whole. Religions do arise, though, to illustrate differing social formations. While 'Nomadology' is chiefly concerned with the relation between the state-form and nomadic social formations, 'Apparatus of Capture' introduces urban and ecumenical or international social formations. In this respect their touchstone is Marx. Crucially, however, they distinguish themselves from Marx by arguing that social formations are not defined by modes of production but by 'machinic processes (Deleuze and Guattari 1987: 435). As an overview of the plateau we can schematize the different social formations along with their defining machinic processes (Table 1.1):

Table 1.1 Social formations and machinic processes

Social formation	**Machinic process**
Primitive societies	Mechanisms of prevention-anticipation
State societies	Apparatuses of capture
Urban societies	Instruments of polarization
Nomadic societies	War machines
International/ecumenical organizations	Encompassment of heterogeneous social formations

Of the different social formations, notice that 'religion' is not among them. The reason for this is that religion is not a unique social formation but may arise in any one of these social formations. Or, to put the matter as succinctly as possible: different kinds of territories will produce different kinds of religions. Even more to the point, while Deleuze and Guattari do not argue for it, differences within a given category of social formation will produce differences in religion. Thus, as evidenced by the Pauline Epistles, the Christianity of Rome differs from the Christianity of Corinth. This claim is even further complicated by the fact that for Deleuze and Guattari the different types of social formation are only separable in principle not in fact. Any given social formation will be some combination of any or all of these social formations in some ratio. Differences in combination and ratio will, of course, affect the religion or religions that arise in a territory and which ones are able to take hold and achieve some measure of stability.

Within the context of 'Nomadology' Deleuze and Guattari are primarily interested in distinguishing nomadic societies from state societies. It is important to remember that both nomads and states are ideal types, not unlike order and chaos. That is, each one represents opposed tendencies for social formations. As is often the case, Deleuze and Guattari describe this difference in terms of different ways of thinking about space, namely the smooth and the striated. In terms that we've already discussed above, a good way to think about this difference is in terms of intensive and extensive. Smooth space is an intensive space with no discrete points to constitute direction or dimension. Striated space is extensive space composed of discrete points that orient and constitute dimension. Both kinds of space produce very different territories. Striated space produces a numbered and divided territory that is parcelled out on the basis of an organizing principle – the laws of the state, for example.

Smooth space produces an open territory that is constituted by the number that occupies it – Mongols riding across the steppe, for example.

Striated space produces what Deleuze and Guattari call the 'relative global'. Striated space is relative because it is limited and limiting. At the same time it is global because it seeks to extend these striations everywhere. The state-form is fundamentally imperial in its inception. In contrast, smooth space is not relative and global but a 'local absolute'. It is absolute because it is not delimited by striations. Smooth space is constituted 'on the fly' as the nomads move through it. Insofar as it is constituted on the fly the operations that create smooth space are always local. The operation of smooth space is always fundamentally anti-imperial, even if in practice nomads are captured by the state-form and converted from a war machine into the military arm of the state.

Religion arises again at precisely this point: 'Making the absolute appear in a particular place – is that not a very general characteristic of religion ...?' (Deleuze and Guattari 1987: 382). Deleuze and Guattari thus make an initial connection between the local absolute of smooth space and religion. As we saw above, religion is the regrouping of forces that follows from territorialization. In keeping with that understanding, what is highlighted here is the intensive forces that are grouped. This is a localization of chaos. As with the child's song, though, the goal is to code (i.e. make extensive) the forces so that any decoded forces remain outside. 'The absolute of religion is essentially a horizon that encompasses, and, if the absolute itself appears at a particular place, it does so in order to establish a solid and stable centre for the global' (Deleuze and Guattari 1987: 382). This is the move from the child's song to home. The calm centre is stabilized (striated) in order to form a boundary between inside and outside. As Deleuze and Guattari show in 'The Smooth and the Striated' the extension of striated space happens in two stages. First, smooth space is treated as an 'encompassing horizon'. In particular here we can think of Anaximander's *apeiron*, the unbounded that encircles and defines the bounded. Second, encompassed (striated) space is separated from encompassing space. The mixture is purified and encompassing space is relegated to an inaccessible outside, Tartarus or the trackless desert, that lies beyond civilization (Deleuze and Guattari 1987: 294–295). This domestication of smooth space happens not only in philosophical and political contexts; it also happens in religious contexts. 'In short, religion converts the absolute' (Deleuze and Guattari 1987: 382), that is, religion converts a local absolute into the relative global.

This conversion of a local absolute into the relative global not only mirrors the confrontation between the state-form and nomadic societies; it is, in fact, the same process. 'Religion is in this sense a piece in the State apparatus' (Deleuze and Guattari 1987: 382). Several points need to be made here. First, it is important to keep in mind that Deleuze and Guattari are speaking of monotheism. They are not making the claim that all religions are a piece of the state apparatus. What they are saying is that monotheisms tend to establish imperial hierarchies, whether theologically or in practice. Second, we will also see that even in monotheisms there is a countervailing tendency away from the state-form. Third, religions can become part of any social formation and consequently effectuate the machinic processes of those differing formations. Religion can be nomadic and become a war machine. Religion can be ecumenical and encompass heterogeneous social formations. Historically, though, Deleuze and Guattari would be remiss if they did not also note that religion is often tied to the state-form.

The additional complication that Deleuze and Guattari introduce here is that religions are not static. They can undergo becoming just as any assemblage can. This is no less true of monotheisms, which can transform from an imperial state-form into something more nomadic. Thus, Deleuze and Guattari write,

> it does not exhaust the question to establish a simple opposition between two points of view, religion-nomadism. For monotheistic religion, at the deepest level of its tendency to project a universal or spiritual State over the entire ecumenon, is not without ambivalence or fringe areas; it goes beyond even the ideal limits of the State, even the imperial State, entering a more indistinct zone, an outside of States where it has the possibility of undergoing a singular mutation or adaptation. (Deleuze and Guattari 1987: 383)

Any assemblage, religions included, is a ratio of tendencies towards stasis and change. For the most part religions, particularly monotheisms, are composed of tendencies towards stasis. In the case of monotheism, this tendency towards stasis manifests itself in terms of the imperial state-form. These tendencies towards stasis, however, do not eliminate the tendencies towards change. These tendencies towards change are relegated to the fringe as much as possible, but even here they might martial sufficient force to change the religion itself. Here we might usefully juxtapose priest and prophet. The priest is the functionary that seeks to preserve the universal, striating tendencies of a religion. Priests constitute the imperial pretensions of a religion. Prophets, on the other hand, always come from the outside. They do not belong to the temple or the palace. They are a 'voice crying in the wilderness'. They argue that the religion of the priests is corrupt and that the people have been led astray. The only solution is to abandon the trappings of priestly religion and seek the absolute beyond the temple walls.

When religions coalesce around a prophetic figure or direction, the tendencies towards change become emphasized and the religion can become a war machine. The becoming-war machine of a religion is best exemplified historically in the Islamic idea of holy war and the Christian idea of a crusade. This is not to say, of course, that in either case Islam or Christianity became pure war machines, pure nomadisms. Assemblages are always de facto mixes. The point here is that with the Crusades or Jihad the typical ratio of stasis to change shifts such that the tendencies towards change become dominant, at least for a little while. Furthermore, these ratios are always in flux. The becoming-war machine of a particular religion may be short-lived. Nevertheless, this tendency towards change present in all assemblages must be thought if we are to understand religion in general.

In addition to nomadisms of territory there can also be nomadisms of thought. Here we can think of the orthodoxy of a religion as its stable centre. At the same time, however, this orthodox centre is surrounded by numerous heterodoxies that lie at various distances from the centre. Various political and social expediencies might require that some of these heterodoxies be labelled heresies. For example, the Trinity was a concept in Christianity centuries in emerging. As a concept it purported to articulate the relation among God the Father, Jesus Christ, and the Spirit of God. As the Trinity migrates towards the orthodox centre and indeed begins to define it, other non-trinitarian conceptual articulations are forced outward, first into heterodoxy, then into heresy. The Arian Controversy in the fourth century CE was definitive in this regard.

Sometimes, however, the centre does not hold and a religion will divide against itself. Such divides occur in all religions, between Sunni and Shi'a Muslims, between Roman Catholicism and Eastern Orthodoxy, between Protestants and Roman Catholics, between Theraveda and Mahayana Buddhism. Of course, the source of the splits is not always doctrinal. Political and geographical factors may be more important, while doctrinal arguments are used as *ex post facto* justification. This was surely the case in the Anglican split from Roman Catholicism. The other issue involved in the creation and diffusion of religions is syncretism. Religions necessarily combine with a whole host of chthonic traditions and each ends up shaping the other in a process of territorialization.

What interests Deleuze and Guattari is precisely this possibility of change, the conditions under which something new might arise. Unlike classical thinkers of religion such as Durkheim, Weber, and Eliade, who define religion solely by its static tendencies, *A Thousand Plateaus* argues that religion has tendencies towards both stasis and change. In line with Puett's argument above, this tendency towards change is, additionally, not something opposed to religion that it acquires accidentally but part of the nature of religion itself. Deleuze and Guattari write,

> religion in general may very well compensate for its specific deterritorializations with a spiritual and even physical reterritorialization, which in the case of the holy war assumes the well-directed character of a conquest of the holy lands as the center of the world. Despite all that, when religion sets itself up as a war machine, it mobilizes and liberates a formidable charge of nomadism or absolute deterritorialization; it doubles migrant with an accompanying nomad, or with the potential nomad the migrant is in the process of becoming; and finally, it turns its dream of an absolute State back against the State-form. And this turning-against is no less part of the 'essence' of religion than that dream. (Deleuze and Guattari 1987: 383–384)

Just as a state has tendencies towards change that may manifest as a war machine, so a war machine has tendencies towards stasis that may manifest themselves in forming a state. Religious war machines are no different. A massive deterritorialization such as the Crusades sends people, language, food, customs, culture, and animals in wildly different directions through a process of invasion, capture, and negotiation. The energy spent in such an undertaking creates a desire to stabilize the gains made. This stabilization occurs on a spiritual level through conversion and the establishment of churches, and it also happens on a political level through the establishment of colonies and protectorates. Deterritorializations are followed by reterritorializations. Change is followed by stasis.

There is more to the story, though, and this is how religion can give rise to something new. This is the dream of an absolute state that turns against the state-form. What Deleuze and Guattari have in mind here is the shift in social formation that can occur in religion from a component of a state, to a war machine, to an ecumenical formation that encompasses heterogeneous social formations. At this level rather than religion being a component of the state, the state becomes a component of religion. Such a possibility for religion is evidenced by the global reach of Roman Catholicism. This is even more explicit if we look at the role that Roman Catholicism played in politics throughout much of Western Europe's history. Similar processes are at work in the history of Islam and remain in effect today, particularly in Iran. In the United States the grassroots mobilization of conservative Christians in an effort to populate local and state governments has shown the way in which a religion can turn against the state-form by encompassing heterogeneous social formations.

4. Religion and philosophy

Within the context provided by *A Thousand Plateaus* we can now look at the seemingly sharp opposition drawn between religion and philosophy in *What Is Philosophy?* Here the distinction that Deleuze and Guattari draw between 'figures', which religion produces, and 'concepts', which philosophy produces, strikingly parallels Hegel's distinction between *Vorstellung* (representation) and *Begriff* (concept). The stark opposition between figure and concept is further mirrored by the planes laid out by each. Figures lay out planes of transcendence and concepts lay out planes of immanence. Deleuze and Guattari write, 'Whenever there is transcendence, vertical Being, imperial State in the sky or on earth, there is religion; and there is Philosophy whenever there is immanence, even if it functions as arena for the agon and rivalry' (Deleuze and Guattari 1994: 43). The claim here reproduces one of the claims from *A Thousand Plateaus*, namely, that religion and the state-form are closely allied. As we saw in our discussion above, this alliance arises from the fact that both the state-form and religion are dependent on the process of territorialization. The process of territorialization is itself a process by which forces are gathered and stabilized. Importantly, though, this process of territorialization does not necessarily result in a plane of transcendence. As we've seen there is a nomadic territorialization that produces a smooth space rather than the striated space of the state-form. Not every regrouping of forces entails transcendence, but wherever there is transcendence there is religion.

It is also at this point that the parallels to Hegel break down. Concepts do not supersede figures for Deleuze and Guattari the way that concepts supersede representations for Hegel. There is no evolution of the concept for Deleuze and Guattari. The development of thought is contingent not necessary. 'The principle of reason such as it appears in philosophy is a principle of contingent reason and is put like this: there is no good reason but contingent reason; there is no universal history except of contingency' (Deleuze and Guattari 1994: 93). What follows from this, then, is not the succession in thought of religion by philosophy as Hegel (or even Durkheim) would have it. Rather, religion and philosophy are opposed tendencies of thought towards stasis and change, and while these tendencies are in principle separable, in actuality they will always be mixed. Spinoza comes closest to a 'pure' philosophy, but it remains for the most part a regulative idea. Deleuze and Guattari are explicit about the de facto mixtures of religion and philosophy when they write,

> Must we conclude from this that there is a radical opposition between figures and concepts? Most attempts to fix their differences express only ill-tempered judgments that are content to depreciate one or other of the terms: sometimes concepts are endowed with the prestige of reason while figures are referred to the night of the irrational and its symbols; sometimes figures are granted the privileges of spiritual life while concepts are relegated to the artificial movements of a dead understanding. And yet disturbing affinities appear on what seems to be a common plane of immanence. (Deleuze and Guattari 1994: 91)

There is a difference between figure and concept, but it is a difference in principle, a way of thinking about the two opposed tendencies present in any assemblage. Here we come face to face with what Deleuze and Guattari call a 'perceptual semiotics' in *A Thousand Plateaus* (Deleuze and Guattari 1987: 23). Perceptual semiotics is a methodology that proposes to see the world differently. The task of this methodology is not to divide the world into two sets of objects: concepts and figures. Rather, the task is to begin with assemblages and ask about the opposed tendencies contained within every assemblage. Thus every assemblage will have figural/religious tendencies and conceptual/philosophical tendencies, that is, tendencies towards stasis and change. This is Deleuze and Guattari's great insight, and this constitutes what they call elsewhere 'schizoanalysis'. The overwhelmingly dominant trend in the history of thought has been to focus the tendency towards stasis to the exclusion of the tendency towards change. What Deleuze and Guattari are proposing is a method by which the tendency towards change can be recognized, and recognized not merely as an adjunct to or privation of stasis but a primary tendency in its own right. The result of this methodology is an account of creation, an account of the new. A perceptual semiotics looks for the deterritorializing edges of any assemblage, the lines of flight, the zones of indiscernibility that indicate becoming. Schizoanalysis does not ask the question, 'What is it?' but 'What might it become?'

This methodology applies as much to religion as anything else. Deleuze and Guattari illustrate this further in *What Is Philosophy?* in discussing the long history of borrowings between philosophy and religion in the West. 'All that can be said is that figures tend toward concepts to the point of drawing infinitely near to them ... Perhaps Christianity does not produce concepts except through its atheism, through the atheism that it, more than any other religion, secretes ... There is always an atheism to be extracted from a religion' (Deleuze and Guattari 1994: 92). As Christianity initially tried to work through the nature of God's transcendence, it was continually caught between the apophatic silence of negative theology in which it could say nothing about God and a kataphatic theology that tended towards a transcendence denying pantheism. The reason for this is clear from Deleuze and Guattari's perspective. The figures of religion are not discrete but promiscuous. Even if their primary tendency is to stabilize and govern a plane of transcendence, they unavoidably have a deterritorializing edge that places a continuous pressure of mutation on them. Often the figures of religion are able to resist this pressure but sometimes the ratio of stasis and change tips over to the change side and the figure becomes a concept, becomes philosophical. This is what happened with Spinoza in relation to Jewish thought (Deleuze and Guattari 1994: 92).

Of course the reverse is also true. The concepts of philosophy can be captured by transcendence and mutate into a figure. 'And if it is true that figures tend toward concepts in this way, the converse is equally true, and philosophical concepts reproduce figures whenever immanence is attributed to something' (Deleuze and Guattari 1994: 92). Philosophical concepts are no more immune to becoming static representations than religious figures are safe from change. The methodological question of schizoanalysis remains the same regardless of the object. What are the lines of flight? Where is becoming blocked? Where is it possible? What heterogeneous connections are being made that might transform this assemblage? Deleuze and Guattari's flat ontology makes the same questions applicable to every assemblage whether conceptual, figural, geographic, or political.

5. Conclusion

Deleuze's theory of religion begins with a particular conception of territory, a conception that is not beholden to geography or law. Rather, this conception of territory is affective, intensive; it concerns the grouping and stabilization of forces. Most importantly, though, it is a conception of territory that does not presuppose the discontinuity of form and content. It is a hylozoic conception of territory. I have argued that this conception of territory makes possible a general theory of religion, a theory of religion that does not reproduce a fundamental dualism in which religion resides solely on the side of order in opposition to chaos. Certainly there is a tendency towards order in religion, which follows from its territorial nature. This tendency towards order, however, is not religion's sole tendency. Religion also has tendencies towards change. Religion surely has historically often been bound up as a component of the state-form, but this is not the only possible expression of religion. Just as territories can take on numerous possible social forms, so can religion.

Religion can transform from a component of the state into a war machine. The war machine can be recaptured by the state, or it can become ecumenical, international, so that the state becomes a component of religion. In keeping with current empirical research about the breadth of religious belief and practice, Deleuze's theory of religion allows for the possibility that every religion contains both the coded forces of order and the decoded forces of chaos. It is only to the degree that both of these tendencies are recognized that the possibilities of religion can be understood. It is only in this way that an analysis of religion can become a schizoanalysis of religion.

Notes

1 See also Lincoln (2012: 109–120).

2 I explore this issue at great length in my *Rethinking Philosophy and Theology with Deleuze: A New Cartography* (2013).

3 For references to Kant, I will use the Cambridge Edition translations. References to the first *Critique* will use the standard A/B references, while citations of Kant's other works will use the volume and page numbers from the *Gesammelte Schriften* Hrsg.: Bd. 1–29.

Bibliography

Adkins, Brent and Paul Hinlicky (2013) *Rethinking Philosophy and Theology with Deleuze: A New Cartography*. London: Bloomsbury.

Deleuze, Gilles and Félix Guattari (1987) *A Thousand Plateaus: Capitalism and Schizophrenia, vol. 2.*, trans. Brian Massumi. Minneapolis: University of Minnesota Press.

Deleuze, Gilles and Félix Guattari (1994) *What Is Philosophy?* Trans. Hugh Tomlinson and Graham Burchell. New York: Columbia University Press.

Henrich, Deiter (1989) 'Kant's Notion of a Deduction and the Methodological Background of the First Critique', in E. Forster (ed.), *Kant's Transcendental*

Deductions: The Three 'Critiques' and the 'Opus postumum'. Stanford, CA: Stanford University, pp. 20–46.

Kant, Immanuel (1992) *On the Form and Principles of the Sensible and the Intelligible World* [Inaugural Dissertation], eds. and trans. David Walford and Ralf Meerbote, Theoretical Philosophy, 1755–1770. Cambridge: Cambridge University Press, pp. 373–416.

Kant, Immanuel (1996) *Religion within the Boundaries of Mere Reason*, in *Religion and Rational Theology*, eds. and trans. Allen W. Wood and George di Giovanni. Cambridge: Cambridge University Press.

Kant, Immanuel (1998) *Critique of Pure Reason*, eds. and trans. Paul Guyer and Allen W. Wood. Cambridge: Cambridge University Press.

Lincoln, Bruce (2012) 'In Praise of the Chaotic', in *Gods and Demons, Priests and Scholars: Critical Explorations in the History of Religions*. Chicago: University of Chicago Press.

Puett, Michael J. (2012) 'Social Order or Social Chaos', in Robert A. Orsi (ed.), *Cambridge Companion to Religious Studies*. Cambridge: Cambridge University Press, pp. 109–130.

2

Schizoanalysis of the Eucharist: From Oedipal Repetition to Liberating Event

Kristien Justaert

1. Introduction: Politicizing the Eucharist

If one member suffers, all suffer together with it;
if one member is honoured, all rejoice together with it.

1 Cor 12: 26

Considered to be the very core of Christian liturgy, and even the 'fount and apex of Christian life' (*Lumen Gentium*, 11), the sacrament of the Eucharist is meant to create a community between the believer and God through the body of Christ. In consuming Christ's body and blood, the Christian believer – whether she is Catholic, Protestant, or Orthodox[1] – can share in the divine life. A reciprocal 'dwelling in each other' of Christ and the believer (Jn 6: 51–59) takes place during the event of the Eucharist. In this, the Eucharist seems to go further than merely making present the grace of God, which is the general function of the sacraments, and further than thanking and praising God, which is the etymological meaning of the word 'eucharist'. Nowadays, however, the Eucharist seems to have lost its charisma and divinizing character. The Catholic Spanish philosopher Xavier Zubiri discerned three problems with the sacrament of the Eucharist (Zubiri 1997).

The first and second difficulties are the *real presence* of Christ in the Eucharist and the *mode* of that presence. Indeed, more and more Christians cannot conceive of the meaning of the Eucharist other than in a (Protestant) metaphorical way, thinking that the bread and the wine merely *symbolize* Jesus' presence in their lives, instead of Jesus Christ being really present *as* bread and wine during the Eucharist, as Catholic Christians affirm with the doctrine of transubstantiation.[2]

The third problem concerns the formal reason for the Eucharist, namely, the possession of eternal life. In a context in which we are aware of our finitude more than ever, in times in which getting older and suffering have become taboos (both are seen as problems to be solved with euthanasia), and in times of outsourcing so many aspects of our lives to others under the pressure of consumption (Illich 1973), life itself (as it was/is expressed by Jesus Christ), let alone eternal life, although eagerly desired, seems far away. In short, the *relation of the sacrament of the Eucharist to life*, and in particular to the life of Jesus, is the core of the problem that I want to tackle in what follows.

In this contribution, I contend that an important reason for the difficulties people are having with the Eucharist nowadays, for the 'lack of life' in the Eucharist, lies in the sacrament being captured in an Oedipal logic of desire, thereby (1) confirming and repeating the patriarchy of the Church and, (2) through the mediation of the sacrament's life-giving power by a priest, preventing the sacrament from expressing and sharing life in an immediate way. Deleuze and Guattari's concept of schizoanalysis as a liberating process will serve as the tool to investigate this hypothesis. In using a 'materialist psychiatry', as Deleuze and Guattari describe schizoanalysis (1983: 22), I choose to highlight the realist and physical character of the Eucharist and of Catholic theology in general: the Eucharist is an event in which the spiritual and the material collide in the body of Christ.[3] However, it goes without saying that applying a concept of Deleuze and Guattari, two notorious anti-theological thinkers, to Christian theology is not self-evident. Indeed, how is it possible to engage a concept from an overtly atheist, immanent, and non-teleological worldview with a sacrament that belongs to an apparently hierarchically structured tradition with a transcendent view of the world? Although at first sight, Deleuze and Guattari's thought and any aspect of Christian theology seem absolutely irreconcilable, I believe that both share a passion for (divine) life and that, as I argued elsewhere (Justaert 2012: 5), there is a message of liberation and 'salvation' even in Deleuze and Guattari's philosophy, a plea for living a 'real' life, for leaving behind the world of representation, hierarchy, and oppression. In that respect, a Deleuzian reading of the Eucharist can be, in my account, 'worthy of the Christ-event'.[4]

Second, I use the process of schizoanalysis here as an *instrument* or a strategy of liberation, affirming Guattari's intuition that schizoanalysis has the potential for becoming a discipline for reading other systems of modelization – not as a general model, but as an instrument for deciphering systems of modelization in various other fields (Guattari 1998: 433). In that sense, Deleuze and Guattari serve as 'mediations' for theology, just as Karl Marx from the 1960s onwards has been a mediation for liberation theologians in their analysis of structures of oppression in Church and society. As a Catholic liberation theologian who considers liberation from any form of oppression to be the core of Christ's message, I'm particularly interested in how schizoanalysis lays bare oppressive dynamics in a phenomenon (such as the Eucharist) and tries to escape from those dynamics, thereby creating an alternative way of life. In this, the presupposition of my attempt is that the Eucharist is in itself a political act with public repercussions, and not a private, intimate communion with God which only concerns the individual believer. Although sharing a meal together is an event that takes place within the household, and although the Eucharist itself, in early Christianity, was also located in the context of the private house, the way we look at food as a product of a controlled industry or as something that nourishes us and gives us life, is an ethics that transcends the walls of our houses or our private life.

Moreover, in sharing his food and his life with his apostles during the Last Supper, Jesus refers to the vision of the kingdom of God *for everyone*. Indeed, as the Spanish theologian Casiano Floristán contends, the Eucharist is more about justice and solidarity than it is about devotion and adoration (Floristán 2007: 242). Given the political character of the act of Jesus himself in the Last Supper, evoking the vision of the kingdom of God that is 'not about food or drink, but about justice, peace, and joy in the Holy Spirit' (Rom 14: 17), leaving the Eucharist in a liturgical and/or institutional niche would be completely missing the point. Robert Karris goes as far as stating that 'Jesus was crucified because of how he ate' (Karris 1985: 47). Not only at the Last Supper, but also during his life before, the way Jesus ate had political consequences. In his sharing of meals with rich and poor, sinners and pagans, he evoked the revolutionary vision of the kingdom of God, transcending all human laws.[5] Using schizoanalysis as an instrument to critically engage with the way the Eucharist is performed will precisely allow me to treat the Eucharist as the political event that it actually is. Indeed, in developing the concept of schizoanalysis, Deleuze and Guattari worked from the conviction that 'the social investments are first in relation to the familial [read: private] investments, which result solely from the application or the reduction (*rabattement*) of the social investments' (1983: 274–275). A schizoanalysis of the Eucharist can therefore help us to transcend the intimate, safe boundaries of the Church.

Of course, there have been other theologians who approach the Eucharist with an agenda of liberation, such as Leonardo Boff (1987), Juan Luis

Segundo (1980), and nowadays especially William Cavanaugh, who pictures the Eucharist as an act of resistance against the contemporary economic globalization that enlarges the gap between the rich and the poor. According to Cavanaugh, the sacrament of the Eucharist produces 'catholicity' (which literally translated means 'on the whole' – a very specific kind of 'globalization') by bringing together the members of the Church, 'regardless of age, race, sex, language, or social class' (Cavanaugh 1999: 190), and is thereby a liberating act of resistance against the logic of global capitalism in which globalization incorporates individualization, competition, and flexibility. The universality expressed in the Eucharist is a local form of universality, centralized around the body of Christ. Cavanaugh refers to Henri de Lubac's reflections on catholicity: '"Catholic" … suggests an idea of an organic whole, of a cohesion, of a firm synthesis, of a reality which is not scattered but, on the contrary, turned toward a center which assures its unity, whatever the expanse in area or the internal differentiation might be' (De Lubac 1982: 174).

Although Cavanaugh's analysis of globalization is, in my view, correct, Deleuze and Guattari would charge him with an inability to escape from the control of desire and life that is performed by global capitalism. The centralized universality that Cavanaugh opposes to economic globalization, and to which he wishes to return, shares in this controlling aspect of global capitalism. Indeed, in the eyes of Deleuze and Guattari, Cavanaugh is right in his analysis of the problem, but his solution would entail a regression to what they call 'the despotic regime' with a strict hierarchy, or worse, it could confirm the capitalist regime by maintaining the Oedipal 'law of the father'.[6] Moreover, Cavanaugh does not respond to the questions posed above about the traditional meaning of the Eucharist – he assumes the 'truth' and effectiveness of the sacrament of the Eucharist as it was agreed upon around the fourth century CE, and 'simply' rethinks, or rather, recontextualizes, its meaning. Nevertheless, Deleuze would (hypothetically) agree with Cavanaugh on the political significance of the (traditionally private event of the) Eucharist. Indeed, as mentioned above, the point of departure of schizoanalysis contains the thesis that structures in society define intimate relations, and not the other way around, as psychoanalysts argue. Even if their worldviews radically differ, Deleuze's and Cavanaugh's alternatives can thus be considered as operating on the same metaphysical level. At this level, Cavanaugh could use Slavoj Žižek's argument to argue against Deleuze and Guattari that, with their immanent, non-hierarchical metaphysics, they lengthen the era of capitalist exploitation rather than fight it, in that they no longer think a centre, a subject that could resist capitalist oppression (Žižek 2004). In Cavanaugh's Catholic narrative, the subject of resistance would be the local community of faith, gathered around the body of Christ. Deleuze and Guattari, however, think that only a collective body (or machine) in the margins that is not hierarchically structured has the ability to 'escape' the dominant logic of capitalism. For them, the subject is always an Oedipal subject whose desires are controlled by the capitalist logic.

My goal here is to bring out the critical potential of the Eucharist, to liberate the sacrament by turning to an approach which has not yet been applied to it, by performing a schizoanalysis of this sacrament. The 'event' of a schizoanalysis (indeed, it is more than an instrument or a method, since it also entails an ethics and a metaphysics) seems to be perfectly suited for a liberation theological approach to the Eucharist. As a revolutionary and liberating movement, schizoanalysis, as I will try to demonstrate, is a fruitful mediation for liberation theology to envision a Eucharist that is truly life-giving.

There is no clear algorithm of a schizoanalysis, or a manual to follow, which has to do with the nature of the task, as will become clear in the following reflections on schizoanalysis. Since the concept of schizoanalysis has been created as an answer to, or rather the creative dealing with, some paramount problems Deleuze and Guattari saw in psychoanalysis, a critique of psychoanalysis as a system of oppression is an important part of schizoanalysis. I will thus analyse four core aspects of psychoanalysis that have been critiqued and taken up and transformed by Deleuze and Guattari into schizoanalysis, namely Oedipus, patriarchy, the unconscious, and repetition. Moreover, these four aspects are all involved in our understanding of the Eucharist. By looking at the Eucharist through these four concepts, first from a psychoanalytical perspective and then within the process of schizoanalysis, the liberating potential of schizoanalysis will uncover how the Eucharist is a political, in addition to a liturgical, reality. By way of conclusion, I will formulate a tentative answer to the problems with the Eucharist formulated in the introduction.

2. Psychoanalysis of the Eucharist

Deleuze and Guattari have developed their schizoanalysis in critical dialogue with psychoanalysis; it would be unsophisticated to state that they have always simply opposed psychoanalysis. As Leen De Bolle states, 'In spite of his detailed and far reaching debates with psychoanalytical theory, Deleuze can hardly be reduced to a critic of psychoanalysis alone' (De Bolle 2010: 7). Their main critique has been that psychoanalysis 'breaks up all productions of desire and crushes all formations of utterances' (Deleuze and Parnet 1987: 77). This is not the place to embark on an analysis of Deleuze and Guattari's relationship with psychoanalysis in all its detail, nor will I use the works of Freud, Lacan, or other known psychoanalysts to refine or correct Deleuze and Guattari's interpretation of psychoanalysis; their critique of psychoanalysis will become clear in our application of it to the Eucharist.

Psychoanalysis can be considered as a liberating movement in itself: the process is meant to liberate women and men from all kinds of self-deception and illusions they hold about themselves, their desires and relations. In this respect, the outcome of a 'psychoanalysis of the Eucharist' will reveal the power dynamics and possible hidden agendas behind the performance of this sacrament. But the consciousness of certain power dynamics doesn't necessarily lead to revolt. 'Psychoanalysts teach infinite resignation, they are the last priests (no, there will be others after them)', says Deleuze and Parnet (1987: 81–82). Although a psychoanalytical account of the Eucharist might point to some insights into how this sacrament works in terms of power relations, it continues to affirm these hierarchy and power dynamics within the Eucharist, making it difficult to escape these dynamics and rethink the Eucharist as a life-giving event instead of a certain formation that controls desire. In what follows, I will try to demonstrate how the Eucharist works according to an Oedipal structuring of the unconscious, thereby confirming patriarchy and endlessly repeating it.

2.1. Oedipus and patriarchy

When linking the Eucharist with the dynamics of the family – which is not so strange since the Eucharist – and liturgy in general – originally took place within the sphere of the household – the Christian believer who receives the Eucharist is put in the place of the child, whereas the father is the priest (or, by extension, the Church) and the mother is God or Christ: the Eucharist is an actualization of the Oedipal triangle. This model, and in particular the not-so-evident identification of the mother with Christ, makes sense from a theological standpoint; in the gospel, believers are often referred to as 'children'.[7] And although Jesus himself referred to God as his father, the institutionalized Church has taken over the role of father, leaving the immediate connection of the believer with God through Christ to the maternal domain.[8] Indeed, throughout the history of theology, nourishment and giving life, in general, are often associated with the mother, especially in the gospels and in the writings of the Church fathers during the first centuries after Christ. Liturgical theologian Teresa Berger points out that whenever Jesus was told in the Bible to feed people, he performed a female task (Berger 2011: 70). The Eucharist, in which Jesus gives his own body as food to his disciples, is the peak of the identification of Christ with the mother: in early Christianity, the blood of Jesus was identified with breast milk, because 'giving one's own body as food is precisely what mothers do when nursing' (Berger 2011: 72), and breast milk was assumed to be the mother's blood 'now heated and thus turned white' (Berger 2011: 72). References have also been found to 'the breasts of God'(!), indicating that 'Christ's body given and his blood shed are understood as a mother's gift of her own body, in nurture of a child's life' (Berger 2011: 85).[9]

After having given all who participate in the Eucharistic event their role in the Oedipal triangle, it's now time to see how the power dynamics of the Eucharist works. From a psychoanalytical perspective, the Eucharist is an oral act, aimed at unification with Jesus Christ. Eating Jesus Christ is a unifying movement that internalizes God, or Life itself,[10] for the believer. The relation between God and the believer can be understood by looking at the pre-Oedipal relation of the child and her mother. In the pre-Oedipal phase, the subject is not yet taken up in the symbolic order of language, law, and representation. In the eyes of Deleuze and Guattari the 'problem' (the territorializing restriction of desire) emerges when the father, or the priest, comes into play and interrupts the bond between mother and child. In order for the child to have a 'healthy' or 'normal' relationship with the symbolic order, she has to pass through the Oedipal phase and solve the Oedipus complex. According to Freud (1913), the Oedipus complex is solved by installing two fundamental laws that lie at the basis of every society, namely the prohibition of incest and the prohibition of parricide. Incest and parricide thus become repressed desires in the unconscious. First, and translated into Eucharistic terms, the prohibition of incest can be interpreted as a movement of preventing the unification with Christ. In this respect, the Church has always been suspicious of mystics as well. Second, the prohibition of parricide confirms the authority of the priest and the Church, an authority that cannot be questioned. Within this logic, Jesus Christ himself is oppressed and relegated to the domain of the unconscious. The one closest to the mother/Christ is, eventually, the father/priest who controls the relation of mother and child, of God and the believer. From this perspective, it is not a coincidence that, in Catholicism at least, there can only be male priests: the male child will eventually identify with his father and follow in his footsteps. In other words, girls are denied access to the divine life (the mother) and access to power (the father), whereas boys can eventually have access to power. Solving the Oedipus complex, that is, becoming a 'good' Christian, introduces the child in the patriarchal order of the Church; the child turns away from the mother-God and accepts the law of the father-church.

Psychoanalysis, in laying bare the power balance within the sacrament of the Eucharist from an Oedipal perspective, affirms the positions of power of the priest and the Church as representations of the symbolic, law-giving order. There is a focus on power and intimate power relations, rather than on divine life. The mother is defined in negative terms, as castrated, as a lesser being (Blake 2009: 18), whereas the divine life can be found in the pre-Oedipal unification with the mother. As Jesus pointed out in the Gospels, it is the children who show us the kingdom of God, and who will be the first to 'arrive' there: 'Truly I say to you, unless you are converted and become like children, you will not enter the kingdom of heaven' (Mt 18:3).[11] Referring to the life of infants, Deleuze described what 'a Life' means to him: pure life is a life without subjectivity, towards which everyone is attracted and yet which itself remains completely neutral, a bundle of possibilities: 'Infants all resemble one another and have hardly any individuality; but they do have singularities – a smile, a gesture, a grimace – such events are not subjective traits. Infants are traversed by an immanent life which is pure power' (Deleuze 2007: 391). The baby does not yet have characteristics; she is an unmediated expression of pure life. From this perspective, it could be argued, even on theological grounds, that the Eucharist should be performed by a *mother*, rather than a priest.

However, the centrality of the figure of Oedipus, and thereby the father, means that the believer's union with Christ always has to be mediated by the law of the Church (the priest) and can never be free and direct. The Eucharist, each time it is performed, reproduces and repeats patriarchy and thereby a form of oppression. Of course, one might say that a child needs this kind of mediation in order to be capable of living within the community of believers (the symbolic order): a law is necessary to develop individuals into independent human beings, and to bind and regulate a community. Initially, however, the Eucharist and the Church shouldn't perform this task. The Eucharist is precisely not directed at the 'child' becoming an independent adult, but at an extreme form of dependence on, or unification with, Jesus Christ. Moreover, according to the gospel narratives, Jesus himself has never hesitated to question and transgress the law.[12] Consequently, the community Jesus envisioned was radically different from what one would usually expect: a community based on a shared identity (e.g. the Jewish community in which Jesus operated, as depicted in the gospels). Jesus formed a community of free human beings who were radically different but who were united through their vision of the kingdom of God. Criticizing the role of the father, the gateway to the symbolic order, is questioning the essence of a community and of life in a society. Psychoanalysis favours the therapy room in which the power dynamics are made explicit: 'Everything that happens in psychoanalysis in the analyst's consulting room is true. What happens elsewhere is derived or secondary' (Deleuze and Parnet 1987: 86). In the same way, when following a psychoanalytical perspective, the event of the Eucharist reveals the truth (of patriarchy) and should be a model for the dynamics of the outside world. But I already mentioned the reversal of schizoanalysis that draws the Eucharist out of its safe niche within the Church and links it inextricably to power dynamics on 'the world'. For Deleuze and Guattari, psychoanalytical logic supports a capitalist structuring of our desires, understood in terms of lack, and in that sense, the Eucharist working according to these patriarchal 'laws' of psychoanalysis also has severe political consequences.

Translated into Marxist terms, Deleuze and Guattari state that the worker becomes alienated from her product because of the dynamics of capitalism, just as the child is separated from her mother because of the intervention of the priest. In other words, the Oedipal relations within a family (here: the Church) are reflections of the relations within a capitalist society:

> The alliances and filiations no longer pass through people but through money; so the family becomes a microcosm, suited to expressing what it no longer dominates. In a certain sense the situation has not changed; for what is invested through the family is still the economic, political, and cultural social field, its breaks and flows. Private persons are an illusion, images of images or derivatives of derivatives. But in another sense everything has changed, because the family, instead of constituting and developing the dominant factors of social reproduction, is content to apply and envelop these factors in its own mode of reproduction. Father, mother, and child thus become the simulacrum of the images of capital ('"Mister Capital, Madame Earth," and their child the Worker'), with the result that these images are no longer recognized at all in the desire that is determined to invest only their simulacrum. The familial determinations become the application of the social axiomatic. The family becomes the subaggregate to which the whole of the social field is applied. (1983: 264–265)

By shedding a psychoanalytical light on the phenomenon of the Eucharist, I have tried to show in what ways the Eucharist captures and controls the power of the life of Christ instead of making it more intense – as a schizoanalysis will try to do. Indeed, performing a schizoanalysis on the Eucharist is not just a game or a non-committal experiment; it performs a critique on the capitalist and Oedipal logic that has pervaded the Church and that is in its core oppressive, not only towards the believer but towards God's very self, who is imprisoned in a forbidden unconscious. To liberate the Eucharist from this logic, thus, at the same time, entails enabling the life of Christ to become present and to form (or even to become) a community of resistance against the capitalist structuring of desire. So whereas Deleuze and Guattari's tactics, and their 'theology' of free desire/life, would be opposed to that of Cavanaugh, their political aim coincides. Christianity imagines an alternative way of structuring desire that is radically opposed to capitalist configurations, and the Eucharist, when schizoanalysed, could be the core of that alternative expression.

2.2. Repetition and the unconscious

An Oedipal structuring of desire results in the reproduction of sameness. This is what Freud called the 'repetition compulsion', which he connected to the death drive. Unresolved conflicts from the past keep on repeating themselves through the course of our lives (1920). Repetition is linked to the unconscious of a subject, to the past of that subject, to the *particular* past of that subject. In the psychoanalytical tradition, the unconscious, a remnant of our pre-Oedipal past, becomes tamed and controlled through the formation of an 'Ego', a subject that functions on the level of representation. Indeed, all forms of immediacy become repressed by the Ego that mediates and represents itself through language in the symbolic order or in culture. From now on, our desires will have to be mediated (and thus represented) by the laws of the symbolic order which install a patriarchal community. Deleuze and Guattari interpret Freud's notion of the unconscious negatively. For them, Freud considers the unconscious as a chaotic pool of perverse desires that needs to be 'civilized' and controlled. In Deleuze's words, 'The fact is that psychoanalysis talks a lot about the unconscious – it even discovered it. But in practice, it always diminishes, destroys and exorcises it. The unconscious is understood as a negative, it's the enemy' (1987: 77). The unconscious needs to be covered up by the formation of a subject who can successfully repress this unconscious. Psychoanalysis dispossesses the unconscious of its productive power and thereby depoliticizes it. 'The productive unconscious makes way for an unconscious that knows only how to express itself – express itself in myth, in tragedy, in dream' (1983: 54). From Deleuze's perspective, the oppressed desire in the unconscious constantly urges the subject into a movement of repetition understood as 'generality', as reproduction of the same.[13]

Already on the first pages of *Difference and Repetition*, Deleuze introduces a different notion of repetition, opposed to one based on remembrance, representation, and resemblance: 'Repetition and resemblance are different in kind – extremely so' (2004: 1). Real repetitions 'do not add a second and a third time to the first, but carry the first time to the "nth" power.... As Péguy says, it is not Federation Day which commemorates or represents the fall of the Bastille, but the fall of the Bastille which celebrates and repeats in advance all the Federation Days' (Péguy 1917: 45, 114 in 2004: 2). This has interesting implications when applied to the Eucharist, giving the Christian event a force worthy of Jesus' own life. Interpreting the repetition of the Eucharist would no longer entail the repetition of an act of Jesus in the past, always using the exact same words that can only be uttered by a person given the authority to do so, that is, the priest. Paraphrasing Deleuze, we could say that it is not the Eucharist which commemorates and repeats the event of Christ, but the event of Jesus Christ's life, death, and resurrection which celebrates and repeats in advance all Eucharists (Justaert 2012: 83). In the next section, I will explore the consequences of this understanding more thoroughly.

3. Schizoanalysis of the Eucharist

In *Anti-Oedipus*, Deleuze and Guattari write as follows: 'Our definition of schizoanalysis focused on two aspects: the destruction of the expressive pseudo forms of the unconscious, and the discovery of desire's unconscious investments of the social field' (1983: 167). A schizoanalysis of the Eucharist thus has as its aim to (1) detect forms of oppression of the unconscious desire, and (2) to analyse the investment of desire in the Eucharist (i.e. the way the believer shares in the life of Jesus Christ) on a political level. A mediated form of connection with Christ on the level of representation that is controlled by the priest reflects a capitalist structuring of desire, whereas an immediate sharing of life with Christ could create a community[14] that is able to escape and resist the controlling logic of capitalism, producing new forms of life.

3.1. Escaping Oedipus: The rhizomal production of desire

While an Oedipal account of the Eucharist reduces the sacrament to a form of inner transformation (as psychoanalysis does), escaping the Oedipus complex entails a politicization, an externalization, of the flows of desire involved in the Eucharistic sacrament. Desire is no longer something that needs to be oppressed in the darker domains of the unconscious, controlled and mediated by the Church; it expresses the intensity of the life of Jesus Christ within the community of Christian believers. Deleuze and Guattari understand desire as a force, as life itself – a collective flow, a form of production and intensification of life. Desire is an immanent, horizontal 'workplace' (De Bolle 2010: 16) where new connections can be made that express the power of life. Interpreting desire as a lack, as psychoanalysis does, results in a hierarchical power dynamics which affirms controlling laws and strictly regulates and mediates the flows of desire. Applied to the Eucharist, a psychoanalytic understanding of desire (which appears to be quite common in Christian tradition) prevents the believer from having direct contact with the divine (the free flow of desire). Schizoanalysis not only liberates the believer from the patriarchal construction she is forced into but also liberates Jesus (Life itself) from the golden cage into which he has been put by the laws of the Church. Ecclesial hierarchy (the 'tree'), executing sacraments on the level of representation, is replaced by direct connection with Jesus Christ on a horizontal level (the 'rhizome') – 'performing' the sacrament. Indeed, within the context of schizoanalysis, one cannot talk any longer about 'unification' with Christ.

Against the logic of psychoanalysis, Deleuze and Guattari reject the idea of a primordial unity (of the child and the mother within the Oedipal triangle): 'We no longer believe in the myth of the existence of fragments that, like pieces of an antique statue, are merely waiting for the last one to be turned up, so that they may all be glued back together to create a unity that is precisely the same as the original unity. We no longer believe in a primordial totality that once existed, or in a final totality that awaits us at some future date' (1983: 42). This is why the figure of Jesus Christ is problematic for Deleuze and Guattari – they call him despotic: within their metaphysics, there is no qualitative difference between Christ and ourselves – there could only be a quantitative difference concerning the degree of intensity running through us. In a rhizome, there is no hierarchy. During a schizoanalysed Eucharist, Jesus Christ becomes the community and the other way around: the community becomes Jesus Christ in its sanctioning of desires to flow freely. So although it might seem at first sight that doing away with the mediation of the Church makes the Eucharist into a very intimate, private event of unification, seen from a Deleuzian standpoint, this is not at all the case. Liberating oneself from Oedipus and the law of the father opens up an impersonal field of desires which no longer belong to individuals, so that the 'most intimate' equals the 'most universal'. Mysticism is allowed again, and the sacrament of the Eucharist expresses what Origen calls the 'Logos', the differentiating power of God, mapping out the soul's transformative 'becoming-divine' (Higgins 2010).

3.2. Repetition and the unconscious

The unconscious no longer belongs to a single individual. With their critique of the Oedipal logic, Deleuze and Guattari wanted 'to discover beneath the familial reduction the nature of the social investments of the unconscious' (1983: 271). As already pointed at above, the Oedipal logic is intrinsically linked to capitalist social investments (the latter coming first for Deleuze and Guattari), indicating that to escape from the Oedipus complex opens up the ability[15] to escape from capitalism and to 'produce' another kind of community or (in Deleuzian) assemblage. The unconscious doesn't need to be repressed, nor should it be represented – it should be produced (1987: 78). And production is created through repetition.

Deleuze has a particular understanding of repetition, influenced by Bergson and Nietzsche, and opposed to Freud's conception of it. Repetition for Deleuze is not the reappearance of sameness – as would be the case in the Eucharist if one focuses on the visible laws of the liturgy, namely, that every time the Eucharist is performed, the exact same words come out of the mouth of a priest. In Deleuze's understanding of repetition, what is stressed is the *productivity* of the repeated event, rather than the *conservation*. So what is repeated in Deleuze's repetition is not the particularity of a certain event, but the *productive power* of it, the intensity of it. If the event of Jesus Christ was powerful enough, that is, if Life was expressed in the life of Jesus Christ, if there was a free flow of desire in him, then that power will be repeated each time we tune in on his wavelength during the Eucharist, transcending the patriarchal laws and prescriptions which the Church holds on to concerning this sacrament. Contrary to a Eucharistic sacrament dictated by laws, Deleuze would appear to bring the Eucharist back to what it really is: a miracle (Justaert 2012: 83):

> If repetition is possible, it is due to a miracle rather than to law. It is against the law: against the similar form and the equivalent content of law. If repetition can be found, even in nature, it is in the name of a power which affirms itself

> against the law, which works underneath laws, perhaps superior to laws. If repetition exists, it expresses at once a singularity opposed to the general, a universality opposed to the particular, a distinctive opposed to the ordinary, an instantaneity opposed to variation and an eternity opposed to permanence. In every respect, repetition is a transgression. It puts law into question, it denounces its nominal or general character in favour of a more profound and more artistic reality. (2004: 3)

The eternal life that is being given to the believer during the Eucharist is not a particular life, but a singular life – the universal Life that she shares with Jesus and with everyone. This is not some kind of vague power. Indeed, the life expressed by Jesus was and remains very concrete. In the process of a repetition, the universal and the singular are being united, 'which dethrones every general law; dissolves the mediations and annihilates the particulars subjected to the law' (2004: 8).

When schizoanalysed, the Eucharist becomes an event of immediate sharing with the life (of Jesus Christ), a 'becoming-Jesus' or 'becoming-divine', as Deleuze and Guattari might call it. The transformation that occurs during the Eucharist affects all parties participating in it: it is not an inner transformation, but an ethical or political one, as radical as going from vertical hierarchy to horizontal community. It entails a giving up of our particular desires in order to liberate a greater, impersonal desire in the movement of becoming-divine.

4. Conclusion: Elements of a liberation theology of the Eucharist

By way of conclusion, I will revisit the problems with the Eucharist indicated by Zubiri that I discussed at the beginning of this text and formulate some concluding reflections on them. I do so by entering into the perspective of the schizoanalytical approach, which I have shown is a preferred paradigm through which to interpret the Eucharist.

Concerning the problem of the real presence of Jesus Christ during the Eucharist and its mode (problems one and two), it is possible to affirm both a material and a spiritual presence of Jesus Christ from a Deleuzian perspective. Indeed, during the Eucharist, in repeating the intensity of Jesus' life, the community becomes Jesus Christ as Jesus Christ becomes the community. The community incarnates the intensity of the divine life expressed in Jesus. It is not a coincidence that *anamnesis*, the Greek word for 'remembrance', as expressed by Jesus during his Last Supper when he told his disciples to 'do this in remembrance of me' (Lk 22:19), actually means the *making present* of a past event. The Eucharist not only makes us contemporaries with Christ; it makes us Christ. Since Jesus spoke these words right before he was killed by the political powers of his time, Cavanaugh rightly points out that 'the Eucharist becomes a ritual maintenance of the "dangerous memory" of Jesus' confrontation with the powers' (Cavanaugh 2001: 182). The Eucharist, being a political act, thus invites us to discern oppressive powers in our lives and to liberate God from them, feeding the divine life just in the way Jesus Christ has done. As Augustine wrote in his *Confessions*, 'I am the food of the fully grown; grow and you will feed on me. And you will not change me into you like the food your flesh eats, but you will be changed into me' (Confessions, X 16).

Through this process, eternal life is expressed (problem three). Eternal life, however, is not linked to individual subjects. 'There is no subject of desire, any more than there is an object. There is no subject of enunciation' (1987: 78). Eternal life is the impersonal flow of desire, which can only be expressed by the production of it by communities or, in Deleuze and Guattari's term, machines. A schizoanalysis of the Eucharist transforms the essence of our understanding of a community. The core of a community is a *communion*, a shared but impersonal Life, the divine life, repeated and intensified through each Eucharist, creating the strength to resist and escape from oppressive power dynamics.

Notes

1 That is called the Eucharist in Catholicism, the offering in Orthodox Christianity, and the Holy Supper by Protestants.

2 Transubstantiation is the Catholic doctrine that states that during the Eucharist, the bread is transformed into the body of Christ, and the wine becomes Christ's blood – even if it cannot be perceived by the senses.

3 Aloysius Pieris refers to the Eucharist as a 'bio-social act', see Pieris (1998: 28).

4 See Deleuze (1990: 149).

5 Cf. C. Floristán (2007: 247): '[From the beginnings of the Church] ... Women, slaves, and baptized pagans were present at the eucharistic meals, alongside and therefore equal to men, free persons, and Jewish converts to the Christian faith'. See also Mk 7:8–9, in which Jesus distinguishes human and divine laws, stressing the relativity of human laws and traditions vis-à-vis the transcendent laws of God.

6 In *A Thousand Plateaus*, Deleuze and Guattari indeed refer to Jesus as an example of a paranoid despot (ATP 184).
7 See, for example, 1 Jn 3:2, Mt 5:9; Mt 13:38.
8 Within contemporary Christian theology, the Eucharist can be interpreted as a sacrifice or as a meal. Although both perspectives on the Eucharist can be said to be 'life-giving', I focus on the meal aspect of the Eucharist, thereby connecting to both ancient (Church fathers) and postmodern interpretations. See Lash (1974).
9 See also Berger (2011: 79):

> Taking all these various textual references together (and more could be added), one might say that although the image of God nursing the faithful with mother's milk is sporadic in early Christian writings, the image does appear repeatedly, in diverse contexts, and in key writers – Clement of Alexandria, Irenaeus of Lyons, and Augustine of Hippo are not marginal figures in the Christian tradition.

10 See, for example, Mt 4:4; Jn 6:35; Jn 8:12; Jn 11, 25–26; Jn 14:6.
11 It is in this respect that the French psychoanalyst Julia Kristeva interprets the pre-Oedipal 'eros' as the core of Christianity instead of an understanding of love as 'agape'. See Kristeva (1983).
12 See, for example, Lk 22:37.
13 The French Catholic theologian Henri De Lubac precisely describes the Eucharist as an action in which the Church constantly reproduces itself. De Lubac criticized accounts of the Eucharist which reduce the event to a symbol or a moment of authoritative presence (De Lubac 1949; Pickstock 1999).
14 Deleuze and Guattari would use the concept of 'machine' instead of 'community'. Claire Colebrook defines the machine in contrast to the organism elegantly: 'An organism is a bounded whole with an identity and an end. A mechanism is a closed machine with a specific function. A machine, however, is nothing more than its connections; it is not made by anything, it is not for anything, and has no closed identity.' See Colebrook (2002: 56).
15 See Deleuze and Guattari (1983: 341), 'The schizo is not revolutionary, but the schizophrenic process – in terms of which the schizo is merely the interruption, or the continuation in the void – is the potential for revolution.'

Bibliography

Augustinus, Aurelius (1992) *Confessions, Book I*, trans. H. Chadwick. New York: Oxford University Press.

Berger, Teresa (2011) *Gender Differences and the Making of Liturgical History. Lifting a Veil on Liturgy's Past*. Farnham: Ashgate.

Blake, Kathryn M. (2009) *A Contemporary Feminist Critique of Psychoanalysis through Gilles Deleuze and Félix Guattari* (unpublished thesis, Rutgers, The State University of New Jersey), New Brunswick. http://rucore.libraries.rutgers.edu/rutgers-lib/25764/.

Boff, Leonardo (1987) *Sacraments of Life: Life of the Sacraments*, trans. J. Drury. Oregon: Oregon Catholic Press.

Cavanaugh, William T. (1999) 'The World in a Wafer: A Geography of the Eucharist as Resistance to Globalization', *Modern Theology* 15:2, pp. 181–196.

Cavanaugh, William T. (2001) 'Dying for the Eucharist of Being Killed by It? Romero's Challenge to First-World Christians', *Theology Today* 58:2, pp. 177–189.

Colebrook, Claire (2002), *Gilles Deleuze* (Routledge Critical Thinkers), London: Routledge.

De Bolle, Leen (2010) 'Desire and Schizophrenia', in L. De Bolle (ed.), *Deleuze and Psychoanalysis. Philosophical Essays on Deleuze's Debate with Psychoanalysis*. Leuven: Leuven University Press, pp. 7–32.

De Lubac, Henri (1949) *Corpus Mysticum: L'Eucharistie et l'Eglise au Moyen-Âge*. Paris: Aubier-Montaigne.

De Lubac, Henri (1982) *The Motherhood of the Church*, trans. Sr Sergia Englund. San Francisco, CA: Ignatius Press.

Deleuze, Gilles (1990), *Logic of Sense*, trans. M. Lester and C. Stivale. New York: Columbia University Press.

Deleuze, Gilles (2004), *Difference and Repetition*, trans. P. Patton. London-New York: Continuum.

Deleuze, Gilles (2007) 'Immanence: A Life', in G. Deleuze (ed.), *Two Regimes of Madness. Texts and Interviews 1975–1995*, New York: Semiotext(e), pp. 388–393.

Deleuze, Gilles and Félix Guattari (1983) *Anti-Oedipus: Capitalism and Schizophrenia*, trans. Hurley, M. Seem and H.R. Lane. Minneapolis: University of Minnesota Press (abbreviated as AO followed by page number).

Deleuze, Gilles and Félix Guattari (1987) *A Thousand Plateaus: Capitalism and Schizophrenia*, trans. B. Massumi. Minneapolis: University of Minnesota Press (abbreviated as ATP followed by page number).

Deleuze, Gilles and Claire Parnet (1987) *Dialogues*, trans. H. Tomlinson and B. Habberjam. New York: Columbia University Press (abbreviated as D followed by page number).

Floristán, Casiano (2007) 'The Place of the Poor in the Eucharistic Assembly', in D.G. Groody (ed.), *The Option for the Poor in Christian Theology*. Notre Dame: University of Notre Dame Press, pp. 239–258.

Freud, Sigmund (1913) 'Totem and Taboo', in J. Strachey (ed.), *The Standard Edition of the Complete Psychological Works of Sigmund Freud*, Vol. 13. London: The Hogarth Press and The Institute of Psychoanalysis, pp. 1–100.

Freud, Sigmund (1920) 'Beyond the Pleasure Principle. Group Psychology and Other Works', in J. Strachey (ed.), *The Standard Edition of the Complete Psychoanalytical*

Works of Sigmund Freud, Vol. 18. London: The Hogarth Press and The Institute of Psychoanalysis, pp. 3–66.

Guattari, Félix (1998) 'Schizoanalysis', trans. M. Zayani, *The Yale Journal of Criticism* 11:2, pp. 433–439.

Higgins, Luke (2010) 'A Logos without Organs: Cosmologies of Transformation in Origen and Deleuze-Guattari', *SubStance* 39:1, pp. 141–153.

Illich, Ivan (1973) *Tools for Conviviality*. New York: Harper and Row.

Justaert, Kristien (2012) *Theology after Deleuze*. London and New York: Continuum.

Karris, Robert J. (1985) *Luke: Artist and Theologian*. New York: Paulist Press.

Kristeva, Julia (1983) *Histoires d'amour*. Paris: Denoël.

Lash, Nicholas (1974) *His Presence in the World. A Study of Eucharistic Worship and Theology*. London: Sheed and Ward.

Lumen Gentium. Dogmatic Constitution on the Church (1964) http://www.vatican.va/archive/hist_councils/ii_vatican_council/documents/vat-ii_const_19641121_lumen-gentium_en.html.

Pickstock, Catherine (1999) 'Thomas Aquinas and the Eucharist', *Modern Theology* 15:2, pp. 159–180.

Pieris, Aloysius (1998) *God's Reign for God's Poor. A Return to the Jesus Formula* (2nd revised edition), Kelaniya: Tulana Research Center.

Segundo, Juan Luis (1980) *The Sacraments Today*, trans. J. Drury. Dublin: Gill and Macmillan.

Žižek, Slavoj (2004) *Body without Organs. On Deleuze and Consequences*. New York: Routledge.

Zubiri, Xavier (1997) *Theological Reflections on the Eucharist*, trans. M. D'Ambrosio, http://www.zubiri.org/works/eucharst.htm.

3

Divine Life: Difference, Becoming, and the Trinity

Christopher Ben Simpson

1. Deleuze's divine difference engine

There is no room for God, as traditionally understood, in the Deleuzian chaosmos (Clark 1999: 180). There is in Deleuze's thought, however, another divine, a different absolute, an atheistic sense of the absolute (Deleuze and Guattari 1987: 383). Deleuze's absolute is absolute difference; difference is unknowable, inexplicable, 'transcendent', the sole transcendental (Clark 1999: 190; Milbank 2006: 301, 306). In his pluralist monism there is only 'one' 'thing': difference – a 'many' that dissolves (and constructs) all 'things' – as Daniel Smith describes it: 'a kind of Spinozism *minus* substance, a purely modal or differential universe' (Smith 2001: 175). This 'ontology of difference' as a continuous revolution against any static structures is an axiomatic fundamental ontology 'which fixes its gaze on difference as the condition of possibility for thought and action' (Milbank 2006: 260, 279; Justaert 2011: 533). With being itself (which is never itself) as difference, as 'continuously differentiating force' (Justaert 2011), the univocity of being, what it is, is difference, equivocity (Smith 2001: 179). What is primordial is the 'pure heterogeneity' of difference (Hallward 2006: 12; Milbank 2006: 306). This is why Deleuze so naturally replaced univocity with the logic of 'and' in *A Thousand Plateaux* (Smith 2001: 180). This absolute difference is not Hegelian negativity 'which', as Baugh writes, 'makes "difference" into a passing "moment" of Being "contradicting itself" *via* its multiple determinations in the "Absolute Idea"' but a logic of affirmative difference (Baugh 2009: 130). Difference itself as absolute is not subordinate to any unity, dialectical or otherwise.

This difference, however, is not a mere abstraction; it is a life. Difference and life are fundamentally connected (Dosse 2010: 139). In Deleuze's 'peculiar theology of absolute immanence' (Sherman 2009: 2), a kind of 'life' takes the place of 'God' – the life of the immanent divine game/power/creativity. Instead of the fictional divine or 'God' as standing in opposition to life, as 'the means of depreciating life' (Deleuze 1983: 125, 158, 184) – against 'the transcendentalism of God's judgment', against God as a dominating will (Dale 2001: 135)[1] – Deleuze's absolute or divine is an 'auto-generating' and 'totally unpredictable auto-creative force' or 'nonorganic vitality' (Poxon 2001: 49; Milbank 2010: 74, 2011: 15). Like Nietzsche's Dionysius as the 'god of indestructible life, ecstasy, joy, and power' (Hart 2003: 96), this 'indomitable will to live' (Deleuze 1997: 133) is the virtual non-psychological, non-organic life of 'spirit', that 'grips the world' (Ansell-Pearson 2001: 149). The virtual as 'the (non-)Being of difference', as 'the becoming of Being', is the life of the world, that from which the world lives – 'a kind of cosmic unconscious' (Clark 1999: 192; Pearson 2001: 153; Smith 2001: 179). Central to this virtual life is the dark precursor: a 'primitive' power that is unconscious, invisible, 'impenetrably dark' (Clark 1999: 190).[2] The dark (invisible) precursor is the virtual 'in itself' of difference that is 'at the origin of things' (Deleuze 1997; Dosse 2010: 152).

The virtual, for Deleuze, is a creative power – the constant is the continual creation of the new, the different (Sherman 2009: 3; Milbank 2011: 4). Not entirely unlike process philosophy, being as creativity produces difference (Sherman 2009: 3). There is a power or energy immanent in matter (Albert 2001: 187), a Dionysian 'will to power, a free and unbound energy' (Deleuze 1990b: 107). This divine difference engine – a deified or simply divine impersonal process of becoming (Milbank 2011: 21) – presents 'the order of the Antichrist' in which 'the disjunction (difference, divergence, decentering) becomes as such an affirmative and affirmed power' (Deleuze 1990b: 297). The ultimate is a process of becoming without purpose, without end (Justaert 2009: 532–533). 'God, as the Being of beings', Deleuze writes, 'is replaced by the Baphomet, the "prince of all modifications," and himself modification of all modifications' (Deleuze 1990b: 297). Instead of God as lord, judge, tyrant, ruler – imposing rational order – the absolute is a divine game of chance with no pre-existing rule – 'a pure Idea of play' (Deleuze 1995: 116, 282–283).

2. Deleuzian theologies of life

Various theologies grouped around a secular trajectory present ways of thinking of divinity in terms of a vitalism, a force of creativity inherent in life itself. Taking the late 'Immanence: A Life' essay as a touchstone, Philip

Goodchild sees in Deleuze a presentation of a fundamental, immanent life as transcendental field (Goodchild 2011: 150, 156–157), as the unconscious forces which shape what we are, what we think, and what we do (Goodchild 1996: 359). This immanent power of life (Albert 2001: 188) is not a 'One' as much as a complex underlying cosmic network (Bonta 2010: 67) – as Catherine Keller writes, 'the ecosocial web of all life', the 'self-organizing complexities by which life comes forth' (Keller 2003: 191, 238). Anthony Paul Smith sees in Deleuze the possibility of conceiving of divinity in terms of 'the creative energies of the universe' echoing Bergson's understanding of the 'very process that is living, immanent and indefinite within life' and of the dynamic religion that 'opens itself up to the flow of nature and flows with it' (Smith 2010: 111–113). Such a Deleuzian divinity is a generative power of affirmation and creativity immanent to life itself naming 'the capacity of immanence to produce beyond all limits of propriety' (Barber 2010b: 169; Goodchild 2011: 16) – 'an infinite creativity', as Anthony Paul Smith writes, such that 'our creativity is thus like a divinity within us' (Smith 2010: 112).

This more fundamental life is the collection of unconscious forces, the sources of life, which shape what we are, what we think, and what we do (Goodchild 1996: 359). Clayton Crockett presents the possibility of seeing 'God' as being this sublime unconscious (Crockett 2001: 111). The more fundamental Deleuzian unconscious divine life from which we live, as Clark observes, is 'profoundly *schizoid*' (Clark 1999: 187) such that the divine is understood as 'the Divine Schizophrenic' (Clark 1999: 187), the One that is many, and to think of the divine in this mode is 'a distinctly postmodern avatar of polytheism: a vision of multiple "little divinities" effecting random syntheses of differential elements within an immanent space of possibilities' (Clark 1999: 192; Albert 2001: 188). The plural 'dark' 'divine elements' that make up 'the Divine Schizophrenic' present us with a God 'impenetrably dark' (Clark 1999: 190–191) – unrecognizable, 'as one of H.P. Lovecraft's Outsider abominations' (Bonta 2010: 62, 73).

Against a reductionistic 'dominological Christianity' that would 'evict us from the world', Catherine Keller in her *Face of the Deep* presents the divine of a 'tehomic theology' as the depth of the world – the deep, the *tehom*, chaos, a 'tehomic infinite', an open infinity (Keller 2003: 7, 13, 190). This *tehom* is echoed in Deleuze's *Ungrund* as 'the place of all relations, all virtualities' which Deleuze 'freely translates this bottomless place of places as "chaos"' (Keller 2003: 169). Such a deep chaos is 'not an undifferentiated chaos, but a chaos from which difference unfolds a cosmos' (Keller 2003: xviii). It is 'an alternative order', an '*originary indeterminacy*' that generates the organization of the world, from which order emerges (Keller 2003: 28, 38, 198). Such a divine, chaotic depth is not other to the world but the world's 'radically anti-hierarchical' self-origination (Keller 2003: 216; Bonta 2010: 66).[3]

As an 'explicitly anti-theological' philosophy of nature (where the 'theological' here is understood in terms of a transcendent God) (Albert 2001: 190), Deleuze's immanent God/divinity names the 'surplus of immanence', its capacity 'to produce beyond all limits of propriety' (Barber 2010b: 169–171). Deleuze's divinity reflects Spinoza's God (Goodchild 2011: 153), 'nature naturing', nature itself (*Deus sive natura*) as 'a site of production, metamorphosis, creation' (Albert 2001: 190; Faber 2002: 216, 219, 223). Deleuze thus funds 'a poststructuralist process theology' where, as Keller writes, 'relationality as a beginningless process ... an unoriginated and endless process of becoming' (Keller 2003: xvii, 170) is 'a becoming God' – the *tehom* as process – that makes 'God' 'possible for the anti-theist Deleuze' (Keller 2003: 170, 182, 226). Such a 'becoming God' as the becoming depth of nature is not a fundamentally singular 'God', but rather an 'elohimic multiple', an originating beginning as difference, 'a multiplicity of differences-in-relation, a multiplicity that as such is the relational, might even thaw open the logic of the Christian trinity' (Keller 2003: 10, 172–173, 177). This kind of understanding of God as multiple and becoming also has potential for a postmodern liberation theology, as Kristien Justaert observes, with liberation theology's emphasis on constructed, plural, fluid identities (Justaert 2010: 156).

Finally, a Deleuzian divine is presented as an immanent power of life (Albert 2001: 188) – 'a power', Justaert writes, 'runs through every being' such that our life is an expression of a Life, of Being, that can be understood as God (Justaert 2009: 543; 2011). Thus Crockett proposes thinking of God in terms of '*potentia*' (as enabling, creative power) instead of *postestas* (as dominating, coercive power) (Crockett 2011: 69–75) such that 'God' names 'the virtual *potentia*', the virtual power that exceeds all actual power 'even as it gives rise to it' (Crockett 2011: 61, 75). Here Deleuze's 'pure implex' – his potentiality, 'the virtual' – is the matrix of 'difference itself', 'a heterogeneous and thus differential depth' (Keller 2003: 168). As Daniel Barber writes, 'God here names an unconditioned power', the world's own 'infinite power of existing', 'that exceeds its given expression' – the virtual expressed in and yet exceeding the actual (Barber 2009: 140; 2010a: 39, 42). That which is 'simply the immeasurable itself', as Anthony Paul Smith writes, is 'the [virtual] constitutive power underneath the [actual] organization of power' (Smith 2011: 72).[4] The divine life, the divine energy, the pure dynamism, that is the affirmative force or power of repetition and differentiation (Goodchild 2011: 161, 163), is the life that expresses itself in individuals (Goodchild 2011: 154), the unthinkable underlying modes of existence (Goodchild 1996: 360), the deep source of the events that happen to us (Goodchild 1996: 364).

3. Virtual life and the dark pleroma

The notion of the virtual as a power of which the actual world of our experience is an expression displays the connection between the virtual and 'virtue' in the sense of power – as Hallward notes, 'the older, now archaic meaning of the word, which relates it to the possession of inherent virtues or powers' (Hallward 2006: 30).[5] This can be seen against the background of a genealogy tracing from late medieval voluntarism (focusing on Divine will and power as 'the only explanation for the way things are' (Pickstock 1998: 123; Milbank 2006: 381) to modern focus on the autonomous power and will of the human person to the late modern focus on a thoroughly inhuman impersonal power beneath the human person – such that we, as William Desmond writes, 'participate in living in an organic nature alive with a darker, sublimer energy' (Desmond 2012a). One thinks of Schopenhauer, but also Spinoza, Bergson, and Nietzsche. (I imagine the descent of mad power from the heavens to the proud mortals to the darkly rumbling earth itself beneath them.) As with Wronski's 'creative virtuality' proper to the Absolute as a 'continuous self-differentiation of creative becoming', Deleuze's virtual is a fundamental autogenic power (Kerslake 2009: 176, 182), such that, as Hallward writes, 'existent individuals are simply so many divergent facets of one and the same creative force' or power (Hallward 2006: 16–17). This fundamental movement of power is the divine game – 'that is, the game of unqualified creation as such, behind which there lies only the pure potential of absolute constituent power or play' (Hallward 2006: 54, 143).

Deleuze's thought can be presented as a kind of pantheism, emphasizing the becoming of the divine as, in Desmond's terms, an erotic origin, a divine self-origination, 'self-determining eternity that determines itself in its own temporal productions' (Desmond 2008: 106). Such a 'dialectical monism', as Desmond tells the story, is a version of human self-determining self-transcendence (Desmond 2008: 92). Reflecting, as Hallward observes, 'the notion that the universe and all it contains is a facet of a singular and absolute creative power', Deleuze 'annuls the difference between God and world' – 'in favour of God, not world' (Hallward

2006: 4, 10) – that is, instead of installing a dualism between God and the world, Deleuze sees the world as a function of God, or the divine power or game: 'dualism is therefore only a moment, which must lead to the re-formation of a monism' (Deleuze 1990a: 29).[6] Here Deleuze's philosophy generally parallels Boehme's theosophy in which 'the course of the world', Kerslake writes, is 'understood as the manifestation of a drama taking place in God himself' (Kerslake; Bonta: 2010: 68). In this, Deleuze follows the general thrust of the gnostic narrative of 'the becoming of the perfection of the divine' (O'Regan 2001: 141, 136).

Seeing difference in itself as the divine, unknowable, 'transcendent', and inexplicable – a difference that 'withdraws from thinkability' (Davies 2001: 84) – Deleuze represents, for David Bentley Hart, a postmodern 'narrative of the sublime' for which the unrepresentable (here difference itself) *is* and is more true than the representable (Hart 2003: 52, 56). The visible world is the effect of an invisible potential (Clark 1999: 190). Here, as Milbank writes, the 'ungrounded "mythical" content of difference', Deleuze's positive difference as the sole transcendental, is 'the "original" and continuous variation of a primordial "unity"' as 'always, endlessly, "other" to itself' (Milbank 2006: xiii, 301, 306, 314).[7] Reflecting modern gnosticism's different understanding of difference in the absolute as a change 'in the meaning and function of the Trinity' (O'Regan 2001: 2), Deleuze's fundamental reality is a deified 'non-relational difference' – a self-differing power, 'a differing differs [that] itself by itself' (Hallward 2006: 152–153). With such an absolute, Hallward observes, 'there can be no "substantial" difference between a purely self-differing unity and a purely self-scattering multiplicity, since in either case there is no place for any relational conception of "self"' (Hallward 2006: 156).[8]

The Deleuzian divine is a God rendered unrecognizable (Bonta 2010: 7), in Desmond's terms, a dark origin. Behind Nietzsche's Dionysius, 'the system behind Nietzsche's anti-system',[9] is Schopenhauer's Will – a 'dark self-expressing energy', a dark origin, 'out of which all comes to be and into which all things pass, as into an ultimately inarticulate night' – with which 'there is no point to its striving beyond itself', the apotheosis of the autonomous self into a blind Will at the root of the world (Desmond 2008: 24–46; 2012a). Likewise, Deleuze's axiomatic decision to think difference is a decision for that which 'overreaches thought', which is invisible, imperceptible, immeasurable, and is not thinkable (Davies 2001: 85; Hallward 2006: 36). The will to power in Deleuze as the power of difference itself is indeed a reversed Platonism, with the absolute not as the Sun in the sky above but as that under the ground of the cave – for, Desmond writes, 'Will is no sun, is no good, but a dark original, darker even than the shadow land of representation' (Desmond 2012a: 92). Such a dark divine, 'a dark origin more primordial than the half-light half-darkness of the Cave', is more like Lovecraft's Cthulhu – a madness underneath our shadowy sanities – for in this reversal 'the good God has flipped into its opposite and shows a face more like the evil genius disporting with itself' (Desmond 2012a: 101). The Deleuzian 'One', then, is a chaotic 'One' – a fecund Chaos that 'stands in the place of the One', an eternal becoming that stands in the place of an eternal unity (Balthasar 2003: 45; Hart 2003: 57). Instead of a transcendent divine will violently imposing order upon the world, Deleuze's is an essentially chaotic, problematic, agonistic, 'violent' will or power (Hart 2003: 64; Milbank 2006: 278–279; Sherman 2009: 13–14). This, in Desmond's terms, accords with gnosticism's own 'immanent divine agonistics' as 'an equivocal agon both within the divine as such' (Desmond 2008: 218).

The first narrative episode of O'Regan's Valentinian narrative grammar presents 'the fullness of the divine as both the alpha and the omega of a drama in which the aboriginal integrity of the divine is lost and regained' (O'Regan 2001: 133). Deleuzian life as virtual difference follows the pattern of this becoming divinity. Life in the gnostic Valentinian narrative grammar 'is ascribable to the pleroma and is a property of any being who participates in it' such that the 'extrapleromic realm is the realm of death' (O'Regan 2001: 131). The divine life in Deleuze, likewise, is not as much one being as a domain of being, difference itself, a dark pleroma.

For Deleuze, after Wronski and Warrain, life itself is internally plural, dynamic, problematic, differential – such that life itself as difference itself is the 'vibration', the 'ultimately non-organic pulse of differentiation' of a virtual 'transcendental calculus' (Kerslake 2009: 170–171, 185).[10] 'The endless, goalless, production of Difference' for Deleuze is a fundamental plurality of 'innumerable forces at play' – 'multiple "little divinities" effecting random syntheses of differential elements' (Clark 1999: 192; Bonta 2010: 65).[11] The divine life for Deleuze is a virtual movement of being in itself as an 'infinitely powerful' creativity (Hallward 2006: 1, 4, 8, 10). The internally multiple 'One', the Deleuzian dark pleroma, is virtual difference itself becoming itself in its own creative generation (Hallward 2006: 16, 55, 164).

4. The Trinity and eternal dynamism

In the Christian doctrine of God, in particular, of God as Trinity, one can find an alternative axiomatic mythos regarding the fundamental place of difference – a different ontology, to be sure, but one with the potential to resonate with and attend to Deleuze's radical provocation to think difference in itself (Balthasar 2003: 46; Milbank 2006: 279). With the doctrine of the Trinity, we are speaking of 'a profound mystery', as Herbert McCabe writes, 'which we could not hope to know apart from divine revelation' (McCabe 2002: 36). In Christianity, we are given something like a perspective on the inner life of God, of the '"interpersonal" life within the One' (Burrell 2004: 131). While the Trinity is revealed to us to a degree, the strange and obviously metaphorical language of Father, Son, and Holy Spirit reminds us that, however revealed, we are a long way from getting a handle on the interior life of God – as McCabe writes, it is 'sometimes safer to use clothes that are quite obviously second-hand' (McCabe 2002: 3).

The Trinity as 'the Christian multiple' as 'an absolute that is *itself* difference' (Milbank 2006: 381, 437), named 'divine difference', gives 'the trinitarian name of difference' (Hart 2003: 185, 181). David Bentley Hart and John Milbank have recently presented the Trinity as an alternative understanding of the ultimacy of difference (Hart 2003: 8; Milbank 2006: 435–436). In God is an Ur-space, an Ur-time – 'divine differentiation' of 'original distance' and 'primordial displacement' (Hart 2003: 192, 212, 186). Christian difference here is not between the infinite One and the finite, plural world but as itself the infinite 'One' – God is eternally difference and relation, otherness and relation in Himself. Difference is not the product of the origin but is itself at the origin – as at the beginning of the Gospel of John: the Word was 'with' and 'was' God before all things were made (Hart 2003: 180, 183).

This difference is not a 'Plotinian descent from unity to plurality' but 'God's *perichoresis* as unity and difference', as 'situating the infinite emanations of difference within the Godhead itself' (Hart 2003: 183; Milbank 2006: 435). Difference is not a fall from the divine unity; difference is 'at the origin and is the origin' such that 'created difference "corresponds" to God, is analogous to the divine life, precisely in differing from God' – it is, in its very difference, an expression of divine differentiation (Hart 2003: 180, 183). Here there are unrecognized affinities between Deleuze's pursuit of difference and Christian theology (Davies 2001: 85). 'God', Hart writes, 'is God in supplementation, repetition, variation; and yet the one God'. Thus, 'there is nothing theologically objectionable in, say, Deleuze's desire to speak of difference first and last, or his repeated insistence that there is nothing more "true" than difference' (Milbank 2010: 77, 102).

William Desmond, in his *God and the Between*, sees the ultimate in terms of difference-in-relation – not a mediation that reduces the many to one, but an intermediation as the ultimate (Milbank 2010: 77, 102). The only 'One' is as properly a Between, a Community, a metaxological community – an intermediation 'within the divine' as 'intimately immanent and immanently other, and these all "all at once" ' – such that 'if it has a "unity", would be more like a community: manifestation of agapeic love of the plural as plural' (Desmond 2008: 113, 160, 179). The 'immanent intermediation of Godhead' as a 'social' procession of love is at once personal – for 'to be personal is to be in social relations' – and 'transpersonal' as a community of Persons (Desmond 2008: 191–192, 291). With the Christian understanding of the Trinity, relationality takes a central place in a metaphysic informed by orthodox Christian theology. The relational, the between, the 'immanently communicative', instead of the whole (in Desmond's terms, open whole instead of a closed whole), plays the role of a transcendental principle (Desmond 2008: 160; Milbank 2011: 23, 25).

For Thomas, the Persons of the Trinity are themselves real, substantive, or subsisting (not merely conceptual) relations – though this, as McCabe writes, is something 'mysterious to us; we do not know what it would mean or what it would be like' – our essentialist impulse is to see things as primary and relations as secondary (Aquinas, *Summa Theologica*, 1.28.1; Aquinas, *Compendium of Theology*, I.53; McCabe 2002: 49, 52). Thus, as Milbank writes, 'as much as Deleuze, Christianity places in the *arche* (the Trinity) a multiple which is not set dialectically over against the one, but itself manifests unity' (Milbank 2006: 381). With the understanding of the Triune God as difference-in-relation, as a between, as a metaxological community, one can see why Hart would observe 'that Christian thought has no metaphysics of the one and the many, the same and the different, because that is a polarity that has no place in the Christian narrative' (Hart 2003: 180) – we run into paradox, 'the one is many'/'the many are one' for we do not truly understand oneness/unity or manyness/difference/plurality but that they are revealed to us in the Trinity (as in Kierkegaard's *Philosophical Fragments*, where we do not know what God and humans are but that they are revealed to us in Christ). 'Christianity', Hart concludes, 'has no tale to tell of a division or distinction within being between a transcendental unity and a material multiplicity ... but knows only differentiation and the music of unity, the infinite music of the three persons giving and receiving and giving anew' (Hart 2003: 180). The Trinity is a community, 'difference in harmony', 'an infinite differentiation that is also a harmony' (Milbank 2006: 438, 434).

The Trinitarian God as ultimate is not a static, dead eternity. What is eternal, what is changeless, is an original dynamism – not entirely unlike Deleuze's understanding of the eternal return. With an understanding of 'the dynamic God', of 'the dynamism and differentiation that God is' (Hart 2003: 188, 192), we can affirm with Kierkegaard's pseudonyms that '_Eternity_ is _ the_true _repetition' – what is the same, and what returns, is an ultimate dynamism (Kierkegaard 1983: 221, 305, 1998a: 18, 151; Simpson 2010: 90). It is a 'peculiarity of trinitarian thought' that God's being or *ousia*, as Hart notes, is 'always determined, by the perichoretic dynamism of the Trinity, as *ousia* in transit' (Hart 2003: 181, 252). In God there is 'no stillness prior to relation' (Hart 2003: 185). This eternal movement of the Trinity is a motion of giving and receiving (Hart 2003: 185; Milbank 2006: 381; Desmond 2008: 289–290), of 'the divine persons who have being as that gift that passes from each to the other', 'the perpetual handing over in love of all that the Father is to the Son and Spirit, and the perpetual restoration of this gift' (Hart 2003: 184, 252). In this 'infinite flow of excessive charitable difference', God is understood as *perichoresis* – 'the God whose life of reciprocal "giving way" and "containing" (*chorein*) is also a kind of "dancing" (*choreuien*), and the God who is *terpsichoros*, delighting in the dance' (Hart 2003: 175; Milbank 2006: 381). Thomas describes the essence of God – not as a property or a 'super-essence' – in terms of action (Aquinas, *Summa Theologica*, I.13.7ad1; Burrell 1986: 44). God's being, his 'to be', *esse*, is conceived 'on the analogy of activity' as a 'pure act' – indeed, the 'act which is the source of all activity' (Burrell 1986: 32, 59, 1993: 70). The being of the Trinity is less understood as a static being than as a dynamic living, as life itself (Aquinas, *Summa Theologica*, I.18.2, I.3.3 sed contra; McCabe 2002: 50). The 'termless dynamism' of the Trinitarian divine life, as the 'substance' of God that gives being and life to the world (Hart 2003: 177, 185), has a certain proximity to Deleuze's thought of 'the powerful, non-organic Life which grips the world' as 'a flow of differing difference' that is the 'unconditioned' foundation and the 'hidden ground' of movement (Deleuze 1989: 81–82, 98; 1997b: 66; Colebrook 2001: 45).

The dynamic divine life of the Trinity is supremely characterized as love. God is, in Desmond's terms, an 'agapeic community' – for Thomas, a communicating friendship, an 'adult love' of equals and, for Hart, 'eros and agape at once: a desire for the other that delights in the distance of otherness' (Aquinas, *Summa Theologica*, I.20.2ad3; McCabe 2002: 7; Hart 2003: 20; Desmond 2008: 301). The 'gratuitous donation' of love is the binding (com-) and unitive (-unity) force of the metaxological divine community (Aquinas, *Summa Theologica*, I.20.1ad3, I.38.2). Trinitarian dwelling together in difference is characterized by porosity, intimacy, embracing, letting be, and opening onto – a *perichoresis* or *circumincessio* as 'perfect indwelling, reciprocal "containment", transparency, recurrence, and absolute "giving way"' – a coinherence across 'the interval of appraisal, address, recognition, and pleasure' (Hart 2003: 173, 175). The 'motion of divine love', Hart writes, is the 'divine difference, a shared giving and receiving that is the divine life', a 'primordial generosity' as a genuinely productive desire, that does not arise from lack, 'that requires no pathos to evoke it' (Hart 2003: 180, 185, 167).

In this vein, the changelessness of the dynamic Trinitarian God is, as Kierkegaard states it, 'changeless in love', an 'eternal love'. What is changeless is the constancy, faithfulness, and stability of the original dynamism – the eternal true repetition (Kierkegaard 1998b: 268, 271–272; Kierkegaard 2005: 268). The changelessness of God is the constancy of the movement of divine love – 'what stands with (con-stans), rather than what stands under (sub-stans)' (Desmond 2012b: 198). As infinite 'non-identical repetition', God is less substance than 'the infinite play of active ... self-deriving habit' (Milbank 2006: 309, 2010: 110). The fullness of God, for Desmond, is an infinite reserve – a transcendence completely at home with itself (Desmond 2008: 107, 160) – not lacking, not in need of creation for completion. 'The Trinity', Hart writes, 'is already infinitely sufficient, infinitely "diverse", infinitely at peace' such that 'the "eternal dynamism" of God's immutability, *apatheia*, and perfect fullness' (Hart 2003: 157, 159). Difference and motion for the ultimate is not in terms of opposition and is not negative. God is neither the stasis nor the change that we would commonly understand as defined in opposition to one another, but a changeless, eternally constant movement.[12] God is neither the one nor the many in the way we would commonly understand them, but the one that is three, the different community. To think the aseity of God on the model of eternal return, of repetition, and to think the oneness, the community of God as attentive to the thought of difference itself – can we here begin to think of the Triune God as inherent dynamism?

Notes

1 God, for Deleuze, is like Morgoth in Tolkein's *Silmarillion*: the great enemy of the world.

2 '"Paradoxical instances," "aleatory points," "dark precursors": these, I would suggest, are the only divine elements in the Deleuzian chaosmos, "primitives" in both a methodological and metaphysical sense' (Clark 1999: 191).

3 Keller presents 'Tehom, Elohim, Ruach' as a kind of trinity – 'The Deep, the Difference and the Spirit. The godness of our depths, our differences, our spirits' – 'Womb, Word and Wind. Tiamat, Sophia and Shekhinah' (Keller 2003: 231, 235).

4 The bracketed terms are mine, not Smith's.

5 See the *OED* for 'virtual' and 'virtue'.

6 Hallward writes: 'one of the most characteristic features of Deleuze's work is his tendency to present what initially appears as a binary relation in such a way as to show that this relation is in fact determined by only one of its two "terms"' (Hallward 2006: 156).

7 Milbank notes that Deleuze's philosophy of difference cannot so easily (as with Heidegger or Derrida) fit the claim it is an ontology of violence (Milbank 2006: 314).

8 'By "relation" I mean a process that operates between two or more minimally discernible terms, in such a way as to condition or inflect (but not fully to generate) the individuality of each term. A relation is only a relation in this sense if its terms retain some limited autonomy with respect to each other. A relation is only a relation if it is between terms that can be meaningfully discerned, even if the means of this discernment proceed at the very limit of indiscernment. In other words, the question is: can Deleuze's theory of difference provide a coherent theory of relation between terms' (Hallward 2006: 152).

9 Desmond is here referring to Christopher Janaway's work.

10 'On Warrain's Wronskian architectonic, life is composed of a series of levels of reality, each a rhythmical and dynamic compromise between continuity and discontinuity, each with its own "universal problem" [problème universel] (how to find a dynamic equilibrium for opposing forces), each with its own secret harmonies. For Warrain, this "life" is the true matter of the transcendental calculus' (Kerslake 2009: 185).

11 Kerslake writes: 'Warrain's metaphysics of vibration and rhythm appears to be *both* immanently philosophical *and* esoteric, and suggests a way in which the potential clash of principles between philosophy and the "esoteric" might be resolved. Warrain illustrated his chapter on Wronski's Law of Creation in *Concrete Synthesis* with a diagram which correlates the elements of Wronski's system one-by-one with the cabbalistic sephiroth of Jewish mysticism' (Kerslake 2011: 171).

12 'To attribute stasis to God', McCabe writes, 'is as mistaken as to attribute change to him' (2002: 43).

Bibliography

Albert, E. (2001) 'Deleuze's Impersonal, Hylozoic Cosmology: The Expulsion of Theology', in M. Bryden (ed.), *Deleuze and Religion*. London: Routledge, pp. 184–197.

Ansell-Pearson, K. (2001) 'Pure Reserve: Deleuze, Philosophy, and Immanence', in M. Bryden (ed.), *Deleuze and Religion*. London: Routledge, pp. 141–156.

von Balthasar, H.U. (2003) *Cosmic Liturgy: The Universe According to Maximus the Confessor*, trans. B.E. Daley San Francisco, CA: Ignatius.

Barber, D.C. (2009) 'Immanence and Creation', *Political Theology* 10:1, pp. 131–141.

Barber, D.C. (2010a) 'Immanence and the Re-expression of the World', *SubStance* 39:1, pp. 38–48.

Barber, D.C. (2010b) 'Secularism, Immanence, and the Philosophy of Religion', in A.P. Smith and D. Whistler (eds.), *After the Postsecular and the Postmodern: New Essays in Continental Philosophy of Religion*. Newcastle upon Tyne: Cambridge Scholars Publishing, pp. 152–172.

Baugh, B. (2009) 'G.W.F. Hegel', in G. Jones and J. Roffe (eds.), *Deleuze's Philosophical Lineage*. Edinburgh: Edinburgh University Press, pp. 30–146.

Bonta, M. (2010) 'Rhizome of Boehme and Deleuze: Esoteric Precursors of the God of Complexity', *SubStance* 39:1, pp. 62–75.

Burrell, D. (1986) *Knowing the Unknowable God: Ibn-Sina, Maimonides, Aquinas*. South Bend: University of Notre Dame Press.

Burrell, D. (1993) *Freedom and Creation in Three Traditions*. South Bend: University of Notre Dame Press.

Burrell, D. (2004) *Faith and Freedom*. London: Blackwell.

Clark, T. (1999) 'A Whiteheadian Chaosmos: Process Philosophy from a Deleuzean Perspective', *Process Studies* 28 3–4, pp. 179–194.

Colebrook, C. (2001) *Gilles Deleuze*. London: Routledge.

Crockett, C. (2001) *A Theology of the Sublime*. London: Routledge.

Crockett, C. (2011) *Radical Political Theology: Religion and Politics after Liberalism*. New York: Columbia University Press.

Dale, C. (2001) 'Knowing One's Enemy: Deleuze, Artaud, and the Problem of Judgment', in M. Bryden (ed.), *Deleuze and Religion*. London: Routledge.

Davies, O. (2001) 'Thinking Difference: A Comparative Study of Gilles Deleuze, Plotinus and Meister Eckhart', in M. Bryden (ed.), *Deleuze and Religion*. London: Routledge, pp. 76–87.

Deleuze, G. (1983) *Nietzsche and Philosophy*, trans. H. Tomlinson. New York: Columbia University Press.

Deleuze, G. (1989) *Cinema 2: The Time-Image*, trans. H. Tomlinson and R. Galeta. Minneapolis: University of Minnesota Press.

Deleuze, G. (1990a) *Bergsonism*, trans. B. Habberjam and H. Tomlinson. Brooklyn, NY: Zone Books.

Deleuze, G. (1990b) *The Logic of Sense*, ed. C.V. Boundas, trans. M. Lester and C. Stivale. New York: Columbia University Press.

Deleuze, G. (1995) *Difference and Repetition*, trans. P. Patton. New York: Columbia University Press.

Deleuze, G. (1997a) *Essays Critical and Clinical*, trans. D.W. Smith and M.A. Greco. Minneapolis: University of Minnesota Press.

Deleuze, G. (1997b) *Negotiations 1972–90*, trans. Martin Joughin. New York: Columbia University Press.

Deleuze, G. (with C. Parnet) (1997c) *L'Abécédaire de Gilles Deleuze*, 3 DVDs, Montparnesse: Arte Video. English overview by C.J. Stivale at http://www.langlab.wayne.edu/CStivale/D-G/ABC1.html (accessed 13 September 2011).

Deleuze, G. and F. Guattari (1987) *A Thousand Plateaus: Capitalism and Schizophrenia*, trans. B. Massumi. Minneapolis: University of Minnesota Press.

Desmond, W. (2008) *God and the Between*. Oxford: Blackwell.

Desmond, W. (2012a) 'From under the Ground of the Cave: Schopenhauer and the Philosophy of the Dark Origin', in B. Vandenabeele (ed.), *A Companion to Schopenhauer (Blackwell Companions to Philosophy)*, Oxford: Wiley-Blackwell.

Desmond, W. (2012b) 'Wording the Between', in C.B. Simpson (ed.), *The William Desmond Reader*. Albany: SUNY Press.

Dosse, F. (2010), *Gilles Deleuze & Félix Guattari: Intersecting Lives*, trans. D. Glassman. New York: Columbia University Press.

Faber, R. (2002) 'De-Ontologizing God: Levinas, Deleuze, and Whitehead', in C. Keller and A. Daniell (eds.), *Process and Difference*. Albany: SUNY Press, pp. 209–235.

Goodchild, P. (September 1996) 'A Theological Passion for Deleuze', *Theology* 99:791, pp. 357–365.

Goodchild, P. (2011) 'Deleuze and Philosophy of Religion', in M. Joy (ed.), *Continental Philosophy and Philosophy of Religion, Handbook of Contemporary Philosophy of Religion* Vol. 4. Dordrecht: Springer, pp. 139–164.

Hallward, P. (2006) *Out of This World*. London: Verso.

Hart, D.B. (2003) *The Beauty of the Infinite: The Aesthetics of Christian Truth*. Grand Rapids, MI: Eerdmans.

Justaert, K. (October 2009) 'Gilles Deleuze: Évaluation Théologique', *Laval Théologique et Philosophique* 65:3, pp. 531–544.

Justaert, K. (2010) 'Liberation Theology: Deleuze and Althaus-Reid', *SubStance* 39:1, pp. 154–164.

Justaert, K. (2011) 'Gilles Deleuze and the Transcendence of the Immanent', Unpublished essay.

Keller, C. (2003) *Face of the Deep: A Theology of Becoming*. London: Routledge.

Kerslake, C. (2009) 'Hoëne Wronski and Francis Warrain', in G. Jones and J. Roffe (eds.), *Deleuze's Philosophical Lineage*. Edinburgh: Edinburgh University Press, pp. 167–189.

Kerslake, C. (2011) 'The Somnambulist and the Hermaphrodite: Deleuze and Johann de Montereggio and Occultism', Culture Machine, InterZone, http://www.culturemachine.net/index.php/cm/article/viewArticle/243/225 (accessed 11 August 2011).

Kierkegaard, S. (1983) *Repetition* (published with *Fear and Trembling*), trans. H.V. Hong and ed. E.H. Hong. Princeton, NJ: Princeton University Press.

Kierkegaard, S. (1998a) *The Concept of Anxiety*, trans. R. Thomte and ed. A.B. Anderson. Princeton, NJ: Princeton University Press.

Kierkegaard, S. (1998b) *The Moment and Late Writings*, trans. H.V. Hong and ed. E.H. Hong. Princeton, NJ: Princeton University Press.

Kierkegaard, S. (2005) *Upbuilding Discourses in Various Spirits*, trans. H.V. Hong and ed. E.H. Hong. Princeton, NJ: Princeton University Press.

McCabe, H. (2002) *God Still Matters*. London: Continuum.

Milbank, J. (2006) *Theology and Social Theory* (2nd edition), Oxford: Blackwell.

Milbank, J. (2010) 'The Mystery of Reason', in P.M. Candler Jr. and C. Cunningham (eds), *The Grandeur of Reason: Religion, Tradition and Universalism*. London: SCM Press, pp. 68–118.

Milbank, J. (26 January 2011) 'Immanence and Life', Stanton Lectures at Cambridge University.

O'Regan, C. (2001) *Gnostic Return in Modernity*. Albany: SUNY Press.

Pickstock, C. (1998) *After Writing: On the Liturgical Consummation of Philosophy*. Oxford: Blackwell.

Poxon, Judith (2001) 'Embodied Anti-Theology: The Body without Organs and the Judgement of God', in Mary Bryden (ed.), *Deleuze and Religion*. London: Routledge, pp. 42–51.

Sherman, J.H. (January 2009) 'No Werewolves in Theology? Transcendence, Immanence, and Becoming-Divine in Gilles Deleuze', *Modern Theology* 25:1, pp. 1–20.

Simpson, C. B. (2010) *The Truth Is the Way: Kierkegaard's Theologia Viatorum*. London: SCM Press.

Smith, A.P. (2010) 'Believing in This World for This Making of Gods: Ecology of the Virtual and the Actual', *SubStance* 39:1, pp. 103–114.

Smith, A.P. (2011) 'Judgment of God and the Immeasurable: Political Theology and Organizations of Power', *Political Theology* 12:1, pp. 69–86.

Smith, D.W. (2001) 'The Doctrine of Univocity: Deleuze's Ontology of Immanence', in M. Bryden (ed.), *Deleuze and Religion*. London: Routledge.

4

Deleuze and Guattari's Machinic Animism

Joshua Ramey

All so-called initiatory journeys include these thresholds and doors where becoming itself becomes, and where one changes becoming depending on the 'hour' of the world, the circles of hell, or the stages of a journey that sets scales, forms, and cries in variation. From the howling of animals to the wailing of elements and particles.

Deleuze and Guattari, *A Thousand Plateaus*

Today, it seems interesting to me to go back to what I would call an animist conception of subjectivity, if need be through neurotic phenomena, religious rituals, or aesthetic phenomena. How does subjectivity locate on the side of the subject and on the side of the object? How can it simultaneously singularize an individual, a group of individuals, and also be assembled to space, architecture and all other cosmic assemblages?

Félix Guattari

1. Introduction

By the time of his collaborations with Félix Guattari, it is clear that Gilles Deleuze was deeply invested in developing the logic and metaphysics of what Guattari calls an 'animist conception of subjectivity'. Several of the plateaus of *A Thousand Plateaus* work through such a logic explicitly – most obviously 'November 28, 1947: How Do You Make Yourself a Body without Organs', and '1730: Becoming-Intense, Becoming-Animal, Becoming-Imperceptible …', but also '1837: Of the Refrain', and '10,000 B.C: The Geology of Morals (Who Does the Earth Think It Is?)'. The logic of an animist subjectivity is the logic of a subjectivity that is non-local, a subject that cannot be identified as contained either in individuals or in numerable groups, but rather exists interstitially, across or between individuals and groups. In *A Thousand Plateaus*, Deleuze and Guattari write,

> Becoming can and should be qualified as becoming-animal even in the absence of a term that would be the animal become. The becoming-animal of the human being is real, even if the animal the human being becomes is not; and the becoming-other of the animal is real, even if that something other it becomes is not. This is the point to clarify: that a becoming lacks a subject distinct from itself; but also that it has no term, since its term in turn exists only as taken up in another becoming of which it is the subject, and which coexists, forms a block, with the first. This is the principle according to which there is a reality specific to becoming (the Bergsonian idea of coexistence of very different 'durations,' superior or inferior to 'ours,' all of them in communication). (1987: 238)

The key term here is the final one, *communication*. An animist conception of subjectivity is a conception of communications not exclusively or even primarily between subjects, let alone by subjects 'about' objects, but rather communications by, through, and *as* different modalities of becoming. Provisionally we could define such becoming as the emergence of unforseeable affordances or capacities, where such capacities exist as a shared yet unreproducible or 'transversal' modality. Animist subjectivity is transversal in the sense that it exists *as the crossing* between different individuals, *as the process* of an exchange and a mutual becoming in which they are implicated. But here 'becoming' must not be thought in the ordinary sense of 'development', especially not in the sense of 'evolution', since many modes of becoming alter and mutate individuals in ways that deform, even *inhibit*, traits or powers in both unforeseeable and, from the standpoint of utility or equilibrium, in often 'unproductive' ways.[1] Thus Deleuze and Guattari warn that the sympathies and symbioses that lead us into novel becomings are 'dark assemblages that stir what is deepest within us', and should not be confused with 'organizations such as the institution of the family and the State apparatus' (1987: 242). For what is generated through becoming are not consistent, stable, homogeneous groups and social forms, but 'multiplicities with heterogeneous terms, cofunctioning by contagion ... *assemblages*' (1987: 242).

Part of what fascinated Deleuze and Guattari was not simply how such a dispersed or 'distributed' subjectivity might be located within organic beings, but how inorganic forms such as architectures, geologies, geographies, even machines, and information sets might also be 'singularized' or 'animated' by a subjectivity. This is obviously a difficult and elusive thought, to say the least.

Recently Isabel Stengers explicitly related the problem of 'reclaiming' animism to something like a problem of resurrection.[2] For Stengers, we must become animists again, but this is a matter of resuscitation, of bringing back something dead. It was Freud – veritable inventor of modern subjectivity – who defined subjectivity in contrast to a 'dead' matter, an inanimate, lifeless world. Freud was neither alone nor original in this, but his account of a human subject *opposed by* a dead, inert material world is particularly acute. Freud not only *describes* the subject in contrast with inanimate matter but explicitly warns against the danger of regression (through fantasy) to an animist view of the world. The success of modernity, for Freud, depended upon an effort of will that the modern subject must make to hold animism at bay. In some sense psychic health for Freud is the ability to ward off the narcissistic infantile fantasy of an external world that might communicate with a subject's desire. And of course this slippage in Freud between description and prescription is precisely where something is repressed in his theory, namely, the reality of a universal animation that is much more potent and much more difficult to ward off than the infantile narcissism to which Freud would have it assimilated.[3]

And yet experimentation with a reclaimed animism was at large even while Freud himself was alive and writing. Stengers points out that André Breton's surrealism, for instance, was a step towards the reclamation of animism insofar as it attempted to save the enigmatic and suggestive potencies of animal magnetism from the reductive worldview of scientists and physicians, with their 'polemical verifications dominated by the suspicion of quackery, self-delusion, or deliberate cheating'.[4] And yet Breton's aesthetic liberation of such a suggestive animist potency is also a restriction and recuperation, falling short of reclaiming animism.[5]

> For Breton, the point was not to verify what magnetized clairvoyants see, or to understand enigmatic healings, but to cultivate lucid trances (automatism) in the milieu of art, with the ultimate aim of escaping the shackles of normal, representational perception. The milieu of art would explore the means to 'recuperate our psychical force.'[5]

The danger, for Stengers, is that the modern has here progressed from a scientific to an aesthetic 'inoculation' against the powers of animism, a way of keeping the reality of a non-localized, distributed subjectivity at bay. The problem with Breton is the danger of aestheticism, that with a certain modality of aesthetic experimentation, we have found yet another way to draw the border and enforce the boundary between the human and the non-human, the subjective and the objective, the living and the dead. As Stengers argues, if we are to reclaim animism, we must also be on guard against a metaphysical or logical inoculation (as much as an aesthetic one) against the contagion – the lure and allure – of animism, especially if that inoculation might come, ironically, from the work of Deleuze and Guattari themselves. As she puts it,

> Relating animism to the efficacy of 'assemblages' is a dangerous move, however, because it may well reassure us a bit too easily. It is part of our fabrication as readers, to feel free to ponder without experiencing the existential consequences of our questions. For instance, we may be tempted to understand assemblages as an interesting concept among others, pondering its connections with other concepts – that is, without feeling our intentional stance threatened by its demand …
>
> This is why it may be better to revive more compromised words, which have been restricted to metaphoric use only. 'Magic' is such a word, as we freely speak of the magic of an event, of a landscape, of a musical moment. Protected by the metaphor, we may then express the experience of an agency that does not belong to us even if it includes us, but an 'us' as it is lured into feeling.[7]

To speak bluntly, flatly, *literally* of animist subjectivity is to speak of magic, and to speak of it in a non-metaphorical sense. To affirm animist subjectivity is thus something different from intellectual assent or from conceptual entertainment. It is a political act. On the contrary, to merely 'appreciate' or 'respect' the point of view of someone who *would* experience her agency and desire as enigmatically distributed within an assemblage (an event, a landscape, a tribe, a ritual, a space etc.) is to intellectually colonize that person. It is to quarantine, and to subjugate, her as 'other'.

This is why the anthropologist Eduardo Viveiros de Castro can speak stridently (in a round table dedicated to the topic in the same journal where Stengers' article appears) of animist subjectivity as the core of a decolonized subject, and animism the spirituality of a decolonial politics. As he puts it,

> For me, anthropology is in fact the theory – to sound a bit like Trotsky – the theory of a permanent decolonization. A permanent decolonization of thought. That is anthropology for me. It is not a question of decolonizing society, but of decolonizing thought. How to decolonize thought? And how to do it permanently? Because thinking is constantly recolonized and reterritorialized. I have always thought that the notion of 'a society against the state' is a profound notion and it has to be deepened. And this goes along with the idea of a society without interiority. This means that, finally, interiority is the state. I still like the wordplay: 'the state is the self'. Thus a society without a state is a society

> without the self, without interiority in this sense. This is animism, the idea that the subject is outside. It is everywhere. And that society is not a guard, that the state is neither guarding nor a guard, meaning that the society does not coincide with the state. That is the idea against the state. Against the state means a society without interiority, which only recognizes itself while being outside of itself. This is the idea of a society without a state. What does it mean to live in a society without a state, against the state? We don't have any idea. You have to live there to see how things happen in a world without a state. In a society that is not only lacking the state but, as Clastres thought, is against the state because it is constituted precisely on the absence of the state. Not because of the lack of a state, but upon the absence of the state, so that the state cannot come into existence. And animism has to do with that. Animism is the ontology of societies against the state.[8]

The political stakes here could not be clearer. And for those who might wonder how close Viveiros de Castro is, here to Deleuze and Guattari, one need only trace the proliferating references to Pierre Clastres' *Society against the State* throughout the two volumes of *Capitalism and Schizophrenia*. Clastres is arguably *the* key reference for much of Deleuze and Guattari's account of the state and for how they envision both resistance to and breaks with the state as located in archaic – that is to say animist – modes of subjectivity.[9]

Now that the stakes are clear, I intend to give a kind of archaeology, based on his earlier writings, of how and why Deleuze joins with Guattari's affirmation of animist subjectivity, and of a 'machinic' animism. This begins with an account of how Deleuze's conception of life is of an 'animation' whose model is drawn explicitly from aesthetic experimentation. His affirmations of life are affirmations of aesthetic experimentation, but I would argue that beyond the ambitions of Breton, those affirmations in turn are precisely of the enigmatic healing and clairvoyant potencies around which aesthetic modernism demurs. This affirmation, as a whole, constitutes what I take to be a religiosity or spirituality specific to Deleuze's thinking.

What I am interested in here is not whether Deleuze has a theory of religion (as Adkins shows in this volume, he does) or whether Deleuze's philosophy can affirm or deny theological positions ranging from atheism to process Christology (which other chapters argue it persuasively can be used to do). What I am looking for is a kind of religiosity or spirituality *intrinsic to* thinking in Deleuze. By a spiritual or religious thinking in Deleuze, I mean nothing more elaborate than perhaps the point made by Pierre Hadot (1995) that there is a dimension to thought that is not simply demonstrative, and that cannot be evaluated purely with reference to deliberative norms of coherence or clear reference or logical validity. Spiritual philosophizing is a kind of thinking that expresses and refracts a vision of the world as a world to which the thinker herself is in some sense subject. Such a spiritual or visionary thought bears witness to powers and events, or the power of events that exceed her capacities and yet within which she looks for new affordances and new capacities to emerge.

If Deleuze has a kind of spirituality immanent to his own philosophical practice, and this kind of thinking is not to be made ancillary to another theology (or to an atheism), then that religion and that theology have something to do with Deleuze's distinctive vitalism, an affirmation of life. But this vitalism, I will argue, has something to do with machinic animism. As Claire Colebrook has brilliantly recognized, Deleuze's conception of life as machinic amounts to a 'passive vitalism' in which the meaning(s) of life is primarily in that which exceeds or extends life beyond the auto-poetic or self-replicating powers of an organism (2011). Meaningfulness thus relates, in Deleuze, not to the auto-satisfaction of the organism, but to the various ways in which the powers of vision, touch, and even of the brain itself are activated and extended through technical and artistic means into novel forms of life. On this view, cybernetics is endogenous to life itself, rather than any kind of appendage or artificial overlay. But rather than see such a cyborg vision of life as inherently novel, it is arguable that Deleuze's thought of life extends a long tradition of spiritual discipline, ascesis, and experimentation that has always viewed the body as a microcosm extended into a macrocosmic project of becoming that both exceeds and challenges the integrity of the individual, while allowing the world to be folded back into a subject who becomes capable of transforming it.

This is why, in *The Hermetic Deleuze: Philosophy and Spiritual Ordeal*, I argued that Deleuze's conception of the work of art – of its power as a modality of intuition, of vision, and of expanded perceptual and affective capacities – is an *hermetic* point of view. What I meant by this is that Deleuze's appreciation for the powers of art can only be understood if those powers are appreciated as transformative potencies. Such potencies, variously described as intensities or as folds or lines of flight, are also powers of thought. This means that Deleuze is an hermetic *philosopher*, in the sense that he, like hermetically inclined thinkers before him, develops concepts as a mode of *searching*, in the sense of an alchemical quest, or more generally, in the sense of what I call a 'spiritual ordeal'. From this perspective, his readings of the history of philosophy and of contemporary mathematical, biological, anthropological, architectural, aesthetic, economic, and political theory are not 'neutral' investigations. They are motivated practices of invention: not in the sense that Deleuze distorts or manipulates these materials, but that he is drawn to materials that reanimate the potencies that would otherwise remain dormant or unspecified in his own thought.

This process involves more than reading. It is also hearing and seeing (and presumably touching, tasting, and even smelling) that form the basis of a particular philosophical spirituality that can see, appreciate, name, and engage with the reality of animistic cosmos. This spirituality or spiritual thought is a practice or habit, rooted in elective affinity and grounded on patterns of attraction (and repulsion). It is above all a religion of intuition. Such intuition is grounded in sympathies and empathies, mediated through various modes of abstraction. It is an intuition that goes beyond memory, and beyond Bergson's 'organic' model of vitalism and his notion of duration as continuity. It is a discontinuous, anorganic vitality that is, for Deleuze, 'the meaning of life', and the essence of his particular religiosity. By his specifically philosophical religiosity I mean to point to Deleuze's *devotion*, his *commitment* and his *attachment*, his *desire*. While in *The Hermetic Deleuze* I attempted to locate or situate Deleuze in a peculiar series of hermetic philosophers, I will here focus less on elucidating the general 'type' of Deleuze's hermeticism and rather focus on the specificity of animism as it emerges in Deleuze's aesthetic thought.

Here is a final prefatory remark. Animism is intuitive religion. But Freud was wrong about the simplicity or childishness of intuition. It is not only, or even primarily, to children that the spirits of the wood or the animals speak but to the elders, to those who are capable of the most refined intuitions. Intuition requires experience: a haptic religion.[10]

2. What is called haptic? Religion in the fourth dimension

Modern art reintroduced animism to a disenchanted world when it began to develop, to re-express, the 'barbarian' and 'gothic' possibilities of the haptic. The clue to rationalizing animism or rendering to it the metaphysics worthy of its passion lies in the link between intuition and 'haptic' experiences. What Deleuze calls haptic are 'local spaces of pure connection', such as the sea, the desert, the steppe, and ice floes (1987: 493). Intuition of the uncannily 'subjective' dimension of things, of places, plants, animals, or even objects or machines is dependent upon (and in some sense productive of) what Deleuze calls smooth spaces, non-differentiable zones of space where what one imputes to the communication of another is indistinct from communication by and for another. The message is the connection. Put differently, animist communication, or *sympathy*, is not from oneself to another, but perhaps better described as between unconscious elements, through elective affinity.

The haptic also has a peculiar temporality, linked to intensive movement. Assemblages have a certain temporal index, what Bergson calls a 'duration' (they also have peculiar, intensive spatialities, which we will examine below). The speeds and slownesses of the various processes (movements, metabolisms, perceptions, cognitions, etc.) of assemblages are not themselves attributable entirely to the separate powers of organisms, machines, buildings, places, and cartographies, but are themselves expressions of a 'dimension' that emerges through the transformation of the entities involved. Thus, although becoming-animal is the point of entry for grasping the logic of becoming, through contagion, sympathy, and symbiosis, it is clear that there is nothing either particularly 'organic' or even necessarily 'alive' about such becomings. 'Exclusive importance should not be attached to becomings-animal', Deleuze and Guattari remind us (1987: 248).

Thus becomings are extremely abstract lines, even if they trace the most intimate, excruciating, and poignant effects of contagion and communion. Becomings are no less concrete for being virtual, in the precise sense that the 'virtual' names a non-actualizable, intransitive potency that is expressed in without being reducible to actual entities and states of affairs. And as virtual, such becomings are 'ideas' in a sense that Deleuze articulates at great, if often obscure, lengths in his 1968 *Difference and Repetition*.

It might seem strange to say that becomings are ideas, given the investment of *A Thousand Plateaus* in what seems to be a stridently *materialist* conception of multiplicities as forces, energies, and processes. But Deleuze does not think ideas in opposition to materiality. 'Ideas are genuine objectivities', he writes, 'made up of differential elements and relations and provided with a specific mode – namely, the "problematic"' (1994: 267). Ideas are problematic in the sense that *actual* differences and constituted forms are temporary 'solutions' to or 'resolutions' – in the sense of the way a lens focuses or 'resolves' light – of ideal, virtual patternings, potencies of differentiation. What is important for our purposes here is the way in which a certain *intensive spatiality* is fundamental to the specificity of each idea – whether an idea of the nature of a living being or of the nature of a particular colour.

As we will see, this intensive spatiality is the clue to Deleuze's peculiar take on animism. To articulate his thinking on intensive spatiality, in *Difference and Repetition*, Deleuze evokes the esoteric conception of the world as a cosmic egg, a bounded yet infinitely rich plasma of mutation and mutability, with potencies for development defined by relations of intensive space.

> The entire world is an egg. The double differenciation of species and parts always presupposes spatio-temporal dynamisms. Take a division into 24 cellular elements endowed with similar characteristics: nothing yet tells us the dynamic process by which it was obtained – 2 × 12, (2 × 2) + (2 × 10), or (2 × 4) + (2 × 8)... ? Even Platonic division would lack a rule with which to distinguish the two sides, if movements and orientations or spatial lines did not provide one. Thus, in the case of fishing: entrap the prey or strike it, strike it from top to bottom or from bottom to top. It is the dynamic processes which determine the actualization of the Ideas.

Ideas are inseparable from specific dynamic, material processes. Deleuze insists on calling such process 'ideas' because various spatial (and temporal) sequences or orderings can occur in different ways involving the same elements, or vice versa. That is to say, the dynamic processes that are actualized are not the same as their actualization. So what accounts for the specificity of each and every development or expression? Unlike Aristotle, Deleuze does not place contingency on the side of the actual, but on the side of the ideal, virtual, and differential *power* of the idea (or what Aristotle would call the essential *form*). He thinks of such powers, in *Difference and Repetition*, as *dramas*. The determination of (virtual) ideas in actuality is precisely 'dramatic' in the sense that actors play or *incarnate* roles which could be played by others. Even though 'there is' no actual role until someone plays it (and apart from someone's actually playing it), there is nevertheless a persistence or *insistence* of roles whose potency cannot be reduced to any finite set of reprisals. There is an actual history of roles enacted, habituated, and remembered within a lineage or tradition of acting, but this lineage is defined as much by virtual singularities and ideal, differential relations as it is by actual specifics of the bodies, times, places, societies, politics, and economics. Such historical or material actualities embody differential relational potencies whose changes are more than the actual changes, bearing witness to an ideal drama that, while itself changing, is not reducible to, even while being affected by, actual changes.

What's important here, for the conception of animism emerging from this account of ideas, is that this virtual power of role in excess of actors, or of ideal dramas in excess of dramatization, is that it is, while perhaps clearest in the case of human activity (such as theatre), no less natural or general than it is specifically cultural. Thus Deleuze can extend the thought directly into the behaviour of cellular automata.

> When a cellular migration takes place, as Raymond Ruyer shows, it is the requirements of a 'role' insofar as this follows from the structural 'theme' to be actualized which determines the situation, not the other way round. The world is an egg, but the egg itself is a theatre: a staged theatre in which the roles dominate the actors, the spaces dominate the roles, and the Ideas dominate the spaces. (1994: 216)

Here we arrive at the conception of intensive or what Deleuze will call in this context 'internal' space, the conception that will enable us to connect the idea of intensive space directly to the spatial fourth dimension that was the fascination of many of the early avant-garde artists that were themselves profound inspirations to Deleuze. For his clearest picture of intensive space, Deleuze turns to the nature of colour.

> Furthermore, by virtue of the complexity of Ideas and their relations with other Ideas, the spatial dramatization is played out on several levels: in the constitution of an internal space, but also in the manner in which that space extends into the external extensity, occupying a region of it. For example, the internal space of a color is not to be confused with the manner in which it occupies an extensity where it enters into relations with other colors, whatever the affinity between these two processes ... Everything is even more complicated when we consider that the internal space itself [whether of a color or a living organism] is made up of multiple spaces which must be locally integrated and connected, and that this connection, which may be achieved in many ways, pushes the object or living being to its own limits, all in contact with the exterior; and that this relation with the exterior, and with other things and living beings, implies in turn connections and global integrations which differ in kind from the preceding. Everywhere a staging at several levels. (1994: 217)

In this logic, an interior is in tension with itself because each part is somehow connected to an 'outside' external to the organism as a whole.[11] As mentioned earlier, Colebrook articulates this point as the way in which 'life' in Deleuze is a force of life that renders each actual individual passive with respect to forces that exceed it. It is not an autopoesis of life by means of which organisms primarily are understood as self-replicating. In *A Thousand Plateaus*, Deleuze and Guattari are clear about the existential stakes of this multiplicity internal to the developmental space of the individual, a space that is in a very real sense at odds with itself, an auto-dismembering or internal tension. The reality of each being – living or nonliving, organic or inorganic – is a reality of being 'pushed to its limits' not just by external factors but by its own internal modes of differentiation. The potencies of red or blue *are* an internal tension, a dynamic that is activated or actualized differently relative to the other colours and forms with which a particular red or blue is in contact.

> *It amounts to the same thing to say that each multiplicity is already composed of heterogeneous terms in symbiosis, and that a multiplicity is continually transforming itself into a string of other multiplicities, according to its thresholds and doors*... If we imagined the position of a fascinated Self, it is because the multiplicity toward which it leans, stretching to the breaking point, is the continuation of another multiplicity that works it and strains it from the inside. (1987: 249, author's italics)

In *A Thousand Plateaus*, Deleuze and Guattari primarily utilize references to works of literary fiction in order to render palpable the 'drama' of symbiosis, and the peculiar role of fascination in that becoming. Ahab's fascination with Moby-Dick is a symbiosis masked by a merely apparent opposition and a wholly sympathetic combat with his 'opponent', the white whale. What appears radically external to his nature, his identity, is in fact the symbol of his own psychotic character. H.P. Lovecraft's terrified heroes are drawn inexorably towards the 'unnamed horror' of the unliveable life of cosmic forces that nevertheless constitutes their very own vitality, beyond the scientific pretence to objectivity and rationality. And Carlos Casteneda's 'tales of power' reveal to the sorcerer that he or she is nothing but a bundle of luminous fibres, multiple lines of potential becoming (1974: 249).

But already Deleuze, in *Difference and Repetition*, had argued that when it comes to becoming, not only literature but 'modern art [in general] tends to realize these conditions: it becomes a veritable theater of metamorphoses and permutations' (Deleuze 1994: 56). The experimentation Deleuze is thinking of, here, is quite specific. Based on the references to Proust, Joyce, Beckett, and Artaud in *Difference and Repetition*, Deleuze is thinking of a series of late-nineteenth- and early-twentieth-century avant-garde artists whose aim was to challenge individual forms, to render them from themselves, to show the processes and dynamisms of which they are composed. And although literary and theatrical experimentation has an exemplary role to play, over the course of his career Deleuze increasingly turns to the specific case of the visual image, especially in Francis Bacon, but also in Cezánne, Kandinsky, and Klee.

The question is, what is the specific experimental achievement of modern experimental works of art, in relation to the theory of ideas? Essentially what is at stake is the ability of the modern work to stage or present the forces and events of which individuals are composed, the deeper levels or higher dimensions of force and process that make up the intensive and unconscious interior of subjectivity. What is crucial is that such forces and processes are never directly represented, but can only *be* as represented through forms, shapes, and characters that only partially reveal the virtual potencies they express. (One of the peculiar aspects of Deleuze's interest in modern art is that he is much less interested in the abstract expressionism of someone like Jackson Pollock or the abstract music of John Cage, and is much more interested in the painting of Klee or Kandinsky or the music of figures like Edgar Varése or Karlheinz Stockhausen. This is because in these latter artists there is something like a very tense (intense) relation between figure and ground, a dramatization of the ways in which one catches a glimpse of passages or 'lines of flight' drawn between the representable and the unrepresentable, the visible and the imperceptible, the familiar and the cosmic.)

3. Art in the fourth dimension

Linda Dalrymple Henderson's study *The Fourth Dimension and Non-Euclidean Geometry in Modern Art* (2013) may hold the key to a whole series of interlinked obscurities in Deleuze's cryptic attempt to rewrite transcendental philosophy in *Difference and Repetition*. There is not space to undertake a full-scale revisitation of *Difference and Repetition* from this perspective, here, but I can suggest in outline what that undertaking would look like, while focusing for the moment on the particular issue of how it is that a connection between the early avant-garde's interest in the fourth dimension and Deleuze's reconfiguration of the transcendental conditions of experience led Deleuze directly to some of his most enigmatic and esoteric spiritual affirmations, and to an ethical vision that verges on mystical and hermetic modes of ecstatic communion with cosmic forces.

As we have seen, the theory of intensive difference is a theory of differential intensification. It is a theory of process. But Deleuze also insists, paradoxically, that such processes are also 'ideas' in the sense of having virtual 'forms' that insist in actual processes of development without being reducible to them. There are, as it were, 'transcendental forms' of becoming, distinct modes of differential intensification. This is where Linda Dalrymple Henderson's history of the role of the spatial fourth dimension in modern art is crucial for understanding Deleuze's vision of the transcendental. Her fascinating work tells the story of the impact of nineteenth- and early-twentieth-century mathematical and scientific debates about a spatial 'fourth dimension' on the early avant-garde, especially a series of early abstractionists including not only Cubists but Duchamp, Max Weber, Gelett Burgess, Claude Bragdon, Russian Futurism, Suprematism, Malevich, and the early De Stijl.[12]

Non-Euclidean and *n*-dimensional geometry was being worked out over the course of the nineteenth century. This development caused something of a crisis in the then-dominant neo-Kantian philosophy. Kant had argued in the *Critique of Pure Reason* for the ideal, transcendental nature of space, but had also held that the rules of Euclidean geometry were a priori synthetic truths. If geometries of *n*-dimensions or non-Euclidean geometries (geometries that were consistent while certain of the axioms, such as that of the non-intersection of parallel lines, denied) were also consistent, this implied that either the transcendental conditions of experience were not fixed, and could develop or change over time, or that there might be different conditions relative to different empirical frameworks. In either case, there would be no universal transcendental condition for the verification of knowledge claims by experience.

Thinkers who wished to remain faithful to Kant on this point, such as Charles Renouvier, simply held firm and claimed that non-Euclidean space was 'less legitimate' because less intuitive. In this way the Kantians hoped to protect the sanctity (i.e. putative universality) of the transcendental from the vagueries of the empirical. On the other hand, positivists such as Helmholtz insisted that we could in fact intuit non-Euclidean space by imagining, for instance, what it would be like to trace lines from the centre of a sphere to its exterior. Because each 'point' on the surface of a sphere is an infinitesimal 'section' of a curve, lines drawn from the centre of a sphere to any point on the surface are at an infinite remove from every other point. This gives us an imaginative intuition of 'pseudospherical' space. Thus there is, for Helmholtz, an imaginative intuition possible of non-Euclidean, pseudospherical space.

Poincaré had 'resolved' the dispute between idealists and positivists with his 'conventionalist' view of space: space has the dimensions that it is 'convenient' for us to recognize: 'experience does not prove to us that space has three dimensions; it only proves to us that it is convenient to attribute three to it' (1891: 774). To put this in Humean terms, what is 'convenient' does not reflect transcendental conditions, but is rather what a matter of habit. And habits can be changed, even if this is extremely difficult. Henderson notes that Poincaré fully embraced the possibility of developing a sensorium to which higher dimensions of space would be convenient. As she puts it, for Poincaré, 'if, for instance, the two muscular sensations of accommodation and convergence of the eye, which normally function together in one series, were to vary independently of one another, the "complete visual space" to which they give rise would have four instead of three dimensions. Pursuing this line of thought, Poincaré makes a statement that must have intrigued the Cubists and their generation: "From this point of view, *motor space would have as many dimensions as we have muscles*"'.[13]

Fascination with the spatial fourth dimension ran across many intellectual currents in the early twentieth century. E.A. Abbot's *Flatland: A Romance of Many Dimensions by a Square* popularized the idea of space of higher dimensions. Theosophy seized upon the idea as a clue to the reality of spirit. And Charles Howard Hinton developed a 'hyperspace' philosophy that could count even philosophers such as William James among its admirers. In *The Fourth Dimension* (1904) and *An Episode of Flatland* (1907), Hinton explicitly called out experience of space as three dimensions as a fixation rooted in habits and in 'self elements', a claim that has profound resonance with ideas in tantric yoga – ideas that fascinated the young Deleuze – about the need to develop higher states of consciousness in order to overcome the binds of ego-consciousness that cause suffering and malaise. Hinton even developed a tool called a 'tesseract', a set of interlocking coloured cubes, to be used in a 'casting out of self' for the development of consciousness of higher dimensions.

William James corresponded with Hinton, and James' own interests in abnormal psychological states such as clairvoyance and apparitions are articulated in terms of the hypothesis of a 'continuum of cosmic consciousness' to which all human minds are connected.[14] It is this 'spiritual' passion for the fourth dimension expressed in Hinton and in William James, and in the painter Max Weber, that is closest to Deleuze's own ideas about a dynamic transcendental, a conception of spatiality not as a static coordinate of perception, but as a dynamic field within which human transcendental faculties *develop*. But the fourth dimension also influenced science fiction and surrealism, as evidenced in H.G Well's *Time Machine* and the importance of higher dimensional space for Alfred Jarry's 'pataphysics (and Deleuze himself wrote a late essay admiring Jarry's insights).

But the most important expression of interest in the spatial fourth dimension is the connection made by a series of artists between a materiality of higher dimensions and a spirituality of experimental life. Henderson goes to great lengths to demonstrate Duchamp's lifelong fascination with the fourth dimension and to trace the ways in which this interest was extended 'from a "playful physics" to a "playful philosophy" for living' (Henderson 2013: 163). And for an American artist such as Max Weber, experimentation with planes and forms was an attempt 'to evoke with grains of matter the very atoms of color and time' (1916: 69–70).[15]

There is not room here to summarize Henderson's account at greater length. But it is absolutely clear to any careful reader of Deleuze's remarks on painting (in particular, but also on music and cinema) that it is this experimental attempt at provoking a vision of the imperceptible, and the ethical and spiritual stakes of such experimentation, that forms the core of Deleuze's metaphysics. Suddenly much of what is obscure in *Difference and Repetition* and *A Thousand Plateaus* becomes much clearer. The specificities of assemblages, and their 'ideal' or 'virtual' status, seem to have everything to do with something like the intuition of a spatial fourth dimension. The spatial fourth dimension is absolutely precise, but it is totally 'imperceptible', and can only be visualized by utilizing three-dimensional figures. These figures have to be represented, somehow, as if they are in motion *around themselves*. It is as if they are 'unfolding' and/or 'refolding' themselves around some implied but indiscernible axis. Unlike the rotation of a two-dimensional figure around a point, or of a three-dimensional figure around a line, the fourth dimension can only be 'perceived', or better *felt*, by suggesting or *implying* how a three-dimensional figure might rotate around a plane. This is very difficult to portray, and demands a development, an expansion, an ordeal of perceptual faculties. At minimum, it is clear that the interest of the early-twentieth-century avant-garde in the fourth dimension is a way of comprehending what Deleuze's metaphysics is trying to describe. And at most, it could be argued that this aesthetic experimentation is *precisely* what that metaphysics is trying to describe.

In any case, in some very important sense, the spatial fourth dimension may be the clue to why Deleuze ascribes a power of 'transcendental empiricism' to modern art (and by modern Deleuze clearly means late-nineteenth- to early-twentieth-century experimentation with form). In the case of visual art, this experimentation under the heading of transcendental empiricism is a method of properly spatial (or 'hyperspatial') intensification that has an essentially 'temporal' dimension, insofar as it is only the *implied movement* of actual three-dimensional figures that reveals the imperceptible virtual dynamic those figures are capable of expressing. This peculiar temporality of the image is also, of course, what is at stake in Deleuze's reading of cinematic images in terms of their ability to produce a 'time-image': with cinema,

> we constitute a sheet of transformation which invents a kind of transverse continuity or communication between several sheets (sheets of the remembered past or imagined future), and weaves a network of non-localizable relations between them. In this way we extract non-chronological time ... The screen itself is the cerebral membrane where immediate and direct confrontations take place between the past and the future, the inside and the outside, at a distance impossible to determine, independent of any fixed point ... The image no longer has space and movement as its primary characteristics but topology and time. (1989: 123)

4. Political spirituality, animist rationales

By focusing on the importance of aesthetic experimentation with the spatial fourth dimension for Deleuze's metaphysics, the otherwise obscure link between Deleuze's apparently extremely formal and ontological commitment to a system of intensive difference and the existential, ethical, and aesthetic commitments that system is supposed to imply becomes much clearer. Perhaps finally and most crucially, Deleuze's very early interest in the *mathesis* of Johann Malfatti de Montereggio, and in a Western esoteric tradition that appropriates tantric yoga, also begins to make much more systematic sense.[16] Tantric practices (the word means 'continuous' or 'continuity') are aimed at realizing enlightenment not through the renunciation of the world of sense, but by coming to perceive the sensuous world as an *extension* of consciousness. There is an exact and uncanny parallel here between the ancient teachings of tantric yoga on the adjunction of consciousness and embodiment to the avant-garde experimental methods of adjoining intuition of the fourth dimension to experimentation in three dimensions. In tantric teachings, the disciplines and practices of coming to comprehend the continuity between consciousness and experience are all oriented towards creating a body capable of perceiving and inhabiting an intensified spatiality. As contemporary French tantric master Daniel Odier puts it bluntly, absolute consciousness *is* something like an absolute Space. 'Once we penetrate deeply into the human fabric, comparisons with art become vital, because the tantrika's search is precisely to transform life into a work of art – that is to say, into the discovery of the profound relationship of individual humanity to spatiality' (2001: 166). What is significant here is the idea of human life as a work of art not in some general sense, let alone of some mere dandyism, but the highly specific sense that artistic experimentation with the fourth dimension gives to human perception and inhabitation of space. The tantric yogini develops the capacity to *live* what the avant-garde attempted to convey or depict – a complex, enfolded spatiality, an energetic spatiality that is absolutely precise even if in constant flux, change, and perpetual motion.

This is the clue to Deleuze's own attraction to Guattari's machinic animism. If animism, according to Viveiros de Castro, is the religion of the decolonized self, then one can see clearly the political stakes of spiritual thought in Deleuze. Through Deleuze's work one can see clearly a set of metaphysical reflections that fuse aesthetic experimentation, political revolt, and spiritual ordeal in a single clamour of being. When it is recalled that the rise of the early avant-garde was connected to a revival of interest in non-Western modalities of representation, especially in Africa and pre-Columbian America, the postcolonial stakes of Deleuze's later affirmations, with Guattari, of animism and sorcery as fundamental ethical and political problems likewise become much clearer. As a reclaimed spiritual project, passing through but not reducible to aesthetic experimentation, machinic animism is the religion of a society against the state, the battle cry of a decolonized self: *we are not rational animals, but animist rationales.*

Notes

1 William E. Connolly's remarks in *The Fragility of Things* are instructive on this point. Connolly avers with Deleuze that not all the drives in organic lives are drives to survival.

2 Stengers' essay, as well as several others I reference here, is contained in a summer 2012 volume of *e-flux* dedicated to an exhibition on animism curated by Anselm Franke, http://www.e-flux.com/journal/introduction—"animism"/ (accessed 1 April 2015).

3 For more on this point, see my reading contrasting Deleuze to Freud on the uncanny, Deleuze (2013).

4 Isabel Stengers, 'Reclaiming Animism', http://www.e-flux.com/journal/reclaiming-animism/ (accessed 1 April 2015).

5 Ibid.

6 Ibid.

7 Ibid.

8 http://www.e-flux.com/journal/assemblages-felix-guattari-and-machinic-animism/ (accessed 1 April 2015).

9 Clastres plays a key role in *A Thousand Pleateau*'s '1227: A Treatise on Nomadology – The War Machine', and throughout *Anti-Oedipus*, especially in Chapter 3, 'Savages, Barbarians, and Civilized Men'.

10 This mode of consciousness is also a kind of controlled delirium. I have argued in *The Hermetic Deleuze: Philosophy and Spiritual Ordeal* (2012) that there is a specific tradition (a plurality of esoteric traditions roughly known as hermeticism in the West) that takes the necessity of deliriums (ecstatic states, trance states, meditational states, erotic states) seriously enough to form traditions of practice around them. I argue that it is clear that Deleuze was influenced by this tradition and mutates it in his own way. One of the most important aspects of this tradition is a conception of 'life' that includes both the living and the non-living. What is 'machinic' about machinic animism means in some sense a subjectivity beyond the distinction of the living and the non-living. It is not necessary for another to be alive in order to have communion, sympathy, and cooperativity with that other. If we press the point, I would argue for a generalized *necromancy* that can be articulated through Deleuze (and Guattari's) weird spirituality. This is perhaps clearest in Deleuze's *Cinema 2*, where the one capable of receiving the perceptual shocks of film is described as a 'spiritual automata' who can access the repotentiation of time through the shards and shrouds of culture. Such 'belief in the world' is the ability, if not to raise the dead, then to remain with the dead without dying oneself, and to retain the potencies of the dead without melancholy and mourning. Alchemy, as Jung first and then many others have appreciated, provides not only a profound model for machinic animism but also perhaps the tradition to which Deleuze ultimately belongs.

11 For more on this point, see Henry Somers-Hall's excellent account of the difference between Hegel's philosophy of the organism and Deleuze's conception of transversal or meta-individual organizing principles in Somers-Hall (2012).

12 Claude Bragdon's 'The Projections Made by a Cube in Traversing a Plane' (*A Pimer of Higher Space*, Rochester, NY, 1913, Pl. 30) is probably the most fascinating attempt to provide a visual exercise in perceiving the fourth dimension. He specifically calls the cubes 'higher selves' that appear in limited forms to our perceptual apparatus bounded by the 'lower space' or lesser-dimensional world. This is an extraordinarily exact way, it seems to me, to understand relations between the virtual and the actual in Deleuze's system.

13 Henderson, 37. Poincaré, *La Science et l'hypothèse*, ch. 4.

14 James (1909: 589).

15 Weber (1916: 69–70).

16 As Christian Kerslake puts it, in 'The Somnambulist and the Hermaphrodite',

> Malfatti puts Schelling's emphasis on *Erzeugung* [procreation] right at the centre of his system, taking the concept at both sexual and metaphysical levels,

> attempting to find the pathways between the two. He continually focuses on the sexual and ecstatic aspects of Indian mysticism, laying out a vast sexualised ontology, culminating (as in Baader's system) in the 'hermaphroditic' consciousness of the human sexual act. In *Anarchy and Hierarchy* it is as if Schelling's final theosophy comes to completion in a hallucinatory Tantrism, in which the living body of God, in its most complete self-development, itself appears in hermaphroditic form in human sexuality, where the coming-to-divine-consciousness becomes identical to the psychosexual attainment, along Tantric lines, of spiritual 'bisexuality'. This 'system', uncovered by Malfatti, is said to form the basis for all subsequent Eastern and Western esoteric thought, and now furnishes us with the long-lost key to the ultimate system of medicine. (Kerslake 2015).

Bibliography

Casteneda, C. (1974) *Tales of Power*. New York: Simon and Schuster.

Colebrook, C. (2011) *Deleuze and the Meaning of Life*. London: Bloomsbury.

Connolly, W.E. (2013) *The Fragility of Things*. Durham, NC: Duke University Press.

Deleuze, G. (1989) *Cinema 2: The Time-Image*, trans H. Tomlinson and R. Galeta. New York: Continuum.

Deleuze, G. (1994) *Difference and Repetition*, trans. P. Patton. New York: Columbia University Press.

Deleuze, G. (2013) 'Learning the Uncanny', in D. Masny and I. Semetsky (eds.), *Deleuze and Education*. Edinburgh: Edinburgh University Press, pp. 177–196.

Deleuze, G. and F. Guattari (1987) *A Thousand Plateaus*, trans. B. Massumi. New York: Continuum.

Hadot, Pierre (1995) *Philosophy as a Way of Life: Spiritual Exercises from Socrates to Foucault*. New York: Wiley and Blackwell.

Henderson, L.D. (2013) *The Fourth Dimension and Non-Euclidian Geometry in Modern Art*. Cambridge: MIT Press.

James, William. (October 1909) 'The Confidences of a "Psychical Researcher"', *American Magazine*, LXVIII, pp. 580–589.

Kerslake, Christian. (2015) 'The Somnambulist and the Hermaphrodite', http://www.culturemachine.net/index.php/cm/rt/printerFriendly/243/225 (accessed 1 April 2015).

Odier, D. (2001) *Desire: The Tantric Path to Awakening*. Rochester, NY: Inner Traditions.

Poincare, H. (1891) 'Les Geometries non euclidiennes', *Revue General des Sciences Pures et Appliquees*, 2, pp. 769–774.

Somers-Hall, Henry (2012) *Hegel, Deleuze, and the Critique of Representation: Dialectics of Negation and Difference*. New York: SUNY Press.

Ramey, Joshua. (2012) *The Hermetic Deleuze: Philosophy and Spiritual Ordeal*. Durham, NC: Duke University Press.

Stengers, I. 'Reclaiming Animism', http://www.e-flux.com/journal/reclaiming-animism / (accessed 1 April 2015).

Weber, M. (1916) 'The Equilibrium of the Innate', *Essays on Art*. New York: W.E. Rudge.

5

The Apocalyptic Unconscious: Schizoanalysis as Political Theology

Aidan Tynan

In the preface to *Difference and Repetition*, Deleuze writes that 'the task of modern philosophy is to overcome the alternatives temporal/non-temporal, historical/eternal and particular/universal', and adds of his own text that 'it should have been an apocalyptic book' (1994: xxi). The precise nature of Deleuze's apocalypticism is one of his philosophy's great secrets. A concern with eschatological and apocalyptic themes runs throughout his works. He wrote an introduction to the French translation of D.H. Lawrence's *Apocalypse* – an analysis of the Revelation of John – while his reading of Proust argues that the hero of the *Search* apprehends the 'finality of the world' in 'crumbs and chaos' (Deleuze 2000: 50, 111). The end of the world visions of the famous nineteenth-century paranoiac Daniel Paul Schreber were a particular source of inspiration for *Anti-Oedipus*. Indeed, the latter book may well be the apocalyptic one Deleuze felt *Difference and Repetition* should have been. One suggestive definition Deleuze and Guattari offer for schizoanalysis is as an eschatological reengineering of psychoanalysis:

> if materialist psychiatry may be defined as the psychiatry that introduces the concept of production into consideration of the problem of desire, it cannot avoid posing in eschatological terms the problem of the ultimate relationship between the analytic machine, the revolutionary machine, and desiring-machines. (1983: 35)

What is the eschatological politics being suggested in these lines? How do analysis, revolution, and desire find their connection to one another through the ancient category of the eschaton, the end time? What is Deleuze's apocalypticism and what is its relation to the doctrine of judgement against which he so adamantly contrasted the goals of his own philosophy? Addressing these questions allows us to sketch the outlines of a schizoanalytic political theology.

1. The immanent eschaton

In an excellent recent volume, Joshua Ramey observes that 'Deleuze's philosophy has yet to be read as a perspective from which the anxieties of secular culture toward spirituality might be overcome' (2012: 212). He suggests that such an overcoming might take the form of an eschatology: '[Deleuzian] thought traces a path toward the identification of immanence with an eschatological endgame of cosmic scale' (2012: 218). The task of thinking immanence involves what Ramey calls a 'spiritual ordeal' because it reveals a profound complicity of mind and nature that forces thought to think what is beyond it (2012: 13). The ordeal of immanence forces thought beyond any mere representational capacity, compelling it to grasp its real power in a movement of constitutive self-limitation. What Ramey calls the 'immanent eschaton' of Deleuzian thought pushes Kantian critique towards a geophilosophy revealing not a world but a self-grounding desert or scorched earth that is world-destroying (2012: 4).[1] Deleuze spoke of a moment of 'catastrophe' in the genesis of thinking that compromises our ability to represent the world but which thereby reveals the ground that rumbles beneath the tranquillity of our representations (1994: 35). Immanence thus entails a kind of loss of world through a razing of cognitive foundations.

Not all apocalypses are catastrophic *per se*, but they are generally oriented around a passing away of the prevailing social and spiritual order at the hands of something entirely unconditioned by it. Apocalyptic is a formal pattern by which the new can be imagined, and affirmed, from within the middle of things. In *Difference and Repetition*, Deleuze mentions the name of the twelfth-century Italian theologian Joachim of Flora in connection with Nietzsche's doctrine of eternal return. Although the reference is brief, and rarely if ever commented upon in the secondary literature, it is telling with regard to Deleuze's relation to the apocalyptic tradition and how this is borne out in the revolutionary project begun in *Anti-Oedipus*. Deleuze observes that 'cyclical' conceptions of history, such as Nietzsche's but also Vico's, have generally divided history into 'three temporal stages' (1994: 92–93). This pattern originates with Joachim, who divided history into three 'Testaments' corresponding to the Father, Son, and Holy Spirit, the third being marked by a period of transition. Jacob Taubes has argued that the Joachitic view of history 'shatters medieval theocracy' because it transformed the understanding of what realizing God's kingdom on earth might entail, severing the kingdom of God from its Augustinian identification with the authority of the Church which 'withers away' in the revolutionary programme of the *ecclesia spiritualis* (2009: 86, 93). The literal *parousia*, or return of Christ as imperial redeemer, is replaced with the advent of monastic communism, the collective messiah. From Joachim we get Thomas Müntzer, prophet of the peasant rebellions, and John of Leyden's Anabaptist revolutionaries in the sixteenth century. The idea of three ages of history reappears in Lessing, Comte, Hegel, and Schelling, and many have observed that Joachim can be seen as the progenitor of the modern revolutionary tradition.[2]

The three-stage historical scheme of primitive, despotic, and capitalist that Deleuze and Guattari propose in *Anti-Oedipus* is a kind of apocalypse. In *Difference and Repetition*, however, these three stages – glossed as the 'the age of gods, the age of heroes and the age of men' – are interpreted not so much as historical periods but as dramatic archetypes or elements of a form (1994: 93). Deleuze observes that Marx's famous adage about great historical events occurring twice, first as tragedy and then as farce, reverses the traditional understanding of dramatic movement (1994: 91). The tragedy of Oedipus, for example, has a three-stage structure or triple repetition of the same event: there is a 'before', in which Oedipus does not yet know he has killed the king/father, a moment of revelation or 'during', and then an 'after' in which Oedipus is banished to the desert (1994: 92). The 'before' is comic because it implies misrecognition and disguise, a 'comedy of errors' (Faulkner 2006: 104). When the masks fall, there is a transition from the comic to the tragic, but this implies 'a third moment beyond the comic and the tragic' that secures their interdependence, their metamorphosis from one into the other. Marx, however, reverses the chronology and this in effect liberates the 'after' from its role as mediator: 'the comic succeeds the tragic as though the failure of metamorphosis, raised to the absolute, presupposed an earlier metamorphosis already completed' (Deleuze 1994: 92). The moment of revelation is no longer the dropping of masks but the appearance of time in itself, an 'empty form' of time independent of the historical contents that fill it and from the whole representationalist logic of resemblance and (mis) recognition (Deleuze 1994: 91–92).

Deleuze links this to the doctrine of eternal return, which he says is also composed of three parts. He says that *Thus Spoke Zarathustra* is 'clearly a drama, a theatrical work', but that

> the third moment remains absent: this is the moment of the revelation and affirmation of eternal return, and implies the death of Zarathustra. We know that Nietzsche did not have time to write this projected part.... Nietzsche gave us only the past condition and the present metamorphosis, but not the unconditioned which was to have resulted as the 'future'. (1994: 92)

This linking of Nietzsche and Marx serves to raise the problem of a third age defined not by the contents of historical events and their resemblances to one another but by a form capable of grasping the 'condition of historical action itself' (1994: 91). Deleuze argues, following Pierre-Simon Ballanche – who saw history as a series of palingenetic ordeals – that the third age is the age of the plebeian or 'no one', the 'modern Oedipus' (1994: 93). There is a repetition specific to the third age that might abolish the resemblances established in the first two and break the circularity of history by which only the same returns. Again, it is not so much a question of historical events here as of their inscription, their repetition at the level of signs by which an event becomes history. This is precisely where apocalyptic plays a role in Deleuze's thinking. Deleuze quotes Joachim's statement that 'there are two signifying things and one signified'. The eschatological destiny of the first two ages or repetitions is the third: 'the present is the repeater, the past is repetition itself, but the future is that which is repeated'. This is why 'the secret of repetition as a whole lies in that which is repeated, in that which is twice signified.... The third ensures the order, the totality of the series and the final end of time' (Deleuze 1994: 93–94).

This seems consistent enough with Joachim's theology. In his *Liber de Concordia*, he traces parallels between the Old and New Testaments, but he gives concordance an entirely new meaning through the possibility of their historical realization in a third. As R.L. Petersen has shown, Joachim's three states of history are designed to accommodate these concordances as duality to trinity: 'history may be seen as three spiritual states, or as two ages running from Jacob to Christ, then from Christ to the consummation' (1993: 33). The theme of 'two witness' or 'paired heralds foreshadowing a new spiritual age' appears throughout biblical tradition generally; in Joachim's reading of the Revelation of John in *Exposito in Apocalypsim*, 'the witnesses are to be two individuals or two spiritual orders coming in the spirit and power of Enoch and Elijah to preach and fight against Antichrist. Two orders of clerics and monks, modelled on Moses and Elijah, point toward and anticipate the third spiritual state'. Joachim's two witnesses 'are similar to the two olive trees or lampstands of the prophet Zechariah, the raven and dove sent out from Noah's ark after the Flood, and the two women who followed Christ, Mary and Martha' (Petersen 1993: 35).

For Deleuze, however, it is the Antichrist, not the war against him, that functions as the repeated of the third spiritual age. This is what raises the problem of belief that figures so centrally in the schizoanalytic politics of desire. The Antichrist is the product of a belief that has been released from the law of representation or resemblance, 'a parody of belief' that both frees us from belief and allows us to believe without tragic consequences (e.g. the death of God). At stake here is not faith as subjective disposition, as something that haunts a subject divided between conditions and actions, but what faith is capable of realizing, a productive faith that dissolves our tormented duality: 'a different and more mortuary betrothal between the dead God and the dissolved self forms the true condition by default and the true metamorphosis of the agent, both of which disappear in the unconditioned character of the product'. The Antichrist can thus be seen as the agent of grace:

> We have too often been invited to judge the atheist from the viewpoint of the belief or the faith that we suppose still drives him – in short, from the viewpoint of grace; not to be tempted by the inverse operation – to judge the believer by the violent atheist by which he is inhabited, the Antichrist eternally given 'once and for all' within grace. (1994: 95–96)

This is enlightening for our understanding of *Anti-Oedipus* because in that book the political impasses of capitalism are framed in terms of a spiritual emergency identified by Deleuze and Guattari not as the loss of belief but as 'a belief by virtue of nonbelief' or a flight of belief to the unconscious (1983: 107). Our remaining pious after the shattering of belief's objective (representational) edifice is one of the main political issues schizoanalysis sets out to engage: 'how can we continue to be pious? We have repudiated and lost all our beliefs that proceeded by way of objective representations' (1983: 307–8). This diagnosis is clearly indebted to Lacan, who famously stated that 'the true formula for atheism is not *God is dead*... but *God is unconscious*' (1977a: 59), and to Octave Mannoni's formula for the fetishistic structure of disavowal ('I know very well, but all the same ... '), which Žižek has more recently used to define the structure of contemporary ideology.[3] In the passage from *Difference and Repetition* quoted above, however, we can note that the spiritual prescription of the Antichrist is precisely the opposite of the Lacanian diagnosis. Deleuze is suggesting that the operation of grace is not to discern in the atheist the belief that he conceals even from himself but to extract from religion the atheism of its belief, the living principle of a 'belief in this world' that is, however secretly, at work in even the most extreme religious phenomena. The act of faith is always conditioned by atheism, not the other way around, which is why, as Deleuze and Guattari put it in *What Is Philosophy?*, all religion but especially Christianity 'secretes' atheism (1994: 92).

2. Energetics of the sign

Taubes argues that the eschaton is the answer various traditions, ancient and modern, have given to the question, 'what makes an event history?' (2009: 3). History finds definition through a limit. As we will see, the eschatological politics of desire presented in *Anti-Oedipus* are concerned in large part with the role of limits. If the concept of eschaton has proved remarkably enduring in our secular age it is because, as Frank Kermode points out in a classic work on the apocalyptic tradition, 'the image of the end can never be *permanently* falsified' (2000: 17). The failure of the end to come as so frequently prophesied is powerless to dispel it because the limit has become displaceable as a result of certain social and spiritual conditions. Taubes goes so far as to suggest that the history of Christianity is defined by the nonoccurence of the *parousia* and the attempt to understand this as part of some divine purpose (2009: 65–66). With eschatological disappointment comes something like a modern historical consciousness, an awareness that the schemes we use to make sense of history and give meaning to events are themselves historical. The eschaton is thus temporalized even as it continues to function as a limit for a historical series.

Kermode writes that 'already in St. Paul and St. John there is a tendency to conceive of the End as happening at every moment; this is the moment when the modern concept of *crisis* was born ... No longer imminent, the end is immanent' (2000: 25). The Greek term *krisis* means judgement, but it is also related to a distinction or a division. We can distinguish time as simple chronology, as *chronos* – as passing time or waiting time, as *saeculum*, the time that, according to Revelation, 'shall be no more' – from *kairos*, time as transitional turning points or hinges, moments, or occasions (Kermode 2000: 47). *Kairos* is the time into which *chronos* passes, the former being 'contractions' of the latter, as Agamben puts it (2005: 69). The distinction of these two temporalities is what defines crisis and the division of messianic from secular time. To be living in a time of crisis means to be living under God's judgement, when things are in transition, when time is running out.

What Kermode argues, however, is that Joachim makes the moment of transition a historical period in itself, one that belongs neither to the eschaton nor the *saeculum* (2000: 12). But the transition, isolated from the notion of end, can be endlessly drawn out, and the idea that we are living in a time of transition becomes ubiquitous to modern historical consciousness and the political ideologies it breeds. This displacement of the eschaton is fundamental for capitalism, as Deleuze and Guattari argue. What we are thus dealing with is three orders of time, not two, since the immanentization of the eschaton through the notion of an indefinite historical transition that effectively takes its place requires a time between the eternity of the end and the temporality of history. Christian theologians such as Aquinas felt it necessary to arrive at such a third order of time to accommodate the Augustinian doctrine of *creation ex nihilo* to the Aristotelian theory of prime matter and a universe without beginning or end. The result was what Aquinas called *aevum*, the Latin term for what the Greeks called *aion*.

The latter will be familiar to readers of Deleuze's *The Logic of Sense*, which insists on and develops an opposition between *chronos* and *aion* as distinct temporal orders within Stoic philosophy. Deleuze characterizes *chronos* as the infinitely expanding present or the capacity of the present to encompass greater and greater spans of time: the present can mean this minute, this hour, this century, and so on ad infinitum. *Aion*, by contrast, is the infinitely subdividable instant, the 'now' that constantly escapes my grasp by splitting itself between past and future so as to become ineffable and abstract. Instead of time as trinity of past, present, and future we have an opposition between two mutually exclusive understandings of time

> one of which [*chronos*] is always definite, active or passive; the other [*aion*] is eternally Infinitive and eternally neutral. One is cyclical, measures the movement of bodies and depends on the matter which limits and fills it out; the other is a pure straight line at the surface, incorporeal, unlimited, an empty form of time, independent of all matter. (1990: 73)

It has been shown, quite convincingly, that in reality the Stoics held to no such theory of time and that the term *aion* is nowhere used in a technical way in their writings. Marcus Aurelius, for example, can be seen using *aion* and *chronos* interchangeably in his *Meditations*. Deleuze's theory is at best an anachronistic reconstruction (see Sellars 2007 on all these points). In fact, it could be suggested that what Deleuze calls *aion* has more in common with the much later concept of *aevum*, since this denotes a form of duration characteristic of spiritual substances such as angelic bodies and is demonstrative of how temporal things can participate in eternity. For Deleuze, *aion* is not the time in which an event happens but in which it is infinitized, eternalized, in which it is never quite over and done with. For this reason, it is also the time of an inscription that doubles, without resembling, the states of things.

Deleuze defines *aion* as being composed of events or singularities. More precisely, *aion* is the eternal or infinitive aspect of any event, its incorporeal or spiritual double constituting the inexhaustible remainder that is inscribed in a different time than its actualization in matter. Events are 'signs' and, like *kairoi*, constitute 'sublime occasions' when everything happens at once and the totality of time seems to present itself, as if all time were needed for anything to happen (Deleuze 1990: 73; 1994: 190). But *kairos* also denotes the 'propitious moment', which Deleuze defines as being at the origin of the representationalist account of difference that begins with Plato and Aristotle. This is the moment when the eye – the 'Greek eye' – inscribes difference between the too large and the too small, the excess and the default, mistaking thereby the conditions of the world with the adequacy of our representations. This sets the scene for the dogmatism of philosophical judgement that Deleuze never ceased to inveigh against throughout his work. The essence of judgement, he tells us, lies in the notion of the 'best distributed' or best proportioned, the 'just measure' (1994: 32). Deleuze offers a definition of God along these lines: 'God makes the world by calculating, but his calculations never work out exactly [*juste*], and this inexactitude or injustice in the result, this irreducible inequality, forms the condition of the world . . . . The world can be regarded as a "remainder"' (1994: 222).

God is the master of divisions, distributions, and disjunctions, the ultimate judge, but if there's a division between world and God it must be because something escapes his judgement. Deleuze famously echoed Artaud's cry 'to have done with the judgment of God'. But Deleuze's views on God are more subtle that this slogan would have us think. Following Kant, he defines God as the 'sum total of the possible . . . from which the exclusive and complete determination of the concept of each thing is derived through disjunction' (Deleuze 1990: 336). As the 'founding' instance of these disjunctions constitutive of phenomenal reality, God is portrayed here like an undifferentiated surface – a desert – waiting to be cut up. But something escapes divine mastery. An opposition between God and a world, which is nothing other than his own self-division, sets in. The Kantian division of noumenon and phenomenon is the act of a God who cannot securely ground his own creation, and cannot ultimately distinguish himself from the Antichrist since in God all disjunctions are included. God and the world were never equal, but it is the unequal in itself that escapes from into profane reality: 'every phenomenon refers to an inequality by which it is conditioned.... Everything which happens and everything which appears is correlated with orders of differences: differences of level, temperature, pressure, tension, potential, *difference of intensity*' (Deleuze 1994: 222). It is as if the desert of the immeasurable yawned open beneath every petty occurrence, every pot boiling over and every cigarette stubbed out.

If, however, these differences of intensity are not so much part of the world as the conditions of the world, if they are the referents of the phenomena by which the world can be read as so many signs, it is because there is something in them that cannot be cancelled out or equalized in the signification. There is in Deleuze's semiotics an energetic conception of the sign. If we can distinguish two things, two fingers of different length, say, then this distinction refers to a third aspect, the element of difference in itself, purely abstract or ideal, that is not actualized in or incarnated in the two things compared but which is the condition of their comparability. Behind ever resemblance is difference in a pure state – not undistributed but corresponding to different kind of distribution, a time off its hinges – that is not cancelled out or exhausted in things. If this is important for our discussion of eschatology, it is because Deleuze arrives at this conception of signs through a critique of a certain account of thermodynamics that he links with judgement and that he calls 'eschatological' (1994: 224).

Deleuze is sceptical of the notion of thermodynamic equilibrium. The notion of universal heat death is certainly a modern kind of eschatology that is at odds with Deleuze's creative ontology. His main aim, however, is not to critique the science of thermodynamics but to point out how both science and philosophy can coincide to 'satisfy' some desire to judge. A certain 'ideology of the middle classes' was gratified by the energetic theories of classical thermodynamics, which Deleuze glosses in the following way: 'qualities are signs which flash across the interval of a difference. In so doing, however, they measure the time of an equalization – in other words, the time taken by the difference to cancel itself out in the extensity in which it is distributed' (1994: 225, 223). The sign becomes a kind of compensation for a degradation that occurs in the interval in which the sign is produced, and this corresponds to an economic logic that is related in fundamental ways to capitalism. Deleuze claims that certain 'basic principles' were produced on this basis that 'satisfied everybody' at a certain politically decisive point: there was 'for the last time a strange alliance at the end of the nineteenth century between science, good sense and philosophy. Thermodynamics was the powerful furnace of that alloy' (1994: 223).

In many ways, the Freudian theory of the death instinct as the longing to return to the inorganic earth can be seen as part of this late-nineteenth-century alliance. If this was eschatological in its desire to equalize and homogenize everything, to be in the 'between' or the 'middle' while thinking itself to be at the end, to heal the rift between God and world through a judicious distribution and an economic logic of measurable quantities, then Deleuze suggests that there is another death instinct, a 'speculative' as opposed to a purely material one, an eschatology on the side of *aion* as opposed to *chronos* (1990: 239). The immanent critique that *Anti-Oedipus* performs on psychoanalytic reason is thus a kind of eschatology of eschatology, an apocalypse applied to the apocalyptic unconscious itself.

3. A new earth

Anti-Oedipus is often read as an attempt to historicize the Freudian unconscious, to de-universalize it, to place it in its proper (i.e. bourgeois-capitalist) context. Of course, people have been trying to do that ever since Freud first formulated his theory, so schizoanalysis on this count would be nothing very new. It is clear, however, that what really concerns Deleuze and Guattari is something more like the history of the conditions that form historical content. It can't simply be a matter of historicizing since what they call 'Oedipus' is the manner in which the unconscious tends to historicize itself and thereby to replace real historical movement with an 'apparent objective movement', to lay down certain laws of destiny such that it submits itself, apparently without resistance, to an 'aggregate of destination', an end point preordained by its origins (Deleuze and Guattari 1983: 101). This is at the core of the schizoanalytic axiom that desire is perfectly capable of desiring its own repression, of composing the infrastructure of repression directly. Lacan recognized this when he maintained that 'events are engendered in a primary historization.... History is already producing itself on the stage where it will be played out' (1977b: 39). Desire is the mode of this primary historization, but this is precisely what makes it repressible. The manner in which we are said to 'resolve' the Oedipus complex has the ring of prophetic repetition or circularity: by internalizing your father's authority in the so-called healthy way, you will find yourself again confronted with it outside the family in the figures of social authority – the teacher, the boss, the cop, the priest – but this time with no way out (Deleuze and Guattari 1983: 79).

Psychoanalysis is mistaken, however, in confining destiny to the family, as if desire's fate were just a family affair: Oedipus is only a 'pseudo destiny' (Deleuze and Guattari 1983: 62). Deleuze and Guattari thus suggest that desire and the social are in fact related along lines of destinal becoming and that this is what constitutes the proper genealogy of desire (1983: 290). Like Oedipus himself, we can repeat well or badly, but all repetition has a destinal mode (Deleuze 1994: 23). What needs to be accounted for is the means by which capitalism expropriates the destinal in order to insert desire into the mechanisms of social reproduction and thereby to inhibit a truly productive desire from breaking the circle. Schizoanalysis is this analysis of destiny, this *Schicksalsanalyse*.

One of Deleuze and Guattari's central concerns, shared by Freud, can thus be said to be with the category of fate in the modern secular age. No other category conveys the tragic extent to which desire has so easily been led to work against its own interests. The Sophoclean master narrative serves Freud well in this respect: Oedipus falls prey to signs that tell him nothing but the truth and desires that lead only to his undoing. What Freud saw was that, at the level of the unconscious, fate and freedom, belief and production, are the same thing. But how can we accept this in an age without gods? Despite what the various attempts to historicize and politicize Freudian theory may give us to think, psychoanalysis was never innocent of history. Its 'disgrace' in this respect lies in its writing of the history of the unconscious, which it inscribes in the name of the father, in the symbolic of repression, as if the fate of desire itself was to be dispossessed of its own name (Deleuze and Guattari 1983: 102). The sign by which we recognize desire is the law, and history begins with the law, but desire and history must therefore be mutually exclusive. Repressed content and repressing form presuppose one another in a vicious circle – wheels within wheels. But what if desire had a kind of history all its own, a time in which its inscription takes place, which doubles but does not resemble the actuality or the contents of events? The exhaustion of history would be revelatory of this other temporality. Deleuze and Guattari, in short, are looking for a positive history in which desire itself would generate the signs we can know it by. This positive history can only be written as an apocalypse.

Deleuze and Guattari insist that there is, however, an apocalyptic pattern already at work in Freud's reasoning. The law of the father is in fact the law of the dead father, meaning that there is a prehistory of the law – in which the father was killed – conditioning its internalization by the 'society of brothers' (Deleuze and Guattari 1983: 79). But if history is identical with the law, history is thus the time of an expiation, a purgation or digestion of the guilt that accompanies the murder. The unconscious therefore is defined in terms of a before and an afterward, a prehistorical and post-historical, which are effectively rendered impossible but necessary. This apocalyptic pattern informs much of Freud's thinking, especially in *Moses and Monotheism*. History *per se* is the time it takes for the memory of the murder of the father-god to return to consciousness, for latency to exhaust itself in an entropic atonement. It is this Oedipal logic, much more than the notion of the death instinct (which in many ways it underwrites), that constitutes psychoanalytic eschatology. Lacan at least suggests this much when he wrote in his seminar on ethics that 'I have led you to the point of apocalypse' – a fact which is echoed in Deleuze and Guattari's admiration of Lacan for having made psychoanalysis ready for autocritique (Deleuze and Guattari 1983: 268; Lacan 1992: 207). In any case, Deleuze and Guattari insist that the politics of schizoanalysis revolve around a contestation of the meaning of eschatology:

> Oedipus is a limit. But 'limit' has many different meanings, since it can be at the beginning as an inaugural event, in the role of a matrix; or in the middle as a structural function ensuring the mediation of personages and the ground of their relations; or at the end as an eschatological determination. Now we have seen that it is only in this last sense that Oedipus is a limit. This is also the case for desiring-production. But in fact this last sense itself can be understood in many different ways. (Deleuze and Guattari 1983: 175)

The third age, after the primitive and the despotic, is the capitalist. But capitalism bears witness to a return of all the old regimes in a mixed semiotic form that is constantly reviving older semiotic regimes. Capitalist culture is defined by disavowed or repudiated belief, a 'motley painting of everything that has ever been believed' (Deleuze and Guattari 1983: 34). This is how psychoanalytic theory was able to develop: the questions animating Freud's discoveries related to the disjunction of conscious avowal and unconscious desire, to conflicts between actions and the unconscious beliefs conditioning them. If the Freudian unconscious is filled with images from primitive and despotic society, this is because in the capitalist age 'everything returns' but in a repudiated or half-believed way: 'Everything, the myth of the earth, the tragedy of the despot, is taken up again as shadows projected on a stage. The great territorialities have fallen into ruin, but the structure proceeds with all the subjective and private reterritorializations' (Deleuze and Guattari 1983: 308).

This exhaustion of belief, however, marks the culmination of theology. Deleuze says that 'it is our epoch which has discovered theology. One no longer needs to believe in God. We seek rather the "structure," that is, the form which may be filled with beliefs, but the structure has no need to be filled in order to be called "theological"' (1990: 322). The structure, as Kant was the first notice, is precisely the disjunction, the limit that is constantly displacing itself, the God who cannot secure his own divisions. The account of capitalism presented in *Anti-Oedipus* is intimately concerned with limits: 'capitalism tends toward a threshold of decoding that will destroy the socius in order to make it a body without organs and unleash the flows of desire on this body as a deterritorialized field' (Deleuze and Guattari 1983: 33). Capitalism's 'revolutionary' movement tends towards a limit, 'the schizophrenic limit', in a way that threatens the consistency of the social formation with dissolution, but it must also 'displace' this limit, pushing it away and keeping it close in a 'double movement' that defines the perpetually imperilled reproduction of the social body (Deleuze and Guattari 1983: 119). This is what defines capitalism's immanence, the manner it has of internalizing the limits restricting its growth only to redraw them at a further remove. Capitalism goes to the ends of the earth in this way, reproducing itself by internalizing every hitherto 'natural' limit and rendering the absolute relative. But this does not happen without what Deleuze and Guattari call 'decoding', the unravelling of the symbolic or cultural systems that tie us to a social territory. Capitalism quite literally deterritorializes societies by making them globally mobile, but it also decodes our beliefs in order to render behaviours plastic to their environments.

It thus becomes possible to view all prior social formations in the light of capitalism. Deleuze and Guattari maintain, quoting Maruice Godelier, that 'the West's line of development, far from being universal because it will recur everywhere, appears universal because it recurs nowhere else.... It is typical therefore because, in its singular progress, it has obtained a universal result' (1983: 140). Capitalism reveals a certain type of exploitation that is unique in being nakedly economic and dependent on unfettered economic flows. In this sense, it is different from every other social formation – whose forms of exploitation were clothed in a cultural superstructure – while revealing the economic nature of exploitation as such.

But why is the limit towards which capitalism tends eschatological, historically terminal, and not just socially cataclysmic? Why is capitalism 'at the end of history' (Deleuze and Guattari 1983: 153)? Francis Fukuyama famously said this after the end of the Cold War, but for exactly the opposite reasons. Deleuze and

Guattari invert the traditional ethnocentric ideology that identifies history with the genealogy of the civilized West, that conflates history as a whole with the story of Western dominance at the expense of those so-called primitives who are generally deemed, in Eric Wolf's evocative phrase, 'people without history'. Could it not be said that it is precisely we, not the primitives, who are outside history? We global capitalist subjects are the ones who find ourselves without the security of beliefs capable of conferring meaning on events and embedding us in a world. It is odd, perhaps, to call capitalism eschatological for this reason: shouldn't the eschaton function to secure some ultimate meaning or ground of historical experience and was this not its original purpose? Certainly, but what Deleuze and Guattari are suggesting is that the capitalist eschaton is in an important sense at the basis of all the others, that the immanence defining capitalist decoding was somehow foreseen by prior social forms:

> We shall speak of an *absolute limit* every time the schizo-flows pass through the wall, scramble all the codes, and deterritorialize the socius: the body without organs is the deterritorialized socius, the wilderness where the decoded flows run free, the end of the world, the apocalypse .... there is no social formation that does not foresee, or experience a foreboding of, the real form in which the limit threatens to arrive, and which it wards off with all the strength it can command .... When [primitive] societies are confronted with this real limit, repressed from within, but which returns to them from without, they regard this event with melancholy as the sign of their approaching death .... How can this nightmare be imagined: the invasion of the socius by noncoded flows that move like lava? (1983: 176)

The precapitalist eschatological imagination contains the capitalist socius negatively, in the form of myths of social collapse and schism. This may seem fanciful on Deleuze and Guattari's part but they are actually backed up by anthropological research. In a recent book on the origins of our contemporary ideas of debt and money, David Graeber remarks that 'anthropologists have come to understand, over the years, that every society is haunted by slightly different nightmares ... some terrifying potential' (2012: 149). Among the Tiv of West Africa, for example, stories have been reported about a secret college of cannibalistic witches capable of infiltrating and dissolving the social order. Following contact with these perfidious beings the only way to save oneself is to sacrifice family members to the witches' cannibalistic practices (though in the end even this is not enough to sate them). Graeber argues that this was the Tiv's way of understanding the ravages of the Atlantic slave trade. It wasn't, however, slavery as such (a practice as old as civilization itself) that terrorized them; it was the logic of commerce and exchange involved, the 'process that dislodges people from the webs of mutual commitment, shared history, and collective responsibility that make them what they are, so as to make them exchangeable . . . the logic of debt' (Graeber 2012: 163). This process is what Deleuze and Guattari call decoding, which 'haunts all societies' as their common limit (Deleuze and Guattari 1983: 144).[4]

With capitalism this absolute limit is treated not with melancholy or dread but with enthusiasm as well. This is true of many precapitalist societies as well, but the difference is that we no longer have a convincing imaginary to contend with it. Freud saw this well enough, and his account of the death instinct is nothing if not a modern eschatology written for an age that has stopped truly believing in myths. If there is nevertheless an air of obsolescence about the Freudian subject, it is not, as Marcuse thought, because it is still too Victorian but because the unconscious itself is sustained by an 'archaism' with a contemporary function (Deleuze and Guattari 1983: 232). It is not a matter of believing in things such as the little despot Oedipus or the primal horde but of experiencing (or re-experiencing) them at the level of the unconscious and in spite of any conscious avowal: 'It is with the thing, capitalism, that the unavowable begins' (Deleuze and Guattari 1983: 247). It is this condition that gives rise to desiring production's 'eschatological determination', its character of being 'at the limit' of social production (Deleuze and Guattari 1983: 175).

Is it simply a matter of reviving belief in the immanent eschaton that accompanies, and even foresees, all major social change? In order to answer this question we must understand that for Deleuze and Guattari eschatology has two very distinct senses relating to different understandings of time's finality, what a concept of completed time might be. This is no doubt because the notion of limit has several meanings. There is an understanding of completion as the exhaustion of novelty, as the return of the same. When people speak of capitalism as being the 'least worst' economic system, they are suggesting something like this since it implies that all alternatives have been explored. This is what Žižek means when he says that most people today are Fukuyamaist (2009: 88). There is, however, another sense of eschatology that implies something very different. There is an exhaustion of time that breaks the chronological links of past, present, and future, that allows time to become divested of the events that fill it so that it may appear as an 'empty form', as time in itself, transition as such. Kermode argues that the 'the absolutely New is unintelligible' since every new thing is conditioned by past and present (2000: 116). Deleuze, however, is insistent upon the possibility of apprehending the future as the 'unconditioned', and this is the essential thing that defines his apocalypticisim: 'all that returns, the eternal return, is the *unconditioned* in the product... the first two repetitions [of past and present] do not return,... they occur only once and for all,... only the third repetition which turns upon itself returns for all times, for eternity'. Past and present are like two 'signifiers' for the future, two witnesses to its unconditioned rising up. The 'product' of the syntheses is this unconditioned object (Deleuze 1994: 297).

To produce something not conditioned by its production might sound paradoxical, an inversion of normal chronology or cause and effect, but it is at the heart of Deleuze and Guattari's approach. What they call the body without organs is precisely this unconditioned object – what they also call the 'unengendered' – and appears in its 'naked' form only with the advent of capitalism (Deleuze and Guattari 1983: 7, 250). In other words, the limit of society is no longer filtered through the imaginary but becomes part of the economic and infrastructural mechanism. If capitalism is to be defined by its immanence, it is because the limit or beyond of the socius is stripped of the mythological and religious contents through which previous social formations had described it, as through a prism. The body without organs is 'not God, quite the contrary', Deleuze and Guattari say, 'but the energy that flows through it is divine' because the unconditioned or unengendered has the character of totality and of being One-all, the *omnitudo realitatis*, which we generally ascribe to divinity (1983: 13). The body without organs, as unconditioned product, thus *appears* to us as the source of all conditions, a 'divine presupposition' (1983: 10). Capital – as the body without organs of capitalist society – appears as the condition of wealth and not its product. It is well known that Marx was obsessed with the spiritual dimension of the commodity form. But there is something spiritual not simply at the level of the imaginary or of mystificatory content. There is something 'miraculous' – something relating to the objectively divine and not simply to the false consciousness of a mystified mind – by which a thing produced can act as the condition of production. It is only with capitalism that the eschaton ceases to occupy the position of the imaginary and that the possibility of producing an object that is also a divine condition arrives in human history. The entire politics of desire that Deleuze and Guattari offer is based around the revolutionary possibilities this presents.

But what is this eschatology, this unconditioned object? The famous memoirs of the nineteenth-century paranoiac Daniel Paul Schreber, as well as Freud's interpretation of them, are revealing here. Schreber's delirium, as documented in his famous memoir, proceeded in apocalyptic fashion. He writes that from the beginning of his illness

> there predominated in recurrent nightly visions the notion of an approaching end of the world, as a consequence of the indissoluble connection between God and myself. Bad news came in from all sides that even this or that star or this or that group of stars had to be 'given up'; at one time it was said that even Venus had been 'flooded,' at another that the whole solar system would now have to be 'disconnected,' that the Cassiopeia (the whole group of stars) had had to be drawn together into a single sun, that perhaps only the Pleiades could still be saved, etc., etc. (1955: 75)

Elsewhere, Schreber writes that the end of the world would come about by a gradual withdrawal of the sun leading to a glaciation of the Earth, by an earthquake, or by a global epidemic of plague and leprosy, the symptoms of which he could detect on his own body. Freud's interpretation of these apocalyptic visions turns on the idea of a radical and calamitous withdrawal of desire:

> The patient has withdrawn from the people in his environment and from the external world generally the libidinal cathexis which he has hitherto directed on to them. Thus everything has become indifferent and irrelevant to him, and has to be explained by means of a secondary rationalization as being 'miracled up, cursorily improvised'. The end of the world is the projection of this internal catastrophe; his subjective world has come to an end since his withdrawal of his love from it. (1958: 70)

However unpleasant it might have been for him, Schreber's subsequent paranoiac delirium – his perceived persecution by various figures including his doctor – was thus an attempt, Freud argues, to rebuild the world following the catastrophe of its destruction and the revelation of its 'miraculous' character: *the delusional formation, which we take to be the pathological product, is in reality an attempt at recovery, a process of reconstruction* (1958: 71).

This rebuilding upon the decathected, glaciated surface of a dead earth is the aspect of delirium that most interests Deleuze and Guattari because it shows how desire subsists at the very limits of society, threatening at any moment to escape into the desert beyond the city gates, to deterritorialize, to flee the libidinal investments foisted upon desire by both the organs of the body and the machines of social organization. The essential point they wish to make is that desire can only be legitimately described from the point of view of its escape, its line of flight into the wilderness. To write the history of desire, we need a conception of an end of history since desire subsists at the limits of the social. As Deleuze and Guattari write, 'the body without organs is the deterritorialized socius, the wilderness where the decoded flows run free, the end of the world, the apocalypse' (Deleuze and Guattari 1983: 176). This is why they maintain that delirium is the proper mode by which the history of desire can be written. The names of history belong not to people and places, ultimately, but to the affective states or becomings traced in the dust of a desert earth.

The earth is not the same as the world, but the desert earth is not the mere annihilation of the world: it is the positing of a new ground, a new foundation, a 'new earth' (Deleuze and Guattari 1983: 131). This is the authentic eschatological destiny of desiring production once it has been freed from the symbolism or structure that makes the father's corpse the timeless ground of the world and the time of expiation the history that is exhausted by its return to this ground. The withdrawal of libido that precipitated Schreber's delirium is extended by Deleuze and Guattari to account for the universal history of decoding that drains belief and reveals the foundation of every territory to be the deterritorialized, the 'desert of the body without organs' (Deleuze and Guattari 1983: 133). This desert body is between historical and eternal, temporal and atemporal; it is the unconditioned. But the construction of a new world is a sham, as Schreber's indeed was, unless the unconditioned provides a new condition, a new ground on which to build. This is why the enigmatic figure of a new earth, not merely a new world or a new society, is so important to schizoanalysis.

Deleuze and Guattari's issue with the Freudian and post-Freudian account of the unconscious is that the latter is 'supposed' to believe now in the theological structure rather than the contents that fill it, or that have filled it in the past. But it is the structure itself that needs to be produced anew. If 'believing in this world' is our most urgent political task, as Deleuze and Guattari suggest, then it's equally true that the theological structure is not the object of belief but of production. One cannot believe in a structure, only produce it. This is why Deleuze's inversion of the psychoanalytic formula for atheism is so crucial. We need to extract from every belief the atheism that drives it, not the inverse, since it is the atheism of the structure that conditions our beliefs and allows them to be posited. To remake this structure down to its geological and telluric core – 'the "demoniacal" element in nature or within the heart of the earth' – would seem to be the main task of schizoanalytic political theology (Deleuze and Guattari 1983: 35).

Notes

1 Christian Kerslake shows in this respect how Deleuze's concerns with geophilosophy and apocalypse are related: 'Deleuze can be heard responding to the calls by [Eugen] Fink and [Kostas] Axelos for a move beyond the existentialist conception of the "world", and towards an existentialised conception of cosmic history. Although Deleuze and Axelos later broke off their relations, it is instructive to examine Axelos' identification of a kind of "planetary thought" that would transcend Heidegger's notion of "world", and reconnect his later "epochal" history of finite thought with a political impulse – necessarily Marxist, according to Axelos. Influenced by Fink's cosmic Heideggerianism, Axelos declares that there is a "game of thought" proper to our "planetary era" [*l'ère planétaire*], a specifically "planetary" kind of thought that it is essential to master if we wish to push our way out of the age of nihilism' (2009: 250).

2 For Ernst Bloch 'Joachim was the first to set a date for the kingdom of God, for the communist kingdom', while Karl Lowith remarked that Joachitic symbolism inspired both the 'Third International' and the 'Third Reich' (quoted in Gould and Reeves 2001: 2). The conservative political theorist Eric Voegelin identified Joachim as the originator of a 'modern gnosticism' that sought to replace 'transcendent being' with a 'world-immanent order' (Voegelin 1997: 68). Voegelin condemned this mode of historical speculation as the progenitor of totalitarian ideologies in the twentieth century. The Voegelinian slogal 'don't let them immanentize the eschaton' was popularized by Conservative spokesperson William F. Buckley in the 1970s and appeared on T-shirts and badges. In a recent work, John Gray rehashes Voegelin's argument and applies it to the neoconservative ideologies unpinning Bush and Blair's invasion of Iraq in 2003 (Gray 2007).

3 Zizek gives the example of how we treat money: 'The easiest way to detect the effectivity of this postulate is to think of the way we behave towards the materiality of money: we know very well that money, like all other material objects, suffers the effects of use, that its material body changes through time, but in the social effectivity of the market we none the less treat coins as if they consist "of an immutable substance, a substance over which time has no power, and which stands in antithetic contrast to any matter found in nature". How tempting to recall here the formula of fetishistic disavowal: "I know very well, but still ... ". To the current exemplifications of this formula ("I know that Mother has not got a phallus, but still ... [I believe she has got one]"; "I know that Jews are people like us, but still ... [there is something in them]") we must undoubtedly add also the variant of money: 'I know that money is a material object like others, but still ... [it is as if it were made of a special substance over which time has no power]"' (1989: 12). It would be interesting to apply Deleuze's inversion here. What would happen if

instead of diagnosing the disavowed belief that secretly drives our secular capitalist societies, we tried to extract from our religious adherence to the abstractions of money the Antichrist that propels it? Such an operation would undoubtedly be explosive for the theological and perverse structure of our current impasses of belief because it would dissolve our avowed faith in the atemporal permanence of this structure and unleash a productive desire to refashion it according to a different, revolutionary faith. This is precisely what the 'famous' psychoanalytic formula (which Žižek here cites) of 'money = shit' does not allow (Deleuze and Guattari 1983: 29).

4 Despite several interesting overlaps with his argument, Graeber chooses to dismiss Deleuze and Guattari's contribution in a footnote (Graeber 2012: 402).

Bibliography

Agamben, G. (2005) *The Time That Remains: A Commentary on the Letter to the Romans*, trans. P. Dailey. Stanford, CA: Stanford University Press.

Deleuze, G. (1990) *The Logic of Sense*, trans. M. Lester and C. Stivale. London: Continuum.

Deleuze, G. (1994) *Difference and Repetition*, trans. P. Patton. New York: Columbia University Press.

Deleuze, G. (2000) *Proust and Signs: The Complete Text*, trans. R. Howard. Minneapolis: University of Minnesota Press.

Deleuze, G. and F. Guattari (1983) *Anti-Oedipus: Capitalism and Schizophrenia*, trans. R. Hurley, M. Seem, and H.R. Lane. Minneapolis: University of Minnesota Press.

Deleuze, G. and F. Guattari (1994) *What Is Philosophy?*, trans. H. Tomlinson and G. Burchell. New York: Columbia University Press.

Faulkner, K.W. (2006) *Deleuze and the Three Syntheses of Time*. New York: Peter Lang.

Freud, S. (1958) *The Standard Edition of the Complete Psychological Works of Sigmund Freud*, trans. J. Strachey. London: Hogarth Press.

Gould, W. and M. Reeves (2001) *Joachim of Fiore and the Myth of the Eternal Evangel in the Nineteenth and Twentieth Centuries*. Oxford: Oxford University Press.

Graeber, D. (2012) *Debt: The First 5,000 Years*. New York: Melville House.

Gray, J. (2007) *Black Mass: Apocalyptic Religion and the Death of Utopia*. London: Penguin.

Kermode, F. (2000) *The Sense of an Ending: Studies in the Theory of Fiction, with a New Epilogue*. Oxford: Oxford University Press.

Kerslake, C. (2009) *Immanence and the Vertigo of Philosophy: From Kant to Deleuze*. Edinburgh: Edinburgh University Press.

Lacan, J. (1977a) *The Seminar of Jacques Lacan, Book XI: The Four Fundamental Concepts of Psychoanalysis*, trans. A. Sheridan. New York: W.W. Norton and Company.

Lacan, J. (1977b) *Écrits: A Selection*, trans. A. Sheridan. London: Routledge.

Lacan, J. (1992) *The Seminar of Jacques Lacan, Book VII: The Ethics of Psychoanalysis, 1959–60*, trans. D. Porter. London: Tavistock/Routledge.

Petersen, R. L. (1993) *Preaching in the Last Days: The Theme of 'Two Witnesses' in the Sixteenth and Seventeenth Centuries*. New York: Oxford University Press.

Ramey, J. (2012) *The Hermetic Deleuze: Philosophy and Spiritual Ordeal*. Durham, NC: Duke University Press.

Schreber, D.P. (1955) *Memoirs of My Nervous Illness*, trans. I. Macalpine and R.A. Hunter. New York: New York Review Books.

Sellars, J. (2007) 'Âion and Chronos: Deleuze and the Stoic Theory of Time', *Collapse* 3, pp. 177–205.

Taubes, J. (2009) *Occidental Eschatology*, trans. D. Ratmoko. Stanford, CA: Stanford University Press.

Voegelin, E. (1997) *Science, Politics and Gnosticism: Two Essays*. Washington, DC: Regnery.

Žižek, S. (1989) *The Sublime Object of Ideology*. London: Verso.

Žižek, S. (2009) *First as Tragedy, Then as Farce*. London: Verso.

6

The Bricolage of Images: Constructing the Cartographies of the Unconscious

Inna Semetsky

Deleuze considered '*an unconscious of thought* [to be] just as profound as *the unknown of the body*' (Deleuze 1988b: 19, Deleuze's italics). The quality of profundity is significant and relates schizoanalysis (Deleuze and Guattari 1983) as a transgressive mode of production of human subjectivity that includes the realm of the unconscious and unthought, to Jung's depth psychology. Deleuze's conception of the unconscious is closer to Jung's, rather than Freud's, theoretical base (Kerslake 2007). Jung's notion of individuation is akin to Deleuze's concept of becoming-other (Semetsky 2011) as the affective process of encounters with the unconscious. A schizoanalytic practice is related to bricolage (Lévi-Strauss 1966) defined as a spontaneous human action grounded in the characteristic patterns of mythological, savage, thinking – or rather, non-thinking.

For Deleuze, rational Cogito as the sole constituent of thought is insufficient because what is yet non-thought is equally capable of producing multiple effects. The dimension of the 'unthought [is] not external to thought' (Deleuze 1988a: 97) but is being enfolded into 'its very heart' (Deleuze 1988a: 97).

The method of critical thinking is inadequate to reach to the very heart, to the very depth of the unconscious. Deleuze's approach is both critical and clinical (Deleuze 1997). Kerslake (2007: 4) suggests that we suspend the clinical dimension but contends that it is not always possible to separate it from the critical. It should not be, indeed. Deleuze considered philosophers, artists, and writers to be first and foremost semioticians and symptomatologists who can read extralinguistic signs and symbols as *symptoms* of life, therefore literally putting into practice the clinical, non-philosophical (if philosophy is understood reductively as a strictly analytic reason) aspect and therefore capable of potentially healing and transforming this very life. As an example of schizoanalytic, clinical practice, this chapter introduces the bricolage of Tarot images, which speak in the silent discourse (Semetsky 2010) of the esoteric, non-verbal, language that nonetheless can be read and interpreted.

While linguistic propositions are the prerogative of the conscious mind, the language of the unconscious expresses itself in *legible images* (Semetsky 2011, 2013). The unconscious ideas need a means of expression other than a plainly discursive reason; still we can read and interpret such a language as a system of signs. By becoming conscious of the unconscious we articulate as yet silent images as the schizoanalytic 'assemblages of enunciation' (Guattari 1995: 59) and translate them into spoken words. The notion of language *per se* is re-conceptualized. Rather than being reduced to propositional thought and verbal language, it becomes 'the marriage of language and the unconscious' (Deleuze 1990b: xiii). Referring to esoteric languages, Deleuze mentions the 'grand literal, syllabic, and phonetic synthesis of Court de Gébelin' (Deleuze 1990b: 140). It was in 1781 when the French pastor and author Antoine Court de Gébelin introduced his ideas of the Egyptian origins of Tarot as related to the Hermetic philosophy taught by the sage Hermes Trismegistus. De Gébelin's nine-volume encyclopaedia was called *Primitive World* (*Le Monde Primitif*) and devoted to the Golden Age of ancient civilization when people were united by one language and one religion. Indeed, as the Biblical account of Genesis (11:1) tells us, once upon a time the whole earth was of one language and of one speech, united by the same understanding of the nature of the universe.

The unconscious that 'speaks' in esoteric language exceeds the narrow boundaries of the Freudian personal repressed: 'the unconscious belongs to the realm of physics' (Deleuze and Guattari 1983: 283), to the world of nature. Jungian unconscious is collective: it is the objective psyche containing skeletal patterns of typical experiences concealed in humankind's collective memory permeated by archetypes, which 'are not just "in the mind": they are in nature' (Laszlo 1995: 135). They subsist in the virtual field of becoming posited by Deleuze to be as real as the actual plane of manifested phenomena, and an object of experience is considered to be given only in its tendency to exist, that is, in the virtual, potential form. The realm of the virtual is reminiscent of, but not limited to, the Jungian archetype of the Shadow (Semetsky 2013) that hides in the collective unconscious or, on the plane of expression, for Deleuze, in the shadow around the words. The encounter with the shadowy structures hiding in the unconscious leads to making sense of, and creating meaning for, our experiences. For Deleuze, 'Sense is essentially produced' (Deleuze 1990b: 95).

Contrary to reductive empiricism positing an individual as born in the state of blank slate, Deleuze claims that 'one never has a *tabula rasa*; one slips in, enters in the middle' (Deleuze 1988b: 123) amidst the archetypal images comprising the field of the collective unconscious. The unconscious, which is over and above its personal dimension, is conceptualized by Deleuze and Guattari as anti-Oedipal, irreducible to Freud's master-signified. Similar to Jung's collective unconscious, it always deals with social and natural frame and is a virtual 'productive machine ... at once social and desiring' (Deleuze 1995: 144). Deleuze's ontology of the virtual posits the world as consisting not of substantial things but of relational entities or multiplicities, and the production of subjectivity is necessarily embedded amidst the relational, experimental, and experiential dynamics. The dynamics of becoming, when any given multiplicity 'changes in nature as it expands its connections' (Deleuze and Guattari 1987: 8), is a distinctive feature of Deleuzian philosophy. The constant becoming-other constitutes the process of 'individuation [that] precedes matter and form, species and parts, and every other element of the constituted individual' (Deleuze 1994: 38). The process of becoming is grounded in the intensive capacity 'to affect and be affected' (Deleuze and Guattari 1987: xvi) as part and parcel of the schizoanalytic production of subjectivity. Archetypes as virtual tendencies have the potential of becoming actual through the process of multiple different/ciations of the transcendental and 'initially undifferentiated field' (Deleuze 1993: 10) not unlike Jung's field of the collective unconscious.

The virtual and the actual are mutually enfolded, and 'we go from fold to fold' (Deleuze 1993: 17) within the unfolding experience. Says Deleuze, 'I undo the folds ... that pass through every one of my thresholds ... "the twenty-two folds" that surround me and separate me from the deep' (1993: 93). Citing Henri Michaux, he says that children are born with the twenty-two folds which are to be unfolded. Only then can human life become complete, fulfilled, individuated. These twenty-two folds, implicated in subjectivity, correspond to the number of images in the Major Arcana of a typical Tarot deck and which symbolically represent what Deleuze called the world of problems embodied in the archetypal journey from the Fool to the World (Figure 6.1).

Each image is a sign that portends and points to something beyond itself, to the whole gamut of archetypal motifs. A semiotic engagement with experiential milieus enables us 'to bring something to life, to free life from where it's trapped, to trace lines of flight' (Deleuze 1995: 141). The very first Arcanum called the Fool portrays a figure at the edge of abyss just about to make a step – to trace

Figure 6.1 Major Arcana (Note: illustrations are by the artist Pamela Colman Smith from the Rider-Waite Tarot Deck. © 1971 US Games Systems, Inc.).

a line of flight – without which it would have forever remained a literal Fool without the possibility of ever reaching the final Arcanum, the World, also called the Universe in some decks. It is the lines of flight or becoming that lead us into the universe of possibilities: 'Each one of us has his own line of the universe to discover, but is only discovered through tracing it' (Deleuze 1986: 195) – through becoming conscious of the unconscious. The unconscious is embedded in the virtual space of the Deleuzian 'outside' as an unorthodox memory 'animated by peristaltic movements, folds and foldings that together make up an inside: they are not something other than the outside but precisely the inside *of* the outside.... The inside is an operation of the outside:... an inside ... is ... the fold of the outside' (Deleuze 1988a: 96–97).

Like Jung's objective psyche, the virtual space of the outside 'possesses a full reality by itself... it is on the basis of its reality that existence is produced' (Deleuze 1994: 211). Jung commented that Freud 'was blind toward the paradox and ambiguity of the contents of the unconscious, and did not know that everything which arises out of the unconscious has ... an inside and an outside' (Jung 1963: 153) – analogous to Deleuze's semiotics grounded in the folded, a-signifying, relations between the inside and the outside. It is the transversal connection created by the bricolage of laid-down images that functions as Jung's transcendent function: traversing the fold prevents the two realms of 'inside' and 'outside' from remaining forever separated by the supposedly unbridgeable, indeed schizophrenic, gap of Cartesian dualism. The prefix 'trans' is significant: the unconscious dimension is *trans*cended by means of an indirect, *trans*versal, link of a symbolic mediation via the archetypal images, thus establishing 'the bond of a profound complicity between [unconscious] nature and [conscious] mind' (Deleuze 1994: 165) leading to the conjunction and unification of opposites, the mystical *coincidentia oppositorum*, which determines the very threshold of consciousness. Deleuze and Guattari relate mystical participation in the reality of what is produced to the figure of the schizophrenic who, because of his intense connection to the unconscious, lives within the very interface with nature, without, however, being capable of becoming conscious of this very predicament. It is schizoanalysis, such as the bricolage of Tarot, that would have enabled him to integrate the unconscious into consciousness, to become-other rather than being overwhelmed by the 'fractured I of a dissolved Cogito' (Deleuze 1994: 194) forming what Jung called complexes.

Derived from the common archetypal core as well as actual experiences, complexes act similarly to Deleuze's pure affects: they are autonomous and 'behave like independent beings' (Jung CW8, 253) over and above conscious intentionality of the Cartesian subject. Jung argued that 'there are things in the psyche which I do not produce, but which produce themselves and have their own life … there is something in me that can say things that I do not know and do not intend' (1963: 183) because these 'things' act at the unconscious level as signs beyond one's conscious will or voluntary control. Deleuze would have agreed; he says that the 'intentionality of being is surpassed by the fold of Being, Being as fold' (Deleuze 1988a: 110). It is multiple signs comprising the objective psyche that continuously create novel relations in our real experience because as dynamic, archetypal forces, they are capable of affecting and effecting changes, thus deterritorrializing and reterritorializing subjectivities in accord with the unfolding dynamics of the Fool's individuation. The unconscious perceptions are implicated as subliminal, or micro-, perceptions (Deleuze 1993); as such, they become part of the cartographic microanalysis – schizoanalysis – of establishing 'an unconscious psychic mechanism that engenders the perceived in consciousness' (Deleuze 1993: 95).

Cartography, by definition, is a mode of graphic communication capable of transmitting visual messages such as those encoded in the hieroglyphic imagery of Tarots. The graphic information may be expressed in the form of a diagram, network, or map, or in the mixed format of a cartogram, that is, a diagram superimposed on a map. Sure enough, because the production of subjectivity includes the realm of the unconscious, 'the cartographies of the unconscious would have to become indispensable complements to the current systems of rationality of … all … regions of knowledge and human activity' (Guattari, original French, in Bosteels 1998: 155). The cartography of the unconscious is represented by the layout of Tarot signs, symbols, and images; and what I earlier called the Tarot hermeneutic (Semetsky 2011, 2013) is exemplary of Deleuze's philosophy of transcendental empiricism. Deleuze's method is empirical as embedded in the multiple contexts, situations, and events of human experiences; yet it is radically transcendental because the very foundations for the empirical principles are left outside our common faculties of perception so that we have to transcend them in practice, hence ourselves becoming capable of perceiving the seemingly imperceptible.

Transcendental empiricism affirms 'the double in the doubling process' (Deleuze 1988a: 98). 'Doubling' is taken in the sense of unfolding that presupposes a necessary existence of the extra, 'outside', dimension, without which the concept of fold is meaningless. This outside dimension becomes internalized, enfolded; hence 'doubling as the interiorization of the outside [becomes] redoubling of the Other [and] it is a self that lives in me as the double of the other: I do not encounter myself on the outside, I find the other in me' (Deleuze 1988a: 98). The other in me is thus always implicit in the unconscious, the esoteric language of which is to be translated into verbal expressions and made explicit so as to indeed effectuate the process of becoming-other. Expanding on Deleuzian conceptualizations, we can actually *see* the internalization of the outside, which came about by redoubling, not in consciousness as an abstract concept, but with our very eyes as a concrete picture. Just so as to become able to be seen, it would have been re-redoubled; in a way, *transcended*, albeit in the seemingly primitive, savage, mode of spreading the Tarot pictures. Deleuze wants to achieve the means so as to literally 'show the imperceptible' (Deleuze 1995: 45), that is, become capable of bridging the gap between the sensible and the intelligible, matter and mind. The imperceptible affects can be *shown* – made visible, perceptible, sensible – rather than simply thought at the level of rational mind. Perceiving something essentially imperceptible – or making the invisible visible as the major postulate of the Hermetic philosophy – is made possible by means of laying down the plane of immanence. That's how Deleuze and Guattari defined the plane of immanence which is not in any way to be reduced to reason alone:

> Precisely because the plane of immanence ... does not immediately take effects with concepts, it implies a sort of groping experimentation and its layout resorts to measures that are not very respectable, rational, or reasonable. These measures belong to the order of dreams, of pathological processes, esoteric experiences, drunkenness, and excess. We head for the horizon, on the plane of immanence, and we return with bloodshot eyes, yet they are the eyes of the mind. (Deleuze and Guattari 1994: 41)

The construction of the plane of 'immanence [which] is the unconscious itself' (Deleuze 1988b: 29) implies the affective and erotic awakening of the eye of the mind – the *nous* – as opposed to the gaze of the Cogito dispassionately observing a distant world of objects. This awakening is a prerogative of 'the genesis of intuition in intelligence' (Deleuze 1991: 111) due to which we can perceive the imperceptible and become conscious of the unconscious. Everything has 'its cartography, its diagram ... What we call a "map", or sometimes a "diagram" is a set of various interacting lines (thus the lines in a hand are a map)' (Deleuze 1995: 33). If the lines in a hand form a map, so do Tarot cartograms when spread in the rhizomatic network forming a specific layout (Figure 6.2) that reflects a semiotic, extralinguistic structure of the yet unthought:

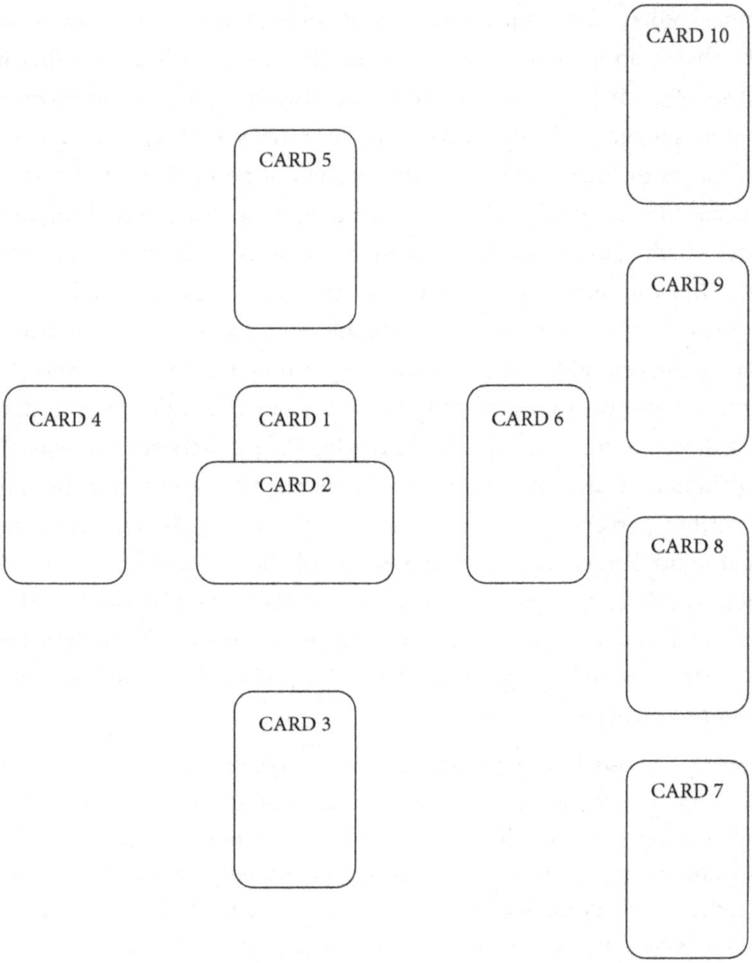

Figure 6.2 The cartograms of Tarot.

Constructing the Tarot map demands 'the laying out of a plane' (Deleuze and Guattari 1994: 36). The layout forms a multiplicity and displays a specific logic. Deleuze's radical empiricism is 'fundamentally linked to a logic – a logic of multiplicities' functioning in accord with 'a theory and practice of relations, of the *and*' (Deleuze and Parnet 1987: viii, 15). Multiplicities always have a middle element, the included 'third which … disturbs the binarity of the two' (Deleuze and Parnet 1987: 131) that are usually presented as opposites in the framework of Cartesian dualism with its separate substances of *res cogitans* and *res extensa*. And as Deleuze and Guattari (1987) pointed out, the 'only way to get outside the dualisms is to be-between, to pass between' (Deleuze and Parnet 1987: 276). A layout of picture is sure in-between: between self and other, consciousness and the unconscious. The logic of the included third, the infamous *tertium* of antiquity, makes the otherwise binary opposites to complement each other, to form a relation as genuine signs are supposed to do. Such triadic, a-signifying semiotics represents a major Peircean inflection in Deleuze's corpus (Semetsky 2006). As 'a being-multiple' (Deleuze and Parnet 1987: viii) multiplicity is a relational and not substantial entity, a genuine sign that defies direct representation but, indirectly and enigmatically, like a hieroglyph to be deciphered, portends and indicates something other than itself. Such are Tarot signs whose implicit meanings are to be deciphered, explicated.

A Tarot 'map does not reproduce an unconscious closed in upon itself; it constructs the unconscious' (Deleuze and Guattari 1987: 12). The exact reproduction would mean a reduction to the excluded middle, to the analytic philosophy of language based on the logical copula 'is', the ideology of direct representation. But the logic of the included middle, of the conjunction 'and', is anti-representational, indirect but mediated as forming extralinguistic, semiotic structures. The 'and' is not a numerical addition but a process of summation that, while suggesting a simple adding of empirical facts, in fact intensifies experience (the multiplicity is intensive!) by means of forming a logical product akin to multiplication, to forming power series. Deleuze is adamant that 'there is not a simple addition, but a constitution of a new plane, as of a surplus value' (Deleuze and Guattari 1987: 313). The addition will have indicated the linearity of the process. But the logic of signs is nonlinear, triadic, interrupted now and then by 'a new threshold, a new direction of the zigzagging line, a new course for the border' (Deleuze 1995: 45) not unlike the movement from one state of human condition to another symbolically represented by the twenty-two paths on the Kabbalistic Tree of Life. Analogously, the twenty-two images of Major Arcana represent an evolutionary dynamics of 'topological and specifically cartographic' (Bosteels 1998: 146) being-as-becoming. The structure of the symbolic Tree of Life, as well the rhizomatic structure of a typical Tarot layout, is 'more like grass than a tree' (Deleuze 1995: 149), and the rhizome's growth – contrary to the growth of a tree – does not proceed from the root up, but is distributed among the multiple, and hidden underground, paths that trace the lines of becoming. Thinking is 'not just a theoretical matter. It [is] to do with vital problems. To do with life itself' (Deleuze 1995: 105).

This true, vitalistic, and enduring, even if invisible and virtual, life is a life as pure immanence (Deleuze 2001) concealed in the transcendental field of the collective unconscious. It thus needs to be unfolded, or revealed from its concealment, like the scroll in the image of the High Priestess (Figure 6.1) that hides in its folds the symbols of secret and esoteric, Gnostic, knowledge. Coincidentally, Jung used the same metaphor of the rhizome as Deleuze:

> The life of a man is a dubious experiment.... Individually, it is so fleeting... Life has always seemed to me like a plant that lives on its rhizome. Its true life is invisible, hidden in the rhizome. The part that appears above ground lasts only a single summer. Then it withers away – an ephemeral apparition.... Yet I have never lost a sense of something that lives and endures underneath the eternal flux. What we see is the blossom, which passes. The rhizome remains. (Jung 1963: 4)

The integration of the unconscious into consciousness leads to the 'intensification of life' (Deleuze and Guattari 1994: 74). By means of interpreting Tarot images, we immerse into an affective 'experimentation on ourselves [that] is our only identity, our single chance for all the combinations which inhabit us' (Deleuze and Parnet 1987: 11); these multiple potential combinations expressed by the images of the Major and Minor Arcana combined in a layout.

One is not consciously passing through the line of flight: Deleuze insists that 'something [is] passing through you' (Deleuze 1995: 141) at the yet unconscious, subtle level and materializing in the constellation of images occupying this or that position in the layout (Semetsky 2011). It is via laying out the plane of immanence formed on the material plane by Tarot images that we can become aware of the unconscious and, like the Hermetic Magi, participate in making the invisible visible. The mode of transversal communication created by Tarot hermeneutic provides an epistemic access to the invisible virtual field representing as such 'a plane of transcendence, a kind of design, in the mind of man or in the mind of a god, even when it is accorded a maximum of immanence by plunging it into the depth of Nature, or of the Unconscious' (Deleuze and Parnet 1987: 91).

The experimentation comprising the process of individuation can reach to the limit-experience exemplified in the Arcanum Death (Figure 6.1) representing 'the harshest exercise in depersonalization' (Deleuze 1995: 6). A symbolic death is a painful, fearful, and lengthy event; time may appear to stand still (Temperance) especially if we remain unconscious of staying in the grip of our old habits (the Devil). So sometimes we have to be hit by symbolic lightning to break the ivory tower of the old outlived values we have imprisoned ourselves in (the Tower). Only then our symbolic rebirth (the Sun) and resurrection (Judgement) become possible so that we can become what in fact we were meant to be all along – even if initially only in the mind of a god (as Deleuze says), inexpressible in propositional thought and verbal language. The explication of the meanings implicit in the rhizomatic network comprising Tarot layout enables one to make sense out of the disparate bits and pieces of confusing issues that are symbolically represented in images, to become conscious of the unconscious ideas, to transform and re-create oneself via 'an intrinsic genesis, not an extrinsic conditioning' (Deleuze 1994: 154). Our ideas are often so enveloped or enfolded 'in the soul that we can't always unfold or develop them' (Deleuze 1993: 49) by means of our cognitive tools alone, unless experience itself becomes saturated with affective, almost numinous, conditions for their unfolding, because this deep inner 'knowledge is known only where it is folded' (Deleuze 1993: 49).

The symbolism of the High Priestess with the scroll of folded knowledge on her lap affirms itself again and again! Such a limit-experience in real life appears to be achieved only by mystics, shamans, magicians or sorcerers (Semetsky 2009; Delpech-Ramey 2010; Semetsky and Delpech-Ramey 2011) who are capable of unfolding her scroll. The experiential world itself is folded – it is, as Charles S. Peirce was saying – perfused with signs! Only as such we are able to

> endure it, so that everything doesn't confront us at once… There's no subject, but a production of subjectivity: subjectivity has to be produced, when its time arrives, precisely because there is no subject. The time comes once we've worked through knowledge and power; it's that work that forces us to frame a new question, it couldn't have been framed before… Subjectification is an artistic activity. (Deleuze 1995: 112–114)

Such creative, schizoanalytic production is a function of time; it is not intentional or volitional but depends on our learning from unfolding experiences so that we can 'frame a new question' precisely because of the evolution of consciousness that brings to our awareness this or that problem, which 'couldn't have been framed before'. The archetypal patterns embodied in Tarot imagery, while making us act unconsciously, lead to learning because their 'structure is part of objects themselves [hence] allowing its positivity and its specificity to be grasped in the act of *learning*' (Deleuze 1994: 64; italics Deleuze's). Such semiotic learning takes us to future territories which are created from the virtual out of which we live.

The actualization of virtual potentialities is 'always a genuine creation' (Deleuze 1994: 212). The Fool's creative becomings exemplified in other Major Arcana accord with 'a theory and practice of relations, of the AND' (Deleuze and Parnet 1987: 15) as the prerogative of the logic of multiplicities – the logic of signs which are *a priori* a-signifying and in a need of the included middle, the conjunction 'and' created by the transversal communication. Semiotics is irreducible to 'the logic of a language. It is a description of the structures that appear when being is understood as the encounter of events and series' (Williams 2008: 23). The logic of verbal language is grounded in identity, but the logic of signs and images is grounded in the 'destruction of identity' (Deleuze 1995: 44). Even as Tarot schizoanalysis 'upsets being' (Deleuze 1995: 44) because of the multiple lines of flight taken by the symbolic Fool, it is along those very lines that 'things come to pass and becomings evolve' (1995: 45).

When mapped onto a pictorial spread, the virtual reality of signs undergoes transformations that 'convey the projection, on external space, of internal spaces defined by "hidden parameters" and variables or singularities of potential' (Deleuze 1993: 16) in our actual experience. Hidden variables become exposed in our very practice: what was buried in the depth of the psyche – hiding, symbolically, in the form of enfolded 'ambiguous signs' (Deleuze 1993: 15) is literally brought to the surface and made available to consciousness. The very depth of the psyche is capable of making sense so that we can discover the deep meanings of our experiences only when it, 'having been spread out became width. The becoming unlimited is maintained entirely within this inverted width' (Deleuze 1990: 9) on the flat surface or plane as a cartographic map that creates 'harmony and interference' (Williams 2008: 163) between matter and mind and reflects on the confluence between Deleuze's thought and the principles of Hermetic philosophy (Ramey 2012) as representative of the 'minor' tradition in philosophy, namely Western esotericism. The priority of signs and relations prevalent in the Hermetic worldview is equally important for Deleuze: 'A *and* B. The AND is ... the path of all relations' (Deleuze and Parnet 1987: 57). It is the conjunction 'and' that connects the opposites, thus suspending the whole dualistic split between the sensible and the intelligible, between rational thought and lived experience, between cognition and sensation, between material and spiritual, between the human and the divine.

A transversal link established by Tarot crosses over the a-signifying gap and connects the dual opposites in one common assemblage. The mode of transversal communication is indirect, mediated by archetypal images, and operates in order 'to bring this assemblage of the unconscious to the light of day, to select the whispering voices, to gather the tribes and secret idioms from which I extract something I call my Self (*Moi*)' (Deleuze and Guattari 1987: 84) as the individuated subjectivity. The process of creating identity anew is a semiotic process of sense-making, and the unconscious is the necessary – and quite often, as Deleuze would say, dark, especially when appearing in the image of the Devil, or the Moon, or the Tower (Figure 6.1) – precursor for individuation, for becoming-other when encountering experiential problems. The embodiment of ideas is a must. We learn when we become aware of the unconscious ideas symbolically presented in the materiality of Tarot because to learn means

> to conjugate the distinctive points of our bodies with the singular points of the objective Idea in order to form a problematic field. This conjugation determines for us a threshold of consciousness at which our real acts are adjusted to our perceptions of the real relations, thereby providing a solution to the problem. Moreover, problematic Ideas are precisely the ultimate elements of nature and the subliminal objects of little perceptions. As a result, 'learning' always takes place in and through the unconscious, thereby establishing the bond of a profound complicity between nature and mind. (Deleuze 1994: 165)

Signs demand 'the corresponding apprenticeship' (Deleuze 2000: 92) in the form of Tarot hermeneutic that ultimately elicits the transformational pragmatics of experience originating 'among a broken chain of affects' (Deleuze and Guattari 1987: 9). Affects are 'becomings that spill over beyond whoever lives through them (thereby becoming someone else)' (Deleuze 1995: 127) within the 'initiatory ordeal' (Ramey 2012: 3) when matter and psyche as two sides of the always already Janus-faced signs fold back on themselves during a self-reflective, critical, and clinical schizoanalytic practice of Tarot readings at the limit of ordinary cognitive capacities of the mind. Becoming-other is described as 'an extreme contiguity within coupling of two sensations without resemblance or, on the contrary, in the distance of a light that captures both of them in a single reflection .... It is a zone ... of indiscernibility ... This is what is called an *affect*' (Deleuze and Guattari 1994: 173). Deleuze purports to show the as-yet-imperceptible by laying down a visible 'map' of the invisible 'territory' via creating the conjunction 'and' between what are customarily considered the dualistic opposites ('without resemblance') of mind and body, *psyche* and *physis*. It is the relational dynamics constituting the logic of the included middle that forms the triad of affects, percepts, and concepts. It is the presence of affect or desire that connects the levels of reality by crossing over, or traversing, the difference between the virtual and the actual and exceeding purely analytic thinking.

Deleuze uses the term 'parallelism' with regard to the mind–body problem and asserts that there must be a threshold that brings thought to the body. One has to 'pursue the different series, to travel along the different levels, and cross all thresholds; instead of simply displaying phenomena or statements in their vertical or horizontal dimensions, one must form a transversal or mobile diagonal line' (Deleuze 1988a: 22), a line of flight or becoming exemplified in Tarot practice. An authentic Tarot reader indeed travels along different levels and crosses the thresholds of the barely liminal, hence bringing to awareness the unthought, unconscious, dimension via the auto-referential relation represented by '*a power to affect itself, an affect of self on self*' (Deleuze 1988a: 101). A Tarot reader is a bricoleur who makes a creative, partaking of demiurgical, synthesis of the material-at-hand. The Tarot signs embody 'levels of sensation ... like arrests or snapshots of motion, which would recompose the movement synthetically in all its continuity' (Deleuze 2003: 35). As Deleuze says,

> A flat image or, conversely, the depth of field, always has to be created and re-created – signs ... always imply a signature .... All images combine the same ... signs, differently. But not any combination's possible at just any moment: a particular element can only be developed given certain conditions .... So there are different levels of development, each of them perfectly coherent. (Deleuze 1995: 49)

The different levels of development showcase themselves in the various constellations of Tarot images. The identity is perpetually contested and re-created in the guise of different Arcana. The unfolding of the unconscious brings forth an element of creativity and presents 'life as a work of art' (Deleuze 1995: 94). Such life, created as an experiment grounded in schizoanalysis, is neutral (Deleuze 2001) – that is, beyond good and evil or any other binary opposites of modern discourse. Coincidentally, Wolfgang Pauli, a physicist and Nobel laureate who was Jung's collaborator on the concept of synchronicity as a meaningful coincidence between *psyche* and *physis*, envisaged the gradual discovery of a neutral language (Meier 2001) that functions symbolically to describe an invisible, potential reality, which is inferable indirectly through its visible effects. Responding to Pauli, Jung pointed out the 'materialization of a potentially available reality, an actualization of the *mundus potentialis*' (Meier 2001: 83) – the archetypal, intermediary, world as mecocosm posited by Henry Corbin – that thus becomes a matter of empirical fact and that we indeed encounter in the material form of Tarot images. Tarot symbolism, in its mediating function, crosses over the psychophysical dualism. Tarot brings forth the neutral, immanent, life expressed in the esoteric language of images. This is 'an impersonal and yet singular life that disengages a pure event freed from the accidents of the inner and outer life, that is from the subjectivity and objectivity of what happens' (Deleuze 1997: xiv). A transversal connection enables us to participate in this singular life by bridging together subjectivity and objectivity, immanence and transcendence so that 'the individual [becomes] able to transcend his form and his syntactical link with a world' (Deleuze 1994: 178).

The syntactical link produced by verbal language grounded in the logic of identity does not include *Sens* as meaning and direction, or the course of practical action. This impoverished syntactic link is transformed into meaningful semiotic connection enabled not by verbal propositions of the conscious mind alone but by the pictorial language of Tarot images and symbols that express the depth of the unconscious. The synthetic method reflects the future-oriented productivity of affect or desire capable of transcending 'spatial locations and temporal successions' (Deleuze 1994: 83). Deleuze refers to the 'levels of profundity' (Deleuze 1991: 59) in the past. The synthetic, and not solely analytic, quality embedded in depth psychology and schizoanalysis alike is oriented to the creative emergence of new meanings, hence bringing in the paradoxical dimension of *future anterior*. Jung emphasized the prospective function of the unconscious or what Deleuze, following Bergson, called the memory of the future that, together with all of the past, is enfolded in the cosmic 'gigantic memory' (Deleuze 2001: 212). These three dimensions of time – past, present, and the potential coming-into-being future – coexist in one and the same Tarot spread (Figure 6.2) with each position denoting a time-element so that, paradoxically, 'everything culminates in a "has been"' (Deleuze 1990b: 159). Deleuze and Guattari say that becoming is an antimemory (1987: 294). Is an antimemory a memory of the future? The enigmatic notion of an *antimemory* relates to the specific synthesis of time as the *future anterior* which is always already projected in the Tarot layout. We head for the future along the line of becoming that, like the witch's flight, escapes the old frame of reference by vanishing through an event horizon, yet appearing anew as if 'willed' by the magic wand in the Magician Arcanum (Figure 6.1) as the very symbol of the transversal link. We thus achieve an expanded perception of time and space, which become 'released from their human coordinates' (Deleuze 1986: 122) that capture space merely in its three dimensions and time as chronological and linear. Our habitual 'space-time ceases to be a pure given in order to become ... the nexus of differential relations in the subject, and the object itself ceases to be an empirical given in order to become the product of these relations' (Deleuze 1993: 89) as a newly created concept.

A virtual event, for Deleuze, is always 'already past and yet in the future, always the day before and the day after' (1990: 77), coexisting on the plane of immanence. In Pauli's 1948 essay called *Modern Examples of Background Physics* (Meier 2001: 179–196), he commented on the doubling of the psyche (not unlike Deleuze's and Foucault's conceptualizations) akin to human birth as a division of the initial unity. Time-wise, the doubling of the time-series is represented by Aion and Chronos with the instance of Kairos in-between. Such moment of Kairos becomes seized under the affective conditions constituting an event of Tarot reading that partakes of mystical experience. Deleuze (1989) equated mystical experience with an event of a sudden actualization of potentialities, that is, awakening of perceptions such as seeing and hearing by raising them to a new power of enhanced perception; a becoming-percept which is future oriented towards a virtual (as yet imperceptible) object. Such 'a vision and a voice ... would have remained virtual' (Goddard 2001: 54) unless some specific experiential conditions necessary for the actualization of the virtual would have been established. It is the desiring-production that enables us to apprehend the deepest symbolic meanings constituting 'the fragments of ideal future [and] past events, which [would] render the problem solvable' (Deleuze 1994: 190; also Kerslake 2007: 109). Such is the apprenticeship in signs (Bogue and Semetsky 2010) that provides us not only with a symbolic diagnosis – that is, reading the signs as the indices of the present – but prognosis as well in terms of evaluating and outlining the rhizomatic structure created by images comprising a particular layout. It is during esoteric experiences such as dreams, déjà-vu, involuntary memories, or Tarot readings that we are able to perceive the level of the virtual enfolded in the grandiose time of coexistence capable of unfolding, or disclosing, it.

The Tarot hermeneutic sure enough brings forth the clinical element in Deleuze's philosophy: 'which of [the rhizomatic lines] are dead-ended or blocked, which cross voids ... and most importantly the line of steepest gradient, how it draws in the rest, towards what destination ... [T]his line has always been there, although it is the opposite of a destiny' (Deleuze and Parnet 1987: 125). It is the opposite of destiny not because fate as such does not exist, but because we can liberate ourselves from its firm grip and become free to choose the line of flight in our experiential journey, thereby potentially changing our very destiny! As Deleuze pointed out, what is called destiny

> never consists in step-by-step deterministic relations.... Consider what we call repetition within a life – more precisely, within a spiritual life. Presents succeed, encroaching upon one another... [and] each of them plays out 'the same life' at a different levels. That is what we call destiny.... That is why destiny accords so badly with determinism but so well with freedom: freedom lies in choosing the levels. (Deleuze 1994: 83)

Tarot gives us freedom to choose different levels by exploring various options concerning alternative courses of action akin to human liberation from fate via *theosis* or *theandry*, that is, an identification of the soul with the divine in our embodied practice, hence naturalizing mysticism.

Deleuze presents us with reversed Platonism: Plato discovered philosophy as spiritual ordeal (cf. Ramey 2012), an examined life; yet he simultaneously restricted its nature that later led to the dogmatic image of thought uncontaminated by paradox or *tertium quid*. But the new image of thought defies dualism because a sign is never 'one [or] two... it is the in-between' (Deleuze and Guattari 1987: 293) in accord with the included middle of the immanent-transcendent 'quality of conjoined opposites' (Jung CW8: 189). The dynamics of signs proceeds in a double movement of different/ciation. An expanded reality of conjoined levels presents the actual and the virtual as a semiotic relation grounded in difference defined as 'the noumenon closest to phenomenon' (Deleuze 1994: 222). The virtual is posited just as a tendency, therefore *no-thing*. Significantly, the numeral corresponding to the very first Arcanum in the deck, the Fool, is Zero or nothing. Virtual tendencies as potentialities or *no-things* become actualized, as though created *ex nihilo* and embodied in the actual *things* partaking of new objects of knowledge as created concepts. The nuance is significant: 'from virtuals we descend to actual states of affairs, and from states of affairs we ascend to virtuals, without being able to isolate one from the other' (Deleuze and Guattari 1994: 160). The Fool-Zero exemplifies the body without organs as symbolic of unlimited freedom of perception and action unrestricted by the limitations of physical organs. Yet, it is a desire for gnosis that propels the as yet disembodied Fool to jump into the abyss so as to connect with the physical world, *this* world. It is such desire 'immanent to a plane which it does not pre-exist' (Deleuze and Parnet 1987: 89) that creates or lays down the plane of immanent consistency in the form of the layout of images.

The topology of Tarot is a precondition for sense-making. For Deleuze, 'typology begins with topology.... We have the truths that we deserve depending on the place we are carrying our existence to, the hour we watch over and the element that we frequent' (Deleuze 1983: 110), that is, a specific context as a singularity of event. What is traditionally called the mystery of *coincidentia oppositorum* is grounded in Deleuze's realist ontology that understands cosmos in terms of virtual reality comprising multiple levels of existence. It is 'the difference between the virtual and the actual [which] requires that the process of actualisation be a creation' (Hardt 1993: 18) – such as the creation of novel concepts and meanings that were imperceptible and unknown prior to being explicated in Tarot images via constructing the plane of immanent consistency. The plane of immanence is enfolded analogous to the Baroque art that expresses the harmonious multiplicity of folds (Deleuze 1993), of ambiguous signs. The function of affect or desire may appear analogous to what Nietzsche called the will to power; according to Deleuze, however, 'there are other names for it. For example, "grace"' (Deleuze and Parnet 1987: 91). Desire, Affect, Eros! Whatever its name, this is what accomplishes the Neoplatonic double movement of ascending and descending, of folding and unfolding. Eros, the mystical son of Poros and Penia, was conceived in an act that has occurred in the middle and muddle of 'groping experimentation … that … belong[s] to the order of dreams, of pathological processes, esoteric experiences, drunkenness, and excess' (Deleuze and Guattari 1994: 41). As a culmination of desire sparked between the two deities, Eros unites the two. The erotic desire deconstructs the Neoplatonic Oneness by means of bringing it (One) down to earth into the multiplicity and diversity of real, flesh-and-blood, human experiences. Hence follows what Deleuze and Guattari (1987) present as a magical formula expressed as 'One = Many' as unity in multiplicity. The symbolic Eros 'does not take as its object persons or things, but the entire surroundings which it traverses' (Deleuze and Guattari 1987: 292) thus establishing transversal communication as a necessary condition for 'the famous mystical principle of *coincidentia oppositorum*, beyond the limit of all human understanding' (Kearney 2001: 104). But it is the desiring-production that transcends the limits of ordinary understanding and intensifies human perception: Tarot hermeneutic represents a definite, albeit schizoanalytic, *method* in the midst of what appears to be the *madness* of mysticism by virtue of creating 'its own terms of actualization. The difference between the virtual and the actual is what requires that the process of actualization be a creation. … The actualization of the virtual … presents a dynamic multiplicity … the multiplicity of organization. … Without the blueprint of order, the creative process of organization is always an art' (Hardt 1993: 18) – the art of Tarot readings.

Here are the key questions: How is an epistemic access to the unconscious (Platonic) ideas made possible? Whence any foundation for moral knowledge? The construction of the plane of immanence grounded in Deleuze's ontology of the virtual enables a glimpse into an 'unconscious psychic mechanism that engenders the perceived in consciousness' (Deleuze 1993: 95). This psychic mechanism functions as the abstract or virtual machine –yet it becomes concrete and actual via its embodiment on the material plane. Immanence is constructivism, and it is the Tarot spread that serves as the surface for the production of sense because signs 'remain deprived of sense as long as they do not enter into the surface organization which ensures the resonance of two series' (Deleuze 1990: 104). The actualization of potentialities is grounded in the same relational dynamics (semiosis) as the unconscious-becoming-conscious when traversing or bridging a gap represented by a 'fundamental distinction between subrepresentative, unconscious and aconceptual ideas/intensities and the conscious conceptual representation of common sense' (Bogue 1989: 59). Wherein the plane of immanence is being constructed, 'the spiritual and the material [as] two distinct yet indiscernible sides of the same fold' (Goddard 2001: 62) do meet. The plane of immanence therefore always presupposes an extra, outside, dimension – as if populated by grace. Being 'located' outside consciousness (non-located, in fact), it can easily appear to us as mystical. For Deleuze, however, it is Nature itself that is essentially 'contingent, excessive, and mystical' (Deleuze 1994: 57). Nature exceeds the observable world of physical objects and includes its own virtual dimension which, however, is never beyond experience, hence ultimate understanding.

The object of experience contains potentialities as virtual or implicit meanings, even if they are not yet actualized or made explicit. A symbolic mediation by Tarot signs creates 'intensity, resonance … harmony' (Deleuze 1995: 86): yet being initially imperceptible it appears to border on a direct mystical contact with the divine. The contact in question is described by means of 'non-localizable connections, actions, at a distance … resonance and echoes' (Deleuze 1994: 83) – yet it is the schizoanalysis of Tarot that localizes what appears to be non-localizable, therefore partaking of the alchemical marriage of the opposites, the *Hierosgamos*. The affectivity and intensity of experience creates the conditions for manifesting a potential human ability to raise 'each faculty to the level of its transcendent exercise [and] to give birth to that second power, which grasps that which can only be sensed' (Deleuze

1994: 165). This potential ability becomes our very actuality during Tarot readings when we witness the play of affects reaching 'a point of excess and unloosening' (Deleuze and Guattari 1987: 134). At this crucial turning point there are two options: a subject must 'either annihilate itself in a black hole or change planes. Destratify, open up to a new function, a diagrammatic function' (Deleuze and Guattari 1987: 134), that is, align yourself with this very transversal link that connects the human with the divine. Similar to the drapes in fabric, things themselves are wrapped up in nature; as for ideas – they are often so enveloped or enfolded 'in the soul that we can't always unfold or develop them' (Deleuze 1993: 49) by means of merely rational thinking but need an embodied schizoanalytic practice within experience saturated with the affective conditions for their unfolding. Deleuze's transformational pragmatics takes place along the vanishing line of flight at the very limit of human understanding – yet within intensified and amplified perception permeated with erotic desire – not over and above it! It manifests at the moment when the potential meaning actualizes itself and becomes expressed by 'the manner in which the existing being is filled with immanence' (Deleuze 1997: 137) along the line of the mysterious conjunction with the transcendental.

Indeed, 'immanence and transcendence [are] inseparable processes' (Williams 2010: 94) of signs-becoming-other-signs across the transversal link that connects both is a paradoxical self-referential manner. The occurrence of the transversal communication therefore always has a numinous, religious element, especially if we read *re-ligio* etymologically as linking backwards to itself and forming an 'echo chamber, a feedback loop' (Deleuze 1995: 139) when we literally look into ourselves during the self-reflective, critical, and clinical Tarot practice. Tarot signs 'imply ways of living, possibilities of existence, [they are] the symptoms of life gushing forth or draining away … There is a profound link between signs, events, life and vitalism' (Deleuze 1995: 143). The shadowy signs appear to be imperceptible, enfolded in the virtual – still at the affective level, in our very skin so to speak, we can sense the silent discourse of the whispering and stuttering voices expressing secret idioms 'defined by a list of passive and active affects in the context of the individuated assemblage … These are not phantasies or subjective reveries' (Deleuze and Guattari 1987: 257–258). These are the expressive instances of the Jungian field of collective unconscious. The practical 'conquest of the unconscious' (Deleuze 1988b: 29) via laying out the Tarot cartographic map becomes imperative for our very life and survival.

The Tarot layout is a sign standing for the reality of the virtual; as such an expert Tarot reader performs 'the supreme act of philosophy: not so much to think THE plane of immanence as to show that it is there, unthought in every plane, and to think it in this way as the outside and inside of thought' (Deleuze and Guattari 1994: 59–60). As the included middle between the inside and the outside, it is being unfolded, picture by picture, in front of our very eyes like 'the pieces of Japanese paper flower in the water' (Deleuze 2000: 90) and represents both opposites in a semiotic relation which is 'holding them in complication' (Deleuze 2000) so that 'Essence [as] the third term that dominates the other two' (Deleuze 2000) finally emerges. Tarot cartographic map is a semiotic machine which 'is installing [itself] transversally to the machinic levels … material, cognitive, affective and social…. It is this abstract [virtual] machine that will or will not give these levels … existence' (Guattari 1995: 35). The embodiment of the transcendental field allows it to merge with its own 'object' that, despite always being immanent in perception, would remain disembodied or virtual and, as such, beyond actual recognition in the absence of reading and interpretation. The self-reference between the levels indicates the univocity of Being. With vocabulary bordering on alchemical, Deleuze and Guattari describe the functioning of transversal communication as 'a transformation of substances and a dissolution of forms, a passage to the limit or flight from contours in favour of fluid forces, flows, air, light, and matter, such that a body or a word does not end at a precise point. We witness the incorporeal power of that intense matter, the material power of that language' (1987: 109). It is because of the desire for gnosis as the 'compulsion to think which passes through all sorts of bifurcations, spreading from the nerves and … communicated to the soul in order to arrive at thought' (Deleuze 1994: 147) that Deleuze's method, compatible with Bergson's intuition, enables the reading of signs, symbols, and symptoms that lay down the dynamical structure of experience. As 'the presentation of the unconscious, [and] not the representation of consciousness' (Deleuze 1994: 192), it is intuition that accesses the transcendental field by means of constructing the plane of immanence and laying down the cartography of the unconscious thus bringing 'into being that which does not yet exist' (Deleuze 1994: 147). Intuition, or noesis as an operation of the *nous*, represents the very depth of human knowledge partaking as such of the universal science of life, mathesis.

Deleuze's 1946 publication called *Mathesis, Science, and Philosophy* (cf. Delpech-Ramey 2010; Semetsky and Delpech-Ramey 2011) appeared as a Preface to the re-issue of the French translation of Johann Malfatti de Montereggio's work titled *Mathesis, or Studies on the Anarchy and Hierarchy of Knowledge.* Malfatti practiced medical science in the tradition of natural philosophy grounded in experimental practice leading to healing through the relational patterns of sympathetic vibrations. In modern times, Leibniz had envisaged a formal *scientia generalis* that would have established a long sought-after unity of knowledge (historically viewed as at once occult and politically subversive). This unified science of all sciences – *mathesis universalis* – would employ a formal universal language of symbols with symbols themselves immanent in life, in nature. Leibniz included pictures and 'various graphic geometrical figures' (Nöth 1995: 274) as a possible medium for such a symbolic language. Deleuze (1994) referred to mathesis in connection with an esoteric usage of calculus, claiming that *mathesis universalis* corresponds to the theory of Ideas as the differentials of thought. Mathesis is not opposed to art, religion, or magic but reconciles them as the unified science of human and post-human natures, thus bringing 'nature and culture together in its net' (Deleuze and Guattari 1987: 236). As Deleuze points out, 'the key notion of mathesis – not at all mystical – is that individuality never separates itself from the universal ... Mathesis is ... knowledge of life' (Deleuze 2007: 146–147) communicated in symbols, signs, and images. This knowledge is achieved via

> the *encounter* of the sensible object and the object of thought. The sensible object is called symbol, and the object of thought, losing all scientific signification, is a hieroglyph or a cipher. In their identity they form a concept .... [T]he mysterious character of mathesis is not directed against the profane in an exclusive, mystical sense, but simply indicates the necessity of grasping the concept in a minimum of time, and that physical incarnations take place in the smallest possible space – unity within diversity, general life within particular life .... If *vocation* defines itself through the creation of a sensible object as the result of a knowledge, then mathesis ... is the vocation of vocations, since its transforms knowledge itself into a sensible object. Thus we shall see mathesis insists upon the correspondences between material and spiritual creation. (Deleuze 2007: 151)

Such correspondence is established via Tarot signs connecting the apparently incommensurable planes or levels in our practice and not only in theory. Incidentally, the symbol for true vocation, emphasized by Deleuze, in the Tarot deck is the Major Arcanum XX called Judgement (Figure 6.1). In the picture, the sound of the trumpet leads to the soul's spiritual awakening, but also to the body's symbolic reincarnation into new experiences and new 'modes of existence' (Deleuze 1986: 114). That is, we are becoming free to act in a new way, thereby making a difference in real life, thus getting closer to becoming individuated selves in the image of the next and final Arcanum called the World, in which a naked feminine figure dances inside an oval garland whose shape partakes of cosmic egg. The image of the World conveys the metaphysics of the universe akin to rhythmic movement and dance: it is world as created in a series of creative acts, not unlike the account of Genesis. The dancing female figure relates to the Dionysian mysteries, to joy and fulfilment, to soul or Anima, which is now fully integrated in the otherwise solely rational, Apollonian, world. The World is a symbol for 'increasingly intimate correspondences' (as Deleuze says referring to mathesis) ultimately achieving the reconciliation between man and nature, the human and the divine. The image of the World can also be related to what liberation theology refers to as the New Jerusalem, a symbol of a harmonious, peaceful world as humanity's futuristic goal. And this goal may very well be within reach: the number of this Arcanum is XXI that, significantly, corresponds to our present twenty-first century in the grand scheme of things and collective experiences.

Mathesis, as the vocation of vocations in its ability to transform knowledge itself into a sensible, visible object, is fully accomplished in the semiotics of Tarot: knowledge is transformed into a sensible object in the form of pictures and images; yet as Janus-faced signs, they partake of the intelligible, invisible, realm of archetypal ideas. It is in this sense that Deleuze used the word 'identity' above; ultimately a sign, as Peirce asserted, is bound to become a sign of itself via the included third of interpretants. The process of reading Tarot images originates in the right hemisphere referred to by Deleuze (2003) as capable of interpreting the 'language of relations, which consists of expressive movements, paralinguistic signs … the analogical language par excellence' (2003: 93). The method of analogy that mystics around the world have practiced for centuries defies the privileged subject position of the Cogito observing the detached world of objects as an independent spectator. Mystics and poets historically played a participatory embodied role in the relational network forming an interdependent semiotic fabric with the world. The language of Tarot images is 'intensive, a pure continuum of … intensities. That is when all of language becomes secret, yet has nothing to hide' (Deleuze and Guattari 1987: 98). The images are hieroglyphic in character, hence taken to be secret or esoteric; still they have nothing to hide but all to expose: their meanings can and should be deciphered or unfolded. The language of Tarot signs functions on the basis of a 'paradoxical code [that] takes analogy as its object' (Deleuze 2003: 95) with analogy-becoming-code in our very experience when the images are narrated, that is, translated into other, verbal, signs.

Deleuze, talking about 'double causality' (1990: 94), maintained that the physics of surfaces demands of events to have both causes and quasi-causes, that is, some other event 'intervening as nonsense or as an aleatory point, and appearing as quasi-cause assuring the full autonomy of the effect' (1990: 95) in its relation to this secondary cause. The very first sign in the deck – the Fool or Zero – seems to signify nothing and is an aleatory non-sensical point which nonetheless is still 'present' in each subsequent Arcanum (zero plus one is still one, etc.). Still, when the cards are distributed on the surface and organized into a semiotic structure, then

> as soon as sense is grasped, in its relation to the quasi-cause which produces and distributes it at the surface, it inherits, participates in, and even envelopes and possesses the force of this ideational cause… This cause is nothing outside of its effect… it maintains with the effect an immanent relation which turns the product, the moment that it is produced, into something productive… Sense is essentially produced. It is never originary but is always caused and derived. (Deleuze 1990: 95)

While representing nothingness or nonsense (non-sense) in the guise of a 'floating signifier' (Williams 2008: 72), the Fool initiates the string of meanings for the series of events. It is nonsense that functions as 'a "donation of sense" … it generates a paradox' (Williams 2008: 72) simultaneously defying the uniformity of meanings: sense is created anew. The meaning of each sign – each Arcanum – is derived in the semiotic, at once associative and inferential, process which is inconsistent with 'the operation of the principle of non-contradiction *as a response to paradoxes*' (Williams 2008: 71; italics in original): its paradoxical semiotic logic is a-signifying and involves two modes: one of 'conscious cogitation and [one] with the unconscious' (Williams 2008: 73). The Tarot plays the role of a paradoxical differentiator, a Janus-faced sign that circulates in both series, hence converging on 'both word and object at once' (Deleuze 1990: 51) via the extension of the mind to the level of the body, the cartography on the surface. Deleuze borrows from Leibniz the notion of differential calculus positing the unconscious ideas to be the '"differentials" of thought… related not to a Cogito… but to the fractured I of a dissolved Cogito' (Deleuze 1994: 194). Recollecting the fractured pieces together is equivalent to becoming, to interpreting Tarot images as signs even if their meanings, just like rhizome whose growth proceeds underground, hide in the depth of the unconscious hence appear imperceptible, invisible to the usual sense-perception.

Tarot hermeneutic reaches out 'to the deepest things, the "arcana", [hence making] man commensurate with God' (Deleuze 1990a: 322). It functions as a semiotic 'bridge, a transversality' (Guattari 1995: 23) capable of making the apparent opposites indeed 'commensurate'. The transversal communication between the levels – virtual and actual, consciousness and the unconscious – created by Tarot signs produces *Sens*, due to which our experience acquires meaning and significance because that's when a 'spark can flash… to make us see and think what was lying in the shadow around the words, things we were hardly aware existed' (Deleuze 1995: 141). Such sparks of the Kabbalistic broken vessels are becoming gathered in the schizoanalysis of Tarot and are symbolically represented in the Arcanum called the Star (Figure 6.1). This is Aurora, the morning star immediately following the Tower Arcanum that, as a symbol of ultimate destruction, is its own *dark precursor* in the natural evolution of signs. As the first feminine figure in the deck stripped from her clothes as though from outlived habits and values, the Star is a symbol for creativity, for hope, for the dawn of the new Golden Age that implies a critical reversal of values (Deleuze 1983).

Deleuze's concept of becoming-woman as 'the key to all other becomings' (Deleuze and Guattari 1987: 277) that can empower even the most phallocratic of us with the creative function manifests in the feminine images in the deck such as the High Priestess, the Empress, and the Star. It was de Gébelin who was the first to associate the image of the High Priestess with the Egyptian Isis, the goddess of the rainbow as a symbolic bridge between heaven and earth, the divine and the human. The High Priestess, while possessing the knowledge of the long-forgotten lost speech used by Adam before the Fall, is reluctant, however, to let her inner knowledge be known to the world. The world, on its side, is to be ready to receive this revolutionary gnosis that went underground when forced out by the developments in positivism (or fundamentalism). It is easy to miss the messages of signs: their discourse is silent! Yet we should become attuned to the warning signs, in nature and culture alike. As Deleuze prophetically asks, 'What is it which tells us that, on a line of flight, we will not rediscover everything we were fleeing?… How can one avoid the line of flight's becoming identical with a pure and simple movement of self-destruction' (Deleuze and Parnet 1987: 38). Destratify or annihilate!

The destratifying, liberating capacity of mathesis is achieved in practice via laying down the Tarot cartographic map that speaks in the bastard language of images and signs. This language nonetheless possesses a semiotic structure never mind being 'an esoteric or even a nonverbal language' (Deleuze in Stivale 1998: 259), and the presence of structure assures intelligibility. Tarot cartography serves as a pragmatic tool to '*read*, find, [and] retrieve the structures' (Deleuze in Stivale 1998: 270; Deleuze's italics) hiding in the unconscious: cartography as a mode of diagrammatic, semiotic reason creates a visual notation for the always already *ens realissimum* ideas that are laid down on the plane of immanence. It is our responsibility to become-women by going beyond taboos and learning to read the bastard language of signs. Deleuze does not locate mathesis in the narrow enclave of some initiated elite; mathesis is egalitarian and democratic, situated in the midst of experiential conditions, and 'to believe that mathesis is merely a mystical lore inaccessible and superhuman, would be a complete mistake ... mathesis deploys itself at the level of life, of living man .... Essentially mathesis would be the exact description of human nature' (Deleuze 2007: 143). The interpreter of signs who engages with mathesis in practice is ultimately a creator, an artist if not a *magus*, an insightful and intelligent symptomatologist who belongs to people to come. These people are themselves produced by virtue of experimentation, of becoming. They comprise 'an oppressed, bastard, lower, anarchical, nomadic, irremediably minor race. [These people] have resistance in common – their resistance to death, to servitude, to the intolerable, to shame, and to the present' (Deleuze and Guattari 1994: 109–110). Resistance to the present means becoming aware of the future, to demonstrate a divinatory potential. And a glimpse into the potential future is afforded by the bricolage of Tarot as a schizoanalytic mapping of the unconscious.

Bibliography

Bogue, Ronald (1989) *Deleuze and Guattari*. London and New York: Routledge.

Bogue, Ronald and Inna Semetsky (2010) 'Reading Signs/Learning from Experience: Deleuze's Pedagogy as Becoming-Other', in Inna Semetsky (ed.), *Semiotics Education Experience* (Educational Futures: Rethinking Theory and Practice 43). Rotterdam: Sense Publishers, pp. 115–131.

Bosteels, B. (1998) 'From Text to Territory: Félix Guattari's Cartographies of the Unconscious', in E. Kaufman and K. J. Heller (eds.), *Deleuze and Guattari: New Mappings in Politics, Philosophy and Culture*. Minneapolis: University of Minnesota Press, pp. 145–174.

Deleuze, Gilles (1983) *Nietzsche and Philosophy*, trans. Hugh Tomlinson. New York: Columbia University Press.

Deleuze, Gilles (1986) *Cinema 1: The Movement-Image*, trans. Hugh Tomlinson and Barbara Habberjam, 2 vols. Minneapolis: University of Minnesota.

Deleuze, Gilles (1988a) *Foucault*, trans. Seán Hand. Minneapolis: University of Minnesota Press.

Deleuze, Gilles (1988b) *Spinoza: Practical Philosophy*, trans. R. Hurley. San Francisco, CA: City Lights Books.

Deleuze, Gilles (1989) *Cinema 2: The Time-Image*, trans. Hugh Tomlinson and R. Galeta, 2 vols. Minneapolis: University of Minnesota.

Deleuze, Gilles (1990a) *Expressionism in Philosophy: Spinoza*, trans. Martin Joughin. New York: Zone Books.

Deleuze, Gilles (1990b) *The Logic of Sense*, trans. Mark Lester and Charles J. Stivale (European Perspectives). New York: Columbia University Press.

Deleuze, Gilles (1991) *Bergsonism*, trans. Hugh Tomlinson. New York: Zone Books.

Deleuze, Gilles (1993) *The Fold: Leibniz and the Baroque*, trans. T. Conley. Minneapolis: University of Minnesota Press.

Deleuze, Gilles (1994) *Difference and Repetition*, trans. Paul Patton. New York: Columbia University Press.

Deleuze, Gilles (1995) *Negotiations, 1972–1990*, trans. Martin Joughin (European Perspectives). New York: Columbia University Press.

Deleuze, Gilles (1997) *Essays Critical and Clinical*, trans. D.W. Smith and M. Greco. Minneapolis: University of Minnesota Press.

Deleuze, Gilles (2000) *Proust and signs*. Minneapolis: University of Minnesota Press.

Deleuze, Gilles (2001) *Pure Immanence: Essays on a Life*, trans. Anne Boyman. New York: Zone Books.

Deleuze, Gilles (2003) *Francis Bacon: The Logic of Sensation*, trans. Daniel W.Smith. Minneapolis: University of Minnesota Press.

Deleuze, Gilles (2007) 'Mathesis, Science and Philosophy', in R. Mackay (ed.), *Collapse III*. Falmouth: Urbanomic, pp. 141–155.

Deleuze, Gilles and Claire Parnet (1987) *Dialogues*, trans. Hugh Tomlinson and Barbara Habberjam (European Perspectives). New York: Columbia University Press.

Deleuze, Gilles and Félix Guattari (1983) *Anti-Oedipus: Capitalism and Schizophrenia*, trans. R. Hurley, M. Seem and H.R. Lane. Minneapolis: University of Minnesota Press.

Deleuze, Gilles and Félix Guattari (1987) *A Thousand Plateaus: Capitalism and Schizophrenia*, trans. Brian Massumi. Minneapolis: University of Minnesota Press.

Deleuze, Gilles and Félix Guattari (1994) *What Is Philosophy?*, trans. Hugh Tomlinson and Graham Burchell. New York: Columbia University Press.

Delpech-Ramey, J.A. (2010) 'Deleuze, Guattari, and the "Politics of Sorcery"', *SubStance* 39, pp. 8–24.

Goddard, M. (2001) 'The Scattering of Time Crystals: Deleuze, Mysticism and Cinema', in M. Bryden (ed.), *Deleuze and Religion*. London and New York: Routledge, pp. 53–64.

Guattari, Félix (1995) *Chaosmosis: An Ethico-Aesthetic Paradigm*, trans. P. Bains and J. Pefanis. Bloomington and Indianapolis: Indiana University Press.

Hardt, Michael (1993) *Gilles Deleuze: An Apprenticeship in Philosophy*. Minneapolis: University of Minnesota Press.

Jung, Carl Gustav (1953–1979) *Collected Works* (Bollingen Series), trans. R.F.C. Hull and eds. H. Read, M. Fordham, G. Adler, W.M.McGuire. Princeton, NJ: Princeton University Press. [cited as CW].

Jung, Carl Gustav (1963) *Memories, Dreams, Reflections*, trans. Richard Winston and Clara Winston. New York: Pantheon Books.

Kearney, R. (2001) *The God Who May Be: A Hermeneutics of Religion*. Bloomington and Indianapolis: Indiana University Press.

Kerslake, Christian (2007) *Deleuze and the Unconscious*. New York: Continuum.

Laszlo, Ervin (1995) *The Interconnected Universe: Conceptual Foundations of Transdisciplinary Unified Theory*, Singapore: World Scientific.

Lévi-Strauss, Claude (1966) *The Savage Mind*, Chicago: University of Chicago Press.

Meier, C.A. (ed.) (2001) *Atom and Archetype: The Pauli/Jung Letters, 1932–1958*. Princeton, NJ: Princeton University Press.

Nöth, Winfried (1995) *Handbook of Semiotics*. Bloomington: Indiana University Press.

Ramey, Joshua (2012) *The Hermetic Deleuze: Philosophy and Spiritual Ordeal*. Durham, NC: Duke University Press.

Semetsky, Inna (2006) *Deleuze, Education and Becoming*. Rotterdam: Sense Publishers.

Semetsky, Inna (2009) 'Virtual Ontology/Real Experiences' [July 18–21, 2009], *Transdisciplinarity in Science and Religion* 6, pp. 169–200.

Semetsky, Inna (2010) 'Silent Discourse: The Language of Signs and "Becoming-Woman"', *SubStance: A Review of Theory and Literary Criticism* 39, pp. 87–102.

Semetsky, Inna (2011) *Re-Symbolization of the Self: Human Development and Tarot Hermeneutic*. Rotterdam: Sense Publishers.

Semetsky, Inna (2013) *The Edusemiotics of Images: Essays on the art~science of Tarot*. Rotterdam: Sense Publishers.

Semetsky, Inna and J.A. Delpech-Ramey (2011) 'Educating Gnosis/Making a Difference', *Policy Futures in Education, Special Issue: Deleuze, Pedagogy and Bildung* 9, pp. 518–527.

Stivale, Charles J. (1998) *The Two-Fold Thought of Deleuze and Guattari: Intersections and Animations*. New York and London: The Guilford Press.

Williams, James (2008) *Gilles Deleuze's Logic of Sense: A Critical Introduction and Guide*. Edinburgh: Edinburgh University Press.

Williams, James (2010) 'Immanence and Transcendence as Inseparable Processes: On the Relevance of Arguments from Whitehead to Deleuze Interpretation', *Deleuze Studies* 4, pp. 94–106.

7

Divine Differentials: The Metaphysics of Gilles Deleuze and Its Significance for Contemporary Theologies

Austin Roberts

It's quite curious to what extent philosophy, up to the end of the 17th century, ultimately speaks to us, all the time, of God... Why is philosophy so compromised with God?... Is it a dishonest compromise or something a little purer?

Gilles Deleuze[1]

1. A Deleuzian turn

Along with Jacques Derrida and Michel Foucault, Gilles Deleuze was part of an influential generation of post-Heideggerian continental philosophers who emerged in the 1960s. Of these three thinkers, Derrida and Foucault have thus far exercised the most wide-ranging influence on the Western philosophical world with their respective 'deconstructive' and 'genealogical' methods. For Derrida in particular, one reason that he has been more influential than Deleuze is due to the fact that his writings were translated into English many years earlier than most of the latter's key texts. While Derrida's *Of Grammatology* was already translated from the original French by 1974, Deleuze's *Difference and Repetition* was not available in English until 1994. As a result, even though there was already a great deal of attention being paid to Derridean deconstruction by the mid-1980s in the English-speaking world, 'it was not until the mid-1990s that major work on Deleuze's thought began to appear in English' (Patton and Protevi 2003: 9). But now in the second decade of the twenty-first century, there has been an explosion of scholarly interest in Deleuze's 'constructivism', giving rise to an increasingly important philosophical trend that can now be identified as a Deleuzian turn.

Beyond Deleuze's growing influence within the world of contemporary philosophy, his ideas have increasingly attracted theologians, some of whom appropriate it as a means of critique, while others have used it in more constructive ways. Especially because Deleuze was so deeply influenced by Nietzsche, he is frequently interpreted as a kind of anti-religious atheist. However, it must also be pointed out that Deleuze employed theological language and concepts in highly creative and suggestive ways throughout his writings. Like Derrida's deconstructive philosophy, which is of course filled with theologically charged ideas about prayer, faith, and the messianic, Mary Bryden explains that Deleuze's constructivism 'can be seen to engage with notions of Godhead, belief, spirituality, cosmology, and biblical research, as well as demonstrating the influence of theist writers and philosophers' (Bryden 2000).

At the same time, Deleuze was certainly not a religious man and he was often intensely critical of academic theology. In fact, his entire philosophical project might be accurately summarized as a revolt against all forms of transcendence. As Philip Goodchild writes, Deleuze's philosophy relentlessly pushes 'thought without transcendence to its furthest limits' (Joy 2010: 139). And for Deleuze, there was a deep connection between transcendence and theology: 'Any organization that comes from above and refers to a transcendence, be it a hidden one, can be called a *theological plan*' (Deleuze 1988: 128). A genuinely immanent philosophy would therefore seem to exclude theology altogether.

So how would this radical French philosopher, who subversively defined theology as the 'science of non-existing entities' and claimed that we 'no longer need to believe in God', nevertheless offer constructive possibilities for religion and theology (Deleuze 1990: 281)? This is the basic question that I will be exploring in what follows, beginning with an exploration of Deleuze's significance for the current return to metaphysics. I will then offer an account of Deleuze's metaphysical perspective and survey some of the recent debates about Deleuze and theology. Finally, I will conclude by pointing to two particularly attractive and plausible styles of Deleuzian theology: one more Nietzschean and the other Whiteheadian.

2. Deleuze and the return to metaphysics

Of particular significance for this inquiry is Deleuze's metaphysics of multiplicity, which is often central to theological appropriations of his thought due to its intensely creative potential when put in relation to traditional perspectives on nature (or creation) and even the divine. While many theologians remain suspicious of metaphysics, it never completely disappeared from academic theology.[2] And now in the light of the environmental crisis, many ecological theologians are increasingly attracted to metaphysical speculation as a way of 'regaining the great outdoors', thus moving beyond the anthropocentrism and anti-realism of so much Western thinking after Descartes and Kant (Shaviro 2014: 9).

This theological return to metaphysics has its counterpart in some corners of contemporary philosophy as well. In fact, it has become increasingly clear that the Deleuzian turn within continental philosophy has played a major role in the recent return to metaphysics after so many philosophers shunned it in the wake of the linguistic turn and Heidegger's attempt to 'overcome' metaphysics. Although not without certain differences, the bold constructions of new metaphysical perspectives by New Materialists like Karen Barad and William Connolly, Neo-Vitalists like Jane Bennett and Rosi Braidotti, and Process Philosophers like Steven Shaviro and Isabelle Stengers owe much to Deleuze's metaphysics. Bruno Latour is an especially prominent thinker out of France who has developed an influential metaphysical perspective, often citing Deleuze as a major influence on his ontology of actants.[3]

In his own time, Deleuze rebelled against the dominant anti-metaphysical phenomenological methods of twentieth-century continental philosophers. Late in his career, he confessed that he never had any interest in 'going beyond metaphysics', unlike many of his contemporaries in France (quoted in Patton and Protevi 2003: 48). He gladly identified himself as a 'pure metaphysician' with the aim of developing an 'antisystematic system', perhaps especially in *Difference and Repetition* (quoted in Simpson 2012: 11–12). While he was a fierce critic of Hegelian metaphysics, he found much of his inspiration in other metaphysicians like Spinoza, Leibniz, and Bergson. Additionally, largely due to the early influence of one of his teachers in France, Jean Wahl, Deleuze was deeply inspired by the process metaphysics of A.N. Whitehead along with the pragmatism of William James (Williams 2008). These radical empiricist metaphysicians formed a school of philosophy that Deleuze affectionately called 'a secret society', singling out Whitehead as 'the last great Anglo-American philosopher before Wittgenstein's disciples spread their misty confusion, sufficiency, and terror' (Deleuze 1992: 76).

As such, while Derrida and Foucault offered radical critiques of totalizing philosophical methods, Todd May explains that Deleuze shared their concerns while moving beyond their anti-metaphysical 'cures' (May 2005: 23). As Daniel Smith asserts, 'if Derrida sets out to undo metaphysics, Deleuze sets out simply to *do* metaphysics' (Patton and Protevi 2003: 50). This is partly a consequence of Deleuze's positive rather than negative dialectical method of doing philosophy: like Whitehead's divine process, he 'affirms incompossibilities and passes through them' (Deleuze 1992: 81). But his interest was not simply to carve up the world into stable categories or to merely 'discover entities' like so many traditional metaphysicians – an impossibility and a fruitless activity for the non-foundationalist Deleuze, to be sure (May 2005: 18–19). He was interested in a more profound metaphysical 'creation of concepts' in order to see what bodies and minds are capable of in a given encounter (Deleuze 1988: 125; Crockett 2013: 48). It is this intentionally creative approach that Deleuze took to philosophy that has injected new energy into the current debates about both continental-styled metaphysics and constructive theology.

In order to engage contemporary Deleuzian theologies, it will first be necessary to have a basic grasp on Deleuze's experimental metaphysics. I will therefore offer a sketch of his complex 'chaosmology' in the following section. While he used a wide variety of potent images to describe his metaphysical constructions – making it especially difficult to interpret his thought in any systematic fashion – I will be particularly interested in showing how he developed three interrelated concepts that are repeated in various ways throughout his work: the virtual, the actual, and the plane of immanence. At least for the present discussion, having a sense of the way that these three concepts function is crucial because they are what many Deleuzian theologians have tended to appropriate. While additional interpretive issues about Deleuze's metaphysics will continue to unfold throughout this chapter, this outline should provide a sufficient starting point for further theological engagement.

3. The Deleuzian chaosmos

One way to interpret Deleuze's metaphysics of difference is as a radicalization of Spinoza's monism, which is grounded in the claim that there is only one infinite substance ('nature naturing') that is expressed in an infinite number of modes ('nature natured') (Deleuze 1988: 92–93). Spinoza developed this monistic pantheism in opposition to both Cartesian dualism and theistic transcendence. For Deleuze, Spinoza was therefore 'the Christ of philosophers' because he 'revealed' a philosophy of immanence without transcendence more than any other Western thinker at the time (May 2005: 26). As Deleuze writes, 'Spinoza belongs to that line of private thinkers who overturn values and constructs their philosophy with hammer blows' (Deleuze 1988: 11).

However, Deleuze diverged from Spinoza's monism because of its reliance on substance metaphysics. In his view, Spinoza did not maintain an immanent philosophy that actually affirms difference, but ultimately resorted to transcendent principles of identity and representation. As Deleuze argues in *Difference and Repetition*, Spinoza's one substance (*Deus sive Natura*) is finally 'independent of the modes, while the modes are dependent on substance'. This means that 'being is said of becoming, identity of that which is different, the one of the multiple, etc' (Deleuze 1994: 40–41). Deleuze was therefore in search of a metaphysics of multiplicity that might realize Spinoza's intentions to fully affirm immanence. To do this, he argued that philosophers must not subject difference to transcendent principles, such as analogy or identity, which 'shackle' differences by forcing them into mediation (Deleuze 1994: 29; Shults 2014: 65). A genuinely immanent metaphysics would result in a 'Copernican revolution, which opens up the possibility of difference having its own concept, rather than being maintained under the domination of a concept in general already understood as identical' (Deleuze 1994: 40–41).

To get beyond Spinoza's limitations, Deleuze found it necessary to turn to other philosophers of immanence and difference, especially Bergson and Nietzsche. As May explains, this trinity of philosophers provided Deleuze with the basic ingredients for his metaphysics: 'Spinoza offers us immanence … Bergson offers us the temporality of duration … and the spirit of Nietzsche [offers] the active and the creative affirmation of difference without recoupment into some form of identity' (May 2005: 26). With this philosophical trinity, Deleuze then developed what we can describe as a type of pluralistic monism. His ultimate goal was in fact to construct a metaphysics that would 'arrive at the magic formula … PLURALISM = MONISM', in which Being is understood univocally and is therefore distributed equally throughout everything in a way that does not eliminate differences (Deleuze and Guattari 1987: 20). As Deleuze explains, the result of this radical commitment to immanence and the univocity of Being is not 'that Being is said in a simple and same sense, but that it is said in a simple and same sense, *of* all its individuating differences or intrinsic modalities' (Deleuze 1994: 36).

Deleuze therefore distributes Being *as* differences, as a multiplicity of singularities (Crockett 2013: 31–33). Pure differences have become primary for him, rather than eternal Platonic essences – or any other concept of identity that would impose transcendence upon thought. For Plato, icons or copies ('the Similar') imitate transcendent models or Ideas ('the Same'). Simulacra, by contrast, are 'false pretenders' or 'illusions'. Differences are thus subordinated to transcendent concepts; becoming is constrained by the being of Ideas (Shults 2014: 54). But with Deleuze's 'inversion' or 'destruction of Platonism', he leaves only differences, only the 'simulacra' in his wake: copies of infinite copies that are absolutely immanent by being entirely groundless (Deleuze 1990: 303). This can be understood as a radicalization of phenomenology, as Colebrook explains, for Deleuze's simulacra do 'not refer to appearances as appearances *of* some world; there will be nothing other than a "swarm" of appearances – with no foundation of the experiencing mind or subject' (Colebrook 2001: 6).

Deleuze therefore constructed an anarchical metaphysics, affirming a chaosmic world of pure differences, of 'jets of singularities' in endless becoming without predetermined goals or foundations (Deleuze 1990: 64). As Deleuze writes, this world 'must be called a divine game, since there is no preexisting rule' (Deleuze 1994: 116). In the Deleuzian chaosmos, there are only endless repetitions, contractions, or syntheses of differences that eternally return in the future. But as Deleuze asserts, 'Eternal return affects only *the new*, what is produced under the condition of default by the intermediary of metamorphosis' (Deleuze 1994: 90).[4] As such, it is not the *same* but only *difference* that returns, which implies an infinite potential for novel becomings (Crockett 2013: 31–33).

Deleuze therefore dissolved Spinoza's one absolute substance into what he variously called a pluralized 'chaosmos', 'the plane of Nature', or 'the plane of immanence'. According to Deleuze, it is 'composed of an infinite number of particles' (Deleuze 1988: 123) and its 'parts vary in an infinity of ways' (Deleuze 1988: 126). He conceptualized the plane of immanence as a kind of duality, as having two sides that '[pass] from one to the other' (Deleuze and Guattari 1987: 269), or 'two ways' in which it is dynamically constructed (Deleuze and Guattari 1987: 265). The plane thus forms a kind of 'frontier' or 'screen' between the two sides, as a kind of 'metaphysical surface' for events (Deleuze 1990: 144). Importantly, the two sides of the plane of immanence are not opposed but mutually and reciprocally determine one another (Williams 2013: 11). They relate not negatively, but positively, which Deleuze imagined as a 'Fold' (Deleuze 1994: 65).

On one side of the plane of immanence is the virtual field, which is the differential source of potentiality that is 'prior to organized matter' (Colebrook 2001: 76). With this concept of the virtual, Deleuze was concerned to emphasize that reality is not exhausted by things that we can actually identify: there is a kind of virtual 'depth' in all actual things (Williams 2013: 11). The virtual field is like a 'chaos' of seething potentialities or singular events that are moving at 'infinite movements and speeds' (Deleuze and Guattari 1996: 42). According to Deleuze, these heterogeneous virtual elements must be carefully defined as 'real without being actual, ideal without being abstract' (Deleuze 1994: 208). As such, virtuals are real potentialities rather than abstract, pre-existing possibilities that would transcend or oppose what is actual.

Virtual differences are also endlessly being folded together by the randomly synthesizing activities of mysterious and unconscious agencies. One name that Deleuze gave to such an agency is 'the dark precursor' (Deleuze 1994: 119). Like the field of virtual singularities that they operate within, these non-intentional folding agents do not 'exist' but 'insist' on the plane of immanence. Their activities ensure 'communication' between what are otherwise heterogonous virtual singularities, putting them into 'immediate relation' to one another. They form virtual Ideas, or 'structures of pure becomings', which are real potentialities for actual becomings (Williams 2013: 15). The dark precursor therefore functions as a principle that limits the infinite ocean of virtual differences (Shults 2014: 105–107). Deleuze thus described it as 'an immanent principle of auto-unification, always mobile and displaced' (Deleuze 1990: 108). As LeRon Shults summarizes, the dark precursor and virtual singularities are concepts that 'refer to the transcendental conditions or sources of genetic determination for the becoming of existing entities' (Shults 2014: 3).

Through the unconscious activities of the dark precursor(s), virtual events or 'molecular' potentialities are then capable of being expressed, 'enveloped', or 'contemplated' by the actual, which is the other side of the Deleuzian plane of immanence (Deleuze 1994: 109). As James Williams explains, 'actual things alter due to their relation to pure differences, or better, to difference itself' (Williams 2013: 11). Through repetitions, virtual events are actualized into 'molar aggregates' or layered 'strata' on a 'plane of organization', forming what we normally experience as sensible matter and relatively stable identities (Deleuze and Guattari 1987: xvii; Kearns and Keller 2007: 256–257). Actual events are therefore syntheses or folds of virtual events, the latter of which are in turn 'determined through reciprocal relations to the actual' (Williams 2013: 15).

As such, the Deleuzian chaosmos is composed of heterogeneous, dynamic processes that are immanently self-creative through relational contractions, a world in which nothing is static and everything is in endless becoming. In the chaosmos, there are no sharp lines between mind and matter, human and non-human, or any other ontological dualism (Deleuze and Guattari 1987: 20). And crucially, seemingly stable identities are in fact effects of infinite virtual differences. Subjects are only relatively stable repetitions of so many differential relations: 'selves are by no means simple… Selves are larval subjects' (Deleuze 1994: 78). The consequence of this Deleuzian logic of multiplicity is that all identities are fractured, including 'my own identity, the identity of the self, the world, and God' (Deleuze 1994: 91). But without the need for a transcendent Creator – which does seem to be excluded by Deleuze's logic – where might one discover the divine in this chaosmos? How are theologians appropriating Deleuze's apparently atheist metaphysics?

4. Exploring Deleuzian theologies

There seem to be three basic ways of answering the question of Deleuze's potential philosophical contributions to theology.[5] As such, I will consider three different styles of contemporary Deleuzian theologies. The first group includes more traditional theologians working with Deleuze whom we can classify as *confessional*. Theologians who operate within this trajectory are those who do not shy away from making claims based on special revelation. They are usually committed to Radical Orthodoxy, a relatively recent theological movement composed primarily of Thomists and Augustinians, engaging continental philosophy. Two important examples within this trajectory include Christopher Ben Simpson, the author of *Deleuze and Theology*, and Catherine Pickstock, who has written theologically about certain connections between Deleuze and sacred music (Pickstock 2012). Both Simpson and Pickstock are orthodox Christian theologians who are critical of much in Deleuze's philosophy, even as they find certain aspects of it to be helpful for thinking through traditional Christian doctrines like the Trinity or theological anthropology. However, Shults rightly points out that the primary concern of such confessional Deleuzians 'seems to be protecting the doctrinal formulations of their coalition from attack or showing that what they find most fascinating in Deleuze can be (or already has been) incorporated into the Christian tradition' (Shults 2014: 193). Fortunately, two additional Deleuzian theological trajectories can be identified that are less protective of traditional positions and remain open to Deleuze's critique of transcendence.

A second group of Deleuzian theologians are those whom we might call *progressives*. Whether Christian or post-Christian, this is an especially creative group of theologians who are willing to take some risks with less tradition-bound theological constructions. It is perhaps especially Deleuze's occasional use of mystical concepts and images that lures these theologians into an engagement with his work. As Shults positively describes this group, 'they are more willing to allow logical reflection, egalitarian concern, or intense contemplative experience to challenge traditional formulations and ecclesial practices' (Shults 2014: 193). They therefore tend to develop Deleuzian theologies that maintain a certain amount of contact with Christian doctrines while reframing their traditional meanings. For example, Kristien Justaert has brilliantly drawn on both Deleuze and liberation theologies to construct an immanently mystical Christology from a progressive Catholic perspective. For her, the 'Christ-event' can offer salvation to humans through ritual 'repetitions' of the 'power' of Jesus' life and death (Justaert 2012: 86). With the help of Deleuze, she then develops an inspiring vision of non-hierarchical and diverse churches that serve as sites of resistance to capitalist exploitation of human and non-human nature (Justaert 2012: 126–130).

Another important example of a progressive approach can be found in the work of the philosopher of religion Philip Goodchild, who has been at the forefront of reading Deleuze theologically since the mid-1990s. Although his work has since moved in more radical and political directions, in his earlier theological readings of Deleuze, Goodchild located the divine *in* and even *as* the virtual side of the plane of immanence. As Simpson notes, this theological interpretation of Deleuze seems to be especially grounded in the latter's essay, 'Immanence: A Life' (Simpson 2012: 65), which employs mystical images that almost seem to personalize the plane of immanence as the 'absolute consciousness' that 'gives' events their 'full reality' (Deleuze 2005: 25, 31). For Goodchild, God after Deleuze therefore becomes a kind of vitalist spirit that animates the world as an immanent '*power* of affirmation and creativity', or even 'a *spirit* of affirmation, a *praise* of creativity' (Joy 2010: 163).[6] In his view, the Deleuzian virtual events 'express themselves' or 'manifest themselves' to produce the actual, thus strongly suggesting that they have a kind of ontological priority over the actual. Indeed, Goodchild claims that everything except virtual ideas is 'mere surface effect'. This would seem to imply that the virtual field is the ground of the actual, and even that there is a kind of idealism in Deleuze's thinking. While recognizing other possible ways of interpreting Deleuze's work that are more thoroughly materialist, he justifies his reading of a vitalizing, divine spirit by pointing out that the Deleuzian plane of immanence is a pluralized alternative to Spinoza's pantheism – and is thus already theological (Joy 2010: 162).

While Goodchild's innovative progressive theology explores important themes in Deleuze's work, his virtual pantheism would seem to confirm the suspicions of philosophers like Alain Badiou, Slavoj Žižek, and Peter Hallward that Deleuze is an idealist philosopher of the One rather than a materialist or a naturalist who celebrates multiplicity. According to Badiou's reading, Deleuze's metaphysics presents us with a 'Platonism of the virtual' by grounding the actual in the virtual and thereby giving ontological '*priority*' to the latter (Crockett 2013: 14). This understanding reintroduces metaphysical transcendence into Deleuze's system and subjects him to the critique that he is a kind of 'quasi-Gnostic' who does not genuinely care for material reality or actual bodies. In this interpretation, Deleuze's philosophy ultimately expresses a desire to escape the actual and ascend to the virtual, and thus he was not a truly immanent philosopher of difference. Žižek even goes so far as to associate Deleuze with fascism because he interprets Deleuze's metaphysics as a 'vitalist philosophy of the immanent One' (Crockett 2013: 13, 23).

This debate brings us to our third trajectory of Deleuzian theologians: the *radicals*. These theologians push against all idealist and vitalist interpretations of Deleuze in favour of reading him more consistently as a kind of non-reductive materialist. This metaphysical position then opens out into a variety of Deleuzian death of God theologies. Unlike the progressive's attempts to reformulate the divine life in a more immanent fashion, the radicals fully embrace the death of every God – which for some might even be understood to be the very core of Christian faith.[7] LeRon Shults has recently offered a powerful argument for an atheist Deleuzian 'iconoclastic theology' that can be located within the radical trajectory. However, in what follows I will primarily focus on the work of Clayton Crockett because of his deep engagement in the debate over idealist and materialist readings of Deleuze.

As Crockett argues in his recent publications, a close reading of Deleuze's work that begins with his most foundational texts does not permit a vitalist or idealist interpretation of his ontology.[8] For Crockett, such interpretations of Deleuze read his work much too closely to Bergson's vitalism. He insists that to 'totally conflate Deleuze with Bergson is to miss what is new and original about Deleuze's thought' (Crockett 2013: 15). Crocket argues that Žižek and Badiou read Deleuze too selectively and thus distort his radically materialist philosophy. Rather than interpreting Deleuze dualistically by giving ontological priority to the virtual, Crockett maintains that the virtual and actual are 'distinguished but not opposed' (Crockett 2013: 14).

Along with James Williams, Crockett contends that the virtual and actual are dynamically related and reciprocally determine one another in an endlessly oscillating movement (Williams 2013: 8–11). The relationship between the virtual and the actual can therefore be understood in terms of a relational 'fold ... which is not simply a static distinction but an operational differenciator' (Crockett 2013: 33). Furthermore, he points out the dynamic tension that Deleuze maintains throughout his work between the *material* genesis of the virtual, whereby virtual singularities are 'effects' of actual 'bodily-material processes-causes', and the *formal* genesis of actual multiplicities out of virtual multiplicities (Crockett 2013: 24). And contrary to what Goodchild, Badiou, and Žižek have emphasized, Crockett explains that Deleuze does not believe that reality is formed simply because the virtual 'affirms' or 'manifests' itself within the actual. Without careful qualification, such a claim implies that the virtual is *more real* than the actual, making the actual little more than a passive moment in virtual 'immutable Being, which is One'. Alternatively, Crockett persuasively argues that it is not the virtual alone but 'the process of *actualization* that constitutes reality' (Crockett 2013: 15).

Crockett's materialist interpretation of Deleuze's philosophy thus implicitly offers a challenge to theological appropriations of his work that reintroduce transcendence into the chaosmos. Theologians cannot simply divinize the Deleuzian virtual field by moralizing or anthropomorphizing it in any way – tendencies that Shults discerns to some extent in Goodchild's earlier Deleuzian theology as well as Justaert's more recent work (Shults 2014: 193–194, 210). After all, Deleuze's virtual singularities are beyond good and evil. As Roland Faber points out, the Deleuzian virtual is completely ambivalent: it is 'both gift *and* theft ... open to *any mixture* of power and love', thereby '*dissipating* any notion of God' (Faber 2014: 502).

Assuming this radical materialist interpretation of Deleuze's ontology, Crockett then argues for a Deleuzian death of God theology. He develops his radical theology in relation to the symbol of resurrection by drawing on the Deleuzian concepts of repetition and eternal return. As I have already noted, Deleuze argues that what eternally returns through repetition is not being or the same but becoming or difference. By repetition, an event 'contracts' virtual singularities through its process of becoming before it perishes into the past. As such, what actually 'exists' is the novel present while the virtual past continuously 'insists' on returning through new 'contemplating' events.[9] This Deleuzian process of repetition is actually very similar to Whitehead's prehension, concrescence, and satisfaction of every actual occasion, which in turn 'perish' into the past and become real potentials for new becomings (Keller 2014: 178; Peterson and Zbaraschuk 2014: 13).

For Crockett's radical theology, what is important about this dynamic process is the insight that repetition endlessly ruptures identities, but then opens out into novel becomings at every moment. As such, the 'death' of every actual event ultimately gives rise to new life, or a 'resurrection'. Crockett therefore theologically interprets Deleuze's concept of eternal return to mean that 'Becoming is becoming differently, becoming in and as difference, and the death of God and self are the only possibilities for resurrection, because that death *is* resurrection itself, which is immediately divine' (Peterson and Zbaraschuk 2014: 152).[10] Because the future brings forth genuine novelty, Crockett also rejects a nihilistic worldview that says that oppressive and violent structures in the present cannot be otherwise. Instead, he affirms a 'hope for a future event' that will, perhaps, result in liberation (Crockett 2011: 143).

While Crockett identifies with 'a radical atheism that converges with radical faith', he also continues to experiment with the language of 'God' as a crucial resource for his work in political theology (Peterson and Zbaraschuk 2014: 152). In strictly non-idealist terms, Crockett's Deleuzian conception of God names the immanent material-energetic 'matrix of organization' or the unconscious and non-teleological 'solvent material khora'. This totally immanent divine is a material process that 'gives space-time a chance' as source of 'potentiality for emergent structure' (Crockett et al. 2014: 280–281). Crockett is thus close to Ernst Bloch's atheistic philosophy of hope, which similarly replaces God with 'matter' as source of 'primordial potentiality'.[11]

Crockett has certainly made a compelling case for a Deleuzian radical theology with powerful political and ethical implications. For some, his position might be the absolute limit of their theological engagements. Professing a humble faith in potentially liberating events of the future, and possibly symbolizing these as divine, might be as far as one is willing to go. But even if traditional theism is indeed indefensible, is radical atheism the only plausible way to theologically engage Deleuze – or might one conceptualize an alternative divine that does not reintroduce transcendence? In the final section of this chapter, I want to suggest such a possibility. Yet I will do so on the grounds of Deleuze's actual writings, which do in fact suggest a position other than a Nietzschean-inspired radical atheism.

5. From Nietzsche to Whitehead

One particularly intriguing way to develop a theology after Deleuze that steers a course between an idealizing pantheism and a radical atheism was already proposed by Deleuze in his late work *The Fold*. In one short chapter, Deleuze approvingly describes Whitehead's process metaphysics in a way that reveals how resonant the two philosophers' views are. I have already noted certain connections between these two great philosophers of immanence, but it is especially significant that Deleuze does not oppose Whitehead's chaosmic divinity.[12] Instead, he affirms it as a necessary correction to Leibnizian theism: 'Even God desists from being a Being who compares worlds and chooses the richest compossible. He becomes Process, a process that at once affirms incompossibilities and passes through them' (Deleuze 1992: 81).

While Crockett recognizes Deleuze's interaction with Whitehead's God-process, he does not develop it in any significant way within his own theological project. He has certainly shown that there are profound ways of theologically engaging Deleuze that do not directly depend on this connection to Whitehead. But this moment in Deleuze's writing does suggest that he was open to a Whiteheadian conception of divinity, even if he did not more explicitly develop such a position in his work. It also provides a way to make sense of Deleuze's surprisingly mystical language that we find in some of his later writings, yet without simply divinizing the virtual plane.

As such, there seem to be two viable options for theologically engaging Deleuze today. One is radical, which we see quite impressively developed in Crockett's work, while the other is closer to a non-idealist form of the progressive trajectory, which I find in the Deleuzian–Whiteheadian process theologies of both Catherine Keller and Roland Faber. While a Deleuzian death of God trajectory begins with Spinoza and moves on to Nietzsche, Faber and Keller attempt to move through Nietzsche to Whitehead in order to develop post-secular alternatives to atheism. Both trajectories insist on univocity and immanence, but they part ways on the question of divinity. Each accepts the death of the transcendent, omnipotent, moralistic, and monotheistic God, but they respond to this divine death differently.

In order to illustrate the constructive potential of a more Deleuzian process theology, I want to conclude with a sketch of the recent projects of both Keller and Faber. By bringing together Deleuze and Whitehead, as well as apophatic and mystical thinkers like Nicholas of Cusa, Keller and Faber have effectively reinvented process theology over the last decade. The significance of this should not be underestimated. After all, process theology is perhaps the 'only vital school' of progressive theology today, as the historical theologian Gary Dorrien has claimed (2006: 190). He elsewhere praises it for making the 'strongest contribution of any theological school to integrating science, culture, ecology, feminism, and postmodernity' (Dorrien 2009: 244). But it was only with the publication of *Process and Difference* in 2002 (which includes important contributions from Keller and Faber) that process theologians truly began to take note of Whitehead's strong resonance with Deleuze's philosophy. Since then, some of the most interesting work within process theology has been both Whiteheadian and Deleuzian, which is increasingly being identified as 'process theopoetics'.

In her most recent work, Keller unfolds an 'apophatic panentheism' through a close reading of both Deleuze and Whitehead (Keller 2014: 68).[13] Unlike some of the more radical Deleuzians, she makes the suggestion that, from her perspective, 'God is not dead but becoming… the generative atheism of Deleuze, close to pantheism, may not so much contradict as *darken* the panentheism of Whitehead' (Keller 2014: 172). As such, she intentionally blurs without completely eliminating the difference between pantheism and panentheism:

> That little *en* encodes the difference of *pan* and *theos* and so, by a certain theologic, difference itself. I want to smudge it apophatically. The world-all, as such, remains as unknown (consider dark energy) as any deity that could enfold it. In other words, the *en* is nothing other than the fold. In the *en*, theos is then not the same or similar to the all, but nonetheless its repetition. (Keller 2014: 186)

Keller is careful to differentiate this apophatic ontology from a more rationalist style of process theology, with its 'particular temptations to objectification' and systematized certainties (Keller 2014: 109). She therefore consistently resists any attempt to simply locate God as a distinct being or entity.

Although it is true that Whitehead named God an 'actual entity' and – rather shockingly – a 'creature', Keller argues that these are 'iconoclasm[s]' answering to theistic transcendence and should be interpreted according to his view of metaphysics as a series of 'metaphors mutely appealing for an imaginative leap'. It is also increasingly apparent that part of what enables her 'apophatic negation' of ontotheology or any straightforward identification of the divine is what she calls 'the Deleuzean tonic' (Keller 2014: 189–190). But this does not ultimately lead her to fully identify God with Whitehead's process of creativity, which she closely relates to Deleuze's virtual plane.[14] Neither does her God become an exception to the univocity of being, but is rather a 'consequence' of the ultimate creativity. As such, 's/he/it' cannot be understood as the transcendent, omnipotent Creator that is 'the first cause or hidden reason behind what happens' (Keller 2014: 190). Drawing on Deleuze's reading of Whitehead's God as a 'Process' (rather than *the* process), she ultimately interprets the divine as 'the *relation* to the infinite process'. Such a 'God does not make the differences; but makes possible – posse ipsum – the difference actualized by every finite creature' (Keller 2014: 188–189).

Faber's Deleuzian reading of Whitehead's divine 'poet of the world' also differs quite radically from many other process theologies. And like Keller, he similarly contrasts his process theopoetics to the secular or radical 'a/theistic disappearance of God-language' (Faber 2014: 45). Taking Deleuze's reading of Whitehead's divine process in *The Fold* as his 'mission statement', he rejects both a simple pantheism and panentheism, which for him are still trapped within the imperialistic logic of the One that a logic of multiplicity deconstructs (Faber 2014: 82). He therefore names his post-monotheistic position 'transpantheism', which maintains a '*strict mutuality*' between the divine process and other processes in the chaosmos: 'a mutual transcendence, mutual otherness, and mutual creativity of God and the world' (Faber 2014: 439).

Faber also resists collapsing divinity into the virtual plane by differentiating God from the infinite creativity, thereby situating the divine within '*a multiplicity of syntheses [as] a synthetic multiplicity*' (Faber 2014: 440). Because both God and the world are '*multiplicities in mutual in/difference*' or '*mutual embodiment*', he argues that God cannot be differentiated from the world by any property (Faber and Fackenthal 2013: 228). As an '*in/finite process*' that never freezes into a simple unity as a substance or being among others, the 'divine manifold' is therefore equally but differently real in relation to the world (Faber 2014: 445). And for Faber, this divine process can only ever '*ex*-sist by *in*-sisting *in* multiplicity' (Faber and Fackenthal 2013: 228). God is thus the powerless love and affirmation of multiplicity that '*initiates* "difference" (principle of concretion) and *collects* "peace"', which Faber names 'polyphilia' and 'theoplicity' (Faber 2014: 380). In this way, the polyphilic divine process does not create the world, but rather saves it from 'stalling into a final state' and 'from being rationalized into subjection to the One' by always insisting 'in/on/as' multiplicity (Faber 2014: 45, 228):

> Divine love... is nothing but *pure* multiplicity. She names the *divine* of the *manifold* as it is a *gift of passage* that *insists on* the baseless fabric of never-was

> and never-will-be. This multiple divine is not 'identical' with the fabric of the multiplicity, but the *poet* of the never-is, of the nonclosure that would be lost in the 'light of clarity,' the salvation that flees finality. (Faber 2014: 12)

In their theopoetic and Deleuzian transformations of Whiteheadian process theology, Faber's mystical transpantheism and Keller's apophatic panentheism present us with exciting possibilities for theologies that will take the risk of seriously engaging post-structuralist philosophy. As viable alternatives to both atheistic radical theology and anti-metaphysical styles of postmodern theology, they can offer fresh inspiration for those who would dare to plunge with them into the often dizzying, but ultimately life-giving Deleuzian manifold.

Notes

1 Deleuze (1980).
2 One important example of metaphysical theology is process theology, which is inspired by the philosophies of Alfred North Whitehead and Charles Hartshorne and was developed in the 1960s by theologians like John B. Cobb, Jr.
3 For a recent discussion on the new metaphysics, see the introduction to Shaviro (2014).
4 My emphasis.
5 I am especially dependent upon the similar typology in Shults (2014: 192–195, 210–212).
6 My emphasis.
7 Citing the radical theologian Peter Rollins, who often makes such a claim (from a Lacanian rather than Deleuzian perspective), Crockett suggests this view of his Deleuzian radical theology in Peterson and Zbaraschuk (2014: 152).
8 Crockett argues that we must interpret Deleuze primarily through *Difference and Repetition* and *The Logic of Sense* before moving on to his writings about individual philosophers, the late essays, or his collaborations with Guattari.
9 On Deleuze's notion of the triple repetition, see chapter 2 of Deleuze (1994).
10 My emphasis.
11 Faber relates Deleuze's virtual to Bloch's primordial potentiality in Faber (2008: 82).
12 On Whitehead's 'insistence on immanence,' see Whitehead (1996: 71).
13 Keller's earliest writings on Deleuze include 'The Process of Difference, the Difference of Process' and 'Process and Chaosmos: The Whiteheadian Fold in

the Discourse of Difference', both of which are in *Process and Difference* (2002). She then went on to explicate a full-fledged Deleuzian–Whiteheadian theology in *Face of the Deep* (2003) and more recently in *Cloud of the Impossible* (2014).

14 To be more precise, Keller connects the Deleuzian virtual plane to Whitehead's creativity and the extensive continuum. See Keller (2003: 167–169, 294).

Bibliography

Bryden, Mary (ed.) (2000) *Deleuze and Religion*. London and New York: Routledge.

Colebrook, Claire (2001) *Gilles Deleuze*. London and New York: Routledge.

Crockett, Clayton (2011) *Radical Political Theology: Religion and Politics after Liberalism*. New York: Columbia University Press.

Crockett, Clayton (2013) *Deleuze beyond Badiou: Ontology, Multiplicity, and Event*. New York: Columbia University Press.

Crockett, Clayton, B. Keith Putt and Jeffrey W. Robbins (eds.) (2014) *The Future of Continental Philosophy of Religion*. Bloomington, IN: Indiana University Press.

Deleuze, Gilles (1980) *Seminar/Spinoza*, 25 November 1980, trans. Timothy S. Murphy, http://www.webdeleuze.com/php/texte.php?cle=17&groupe=Spinoza&langue=2.

Deleuze, Gilles (1988) *Spinoza: Practical Philosophy*, trans. Robert Hurley. San Francisco, CA: City Lights Publishers.

Deleuze, Gilles (1990) *The Logic of Sense*, ed. Constantin V. Boundas, trans. Mark Lester and Charles Stivale. New York: Columbia University Press.

Deleuze, Gilles (1992) *Fold: Leibniz and the Baroque*, trans. Tom Conley. Minneapolis, MN: University of Minnesota Press.

Deleuze, Gilles (1994) *Difference and Repetition*, trans. Paul Patton. New York: Columbia University Press.

Deleuze, Gilles (2005) *Pure Immanence: Essays on a Life*, 2nd edition, trans. Anne Boyman. New York and Cambridge, MA: Zone Books.

Deleuze, Gilles and Félix Guattari (1987) *A Thousand Plateaus: Capitalism and Schizophrenia*, trans. Brian Massumi. Minneapolis, MN: University of Minnesota Press.

Deleuze, Gilles and Félix Guattari (1996) *What Is Philosophy?*, trans. Hugh Tomlinson and Graham Burchell. New York: Columbia University Press.

Dorrien, Gary (2006) *The Making of Modern Liberal Theology: Crisis, Irony, and Postmodernity: 1950–2005*. Louisville, KY: Westminster John Knox Press.

Dorrien, Gary (September 2009) 'Dialectics of Difference: Barth, Whitehead, Modern Theology and the Uses of Worldviews', *American Journal of Theology & Philosophy* 30:3, pp. 244–270.

Faber, Roland (2008) *God as Poet of the World: Exploring Process Theologies*. Louisville, KY: Westminster John Knox Press.

Faber, Roland (2014) *The Divine Manifold*. Lanham, MD: Lexington Books.

Faber, Roland and Jeremy Fackenthal (eds.) (2013) *Theopoetic Folds: Philosophizing Multifariousness*. New York: Fordham University Press.

Joy, Morny (ed.) (2010) *Continental Philosophy and Philosophy of Religion*. New York: Springer.

Justaert, Kristien (2012) *Theology after Deleuze*. New York: Bloomsbury Academic.

Kearns, Laurel, and Catherine Keller (eds.) (2007) *Ecospirit: Religions and Philosophies for the Earth*. New York: Fordham University Press.

Keller, Catherine (2003) *Face of the Deep: A Theology of Becoming*. New York: Routledge.

Keller, Catherine (2014) *Cloud of the Impossible: Negative Theology and Planetary Entanglement*. New York: Columbia University Press.

Keller, Catherine and Anne Daniell (eds.) (2002) *Process and Difference: Between Cosmological and Poststructuralist Postmodernisms*. Albany, NY: State University of New York Press.

May, Todd (2005) *Gilles Deleuze: An Introduction*. New York: Cambridge University Press.

Patton, Paul and John Protevi (eds.) (2003) *Between Deleuze and Derrida*. London and New York: Bloomsbury Academic.

Peterson, Daniel J. and G. Michael Zbaraschuk (eds.) (2014) *Resurrecting the Death of God: The Origins, Influence, and Return of Radical Theology*. Albany, NY: State University of New York Press.

Pickstock, Catherine (2012) 'God and Meaning in Music: Messiaen, Deleuze, and the Musico-Theological Critique of Modernism and Postmodernism', *Imaginatio et Ratio: A Journal of Theology and the Arts* 1:1, pp. 6–26.

Shaviro, Steven (2014) *The Universe of Things: On Speculative Realism*. Minneapolis, MN: University of Minnesota Press.

Shults, F. LeRon (2014) *Iconoclastic Theology: Gilles Deleuze and the Secretion of Atheism*. Edinburgh: Edinburgh University Press.

Simpson, Christopher Ben (2012) *Deleuze and Theology*. London and New York: Bloomsbury T&T Clark.

Whitehead, Alfred North (1996 [1927]) *Religion in the Making*. New York: Fordham University Press.

Williams, James (2008) 'Gilles Deleuze' (1925–1995), in Michel Weber and Will Desmond (eds.), *Handbook of Whiteheadian Process Thought Vol. II*. Heusenstamm, Germany: Ontos Verlag, pp. 645–48.

Williams, James (2013) *Gilles Deleuze's Difference and Repetition: A Critical Introduction and Guide*, 2nd edition. Edinburgh: Edinburgh University Press.

8

The Atheist Machine

F. LeRon Shults

In their first co-authored book, *Anti-Oedipus*, Deleuze and Guattari challenged the psychoanalytic idealization and capitalist appropriation of Oedipus, and set out a plan in which – or a plane on which – a new set of questions could be productively engaged: 'Given a certain effect, what machine is capable of producing it? And given a certain machine, what can it be used for?' (2004a: 3). My focus in this chapter is on what I will call *the atheist machine*, the multiple uses and effects of which are expressed throughout the productions, registrations, and consumptions of Deleuze's literary corpus. Using the language of *A Thousand Plateaus*, we might say that the abstract machine of affirmative atheism produces rhizomic lines of flight whose absolute deterritorialization molecularizes the transcendent pretences of monotheistic molarities. I will argue that the atheist machine is always at work wherever schizoanalysis (or rhizomatics, micropolitics, pragmatics, etc.) proceeds, as long as it proceeds.

In their last co-authored book, *What Is Philosophy?*, Deleuze and Guattari argued that 'Wherever there is transcendence, vertical Being, imperial State in the sky or on earth, there is *religion*; and there is Philosophy only where there is immanence ... only friends can set out a plane of immanence as *a ground from which idols have been cleared*' (1994: 43, emphases added). When it comes to dealing with priestly erections of arborescent icons within a religious Imaginarium, the schizoanalytic task of the Deleuzian Friend is definitely destructive. 'Destroy, destroy. The whole task of schizoanalysis goes by way of destruction' (2004a: 342). As the last few sections of *Anti-Oedipus* make clear, however, this destruction is inextricably linked to the positive and creative tasks of schizoanalysis.

This chapter is an expanded version of a keynote presentation given at the 7th annual International Deleuze Studies Conference in Istanbul, Turkey, in July 2014. Its subsections reflect the general theme of that conference: 'Models,

Machines, and Memories'. I begin by introducing the concept of theogonic (god-bearing) mechanisms: evolved cognitive and coalitional *machines* that engender shared imaginative engagement with supernatural agents. Insights derived from empirical findings and theoretical developments within the biocultural sciences of religion can help us understand how and why gods are so easily born(e) in human minds and groups. We also need to refresh our *memories* about the historical contingencies surrounding the emergence of the (Western) monotheistic idea of 'God' – an infinite supernatural Agent who has a special plan for a particular Group. In the second section, I briefly explain how the advent of this conception, which turned out to be logically, psychologically, and politically unbearable, contributed to the assemblage of the atheist machine during the axial age.

Third, I utilize the conceptual framework outlined in section one as a heuristic *model* for clarifying the dynamics at work within and among the four main social-machines treated in the *Capitalism and Schizophrenia* project (i.e. the territorial, despotic, capitalist, and war machines). As we will see, the atheist machine plays a special role in the creative production of the (revolutionary) war machine. The fourth section demonstrates the explanatory power of this integrated model by examining two case studies – cases selected in part because of their significance in the context of the original conference presentation. The excavation of Çatalhöyük, a well-known archaeological site in south central Turkey, has shed light on the development of significant social-machinic shifts during the Neolithic. Deleuze and Guattari themselves referred to this site in their discussion of the Apparatus of Capture (2004b: 473–474). Istanbul is a contemporary site that exemplifies the tension between religion and naturalist-secularist forces within a complex, pluralistic and globalizing cosmopolitan society.

Finally, I will explore the implications of the integration of these machines, memories, and models for the productive task of *becoming-atheist*, that is, for the experimental construction of bodies without organs on the plane of immanence without any recourse to transcendent religious Figures imaginatively engaged by subjugated groups whose rituals allegedly mediate divine revelation. Elsewhere I have spelled out the conceptual framework of 'theogonic reproduction theory' and its relation to Deleuzian philosophy in more detail (Shults 2014a, 2014b, 2014c, 2014d). In the current context I limit myself to a broad outline of the theory, demonstrating its usefulness for abstracting a Deleuzian atheist machine and extracting its revolutionary force for the schizoanalysis of religion.

1. Atheism and schizoanalysis

The goal of schizoanalysis is 'to analyze the specific nature of the libidinal investments in the economic and political spheres, and thereby to show how, in the subject who desires, desire can be made to desire its own repression… All this happens, not in ideology, but well beneath it' (2004a: 115). One of the goals of *theological* schizoanalysis, I suggest, is to show how subjects come to desire their own *religious* repression. 'All this' does indeed occur 'well beneath' the surface of priestly ideology. As we will see in the next section, evolved cognitive and coalitional mechanisms surreptitiously regulate desiring-production by engendering god-conceptions in human minds and cultures. At this stage, however, our focus is on the way in which schizoanalysis works to challenge the striations and segmentations of the socius effected by priestly figures, whether psychoanalytic or religious (2004b: 171).

Deleuze expresses astonishment that so many philosophers still find the death of God tragic. 'Atheism', he insists, 'is not a drama but the philosopher's *serenity* and philosophy's *achievement*'. The dissolution of God is not a problem. 'Problems begin only afterward, when the *atheism* of the concept has been attained' (1994: 92, emphasis added). Why, then, would the Deleuzian Friend continue to devote attention to religious ideas, such as concepts of God that hold up monotheistic molarities? First of all, chipping away at such repressive representations is valuable in and of itself. But Deleuze suggests another motivation for poking around religious and theological edifices. 'Religions', he argues, 'are worth much less than the nobility and the courage of the atheisms that they inspire' (2007: 364).

Some of Deleuze's most inspiring pages are those in which he attends to sacerdotal stratifications; this makes sense in light of his claim that 'there is always an atheism to be extracted from religion'. In fact, Deleuze singles out Christianity as that religion that *secretes atheism* 'more than any other religion' (1994: 92). This helps to explain his frequent criticism of that long-dominant monotheistic Coalition. However, Deleuze explicitly separates *all* religion from philosophy, art, and science. The latter three require more than the making of 'opinions', which are attempts to protect ourselves from chaos based on the invocation of 'dynasties of gods, or the epiphany or a single god, in order to paint a firmament on the umbrella, like the figures of an Urdoxa from which opinions stem'. Art, science, and philosophy 'cast planes over the chaos… [they] want us to tear open the firmament and plunge into the chaos. We defeat it only at this price' (1994: 202). Each of these struggles with chaos in its own way, 'bringing back' varieties (art), variables (science), or variations (philosophy). Efforts within all three disciplines are always and already bound up in the struggle against *opinion* – especially opinions woven into sacred canopies defended by religious hierarchies.

What does any of this have to do with schizoanalysis? Does Deleuze really link schizoanalysis (and rhizomatics, micropolitics, pragmatism, etc.) to *atheism*? Indeed he does. In *Anti-Oedipus*, Deleuze notes that denying God is only a 'secondary thing', and accomplishes nothing if 'man' is straight away set in God's place. The person who realizes that 'man' is no more central than 'God' does not even entertain the question of 'an alien being, a being placed above man and nature'. Such a person, he observes, no longer needs 'to go by way of this mediation – the negation of the existence of God – since he has attained those regions of an auto-production of the unconscious where the unconscious is no less atheist than orphan – immediately atheist, immediately orphan' (2004a: 65–66). For the schizoanalyst, the unconscious is not mediated by Oedipus or Christ (or any other religious Figure): it is *immediately* orphan *and* atheist.

In his critique of psychoanalysis Deleuze identifies three errors concerning desire: lack, law, and the signifier. These are in fact the same error, an 'idealism that forms a pious conception of the unconscious'. But where did these errors come from? 'These notions cannot be prevented from dragging their *theological* cortege behind – insufficiency of being, guilt, signification ... But what water will cleanse these concepts of their background, their previous existences – *religiosity*?' (2004a: 121, emphases added). In *A Thousand Plateaus* these notions are explicitly linked to the triple curse cast on desire by 'the priest', the most recent figure of which is the psychoanalyst: 'the negative law, the extrinsic rule, and the transcendental ideal' (2004b: 171). The similarity between traditional interpretations of the Genesis myth as a 'Fall' and models of the Oedipal conflict that rely on privative, punitive, and palliative categories is hard to miss: both understand desire in terms of loss, guilt, and idealization – as under the curse of anxiety, prohibition, and displacement from a desexualized paradise (cf. Shults 2014b).

In the plateau on 'Nomadology', Deleuze also explicitly links atheism to the creative war machine that was invented by the nomads. 'It may be observed that nomads do not provide a favorable terrain for religion; the man of war is always committing an offense against the priest or the god ... The nomads have a sense of the absolute, but a singularly *atheistic* one' (2004b: 422, emphasis added). Although the phrase 'war machine' does not appear in *Anti-Oedipus*, we do find references there to a 'revolutionary machine' and to hunters in nomadic space who follow the flows and escape the 'sway of the full body of the earth' (2004a: 354, 163). Atheism and schizoanalysis cannot be separated. 'For the unconscious of schizoanalysis is unaware of persons, aggregates, and laws, and of images, structures, and symbols. It is an orphan, just as it is an anarchist and an *atheist*' (2004a: 342, emphasis added).

This link between atheism and schizoanalysis will come as no surprise to those familiar with Deleuze's earlier single-authored works of philosophical portraiture, in which he consistently hammers away at religious ressentiment and traditional notions of God, and celebrates the atheistic effects of Nietzsche (1983), Spinoza (1990), Hume (1991), and even Kant (1984). In *Difference and Repetition*, he encourages us not to judge the atheist from the point of view of the belief that supposedly drives him, but to judge the believer 'by the *violent atheist* by which he is inhabited, the *Antichrist* eternally given "once and for all" within grace' (1994: 96, emphases added). In *Logic of Sense*, Deleuze insists that there has only ever been one ethics, the *amor fati* of the humour-actor who is 'an anti-God (*contradieu*)' – the Stoic sage who 'belongs to the Aion' and opposes the 'divine present of Chronos' (1990b: 170–171).

Deleuze found atheism a somewhat obvious place to begin. Instead of loitering around the starting line of philosophy, he encouraged us to get moving, to experiment on the plane of immanence by creating concepts. Getting people to the starting line, however, is harder than Deleuze seemed to realize. One of the most important effects (and uses) of an atheist machinic assemblage, I suggest, is the disassembling of the god-bearing machines that reproduce supernatural agents in the human Imaginarium and covertly pressure believers to keep nurturing them through regulated ritual engagement. Unveiling these evolved mechanisms, which operate 'well beneath' theological ideologies, is an important initial step as we begin to have 'the talk' about religious reproduction.

2. Theogonic machines: How gods are born(e)

Where do babies come from? Why do parents keep them around? Archaeologists working at sites like Çatalhöyük do not have to dig around for answers to such questions. As they unearth Neolithic skeletons and artefacts, clearing the ground of 'idols' (or, at least, of 'figurines'), they can confidently assume that the regular arrival and continued nurture of the infants in that community were the result of the same basic sort of coital procedures and mating strategies that were naturally selected during the evolution of *Homo sapiens* in the Upper Paleolithic and that continue to replenish the human population today. Although research on these practices in a cosmopolitan city like Istanbul might yield insight into some interesting variations, cultural anthropologists know enough about the human phylogenetic inheritance and the dynamics of the transmission of social entrainment practices to explain, without additional field work, where Turkish *babies* come from today and why adult Turks keep them around.

A similar confidence is emerging among scholars in the biocultural sciences of religion about the mechanisms by which *gods* are born in human minds and borne in human cultures. During the last quarter century, theoretical proposals based on empirical research within a wide variety of fields such as evolutionary biology, archaeology, cognitive science, moral psychology, and cultural anthropology have been converging around the claim that religious phenomena can be explained by the evolution of *cognitive* processes that overdetect human-like forms in the *natural* world and *coalitional* processes that overprotect culturally inscribed norms in the *social* world. Elsewhere I have summarized many of the major theories within the biocultural study of religion that shed light on god-bearing mechanisms, consolidating them in what I call *theogonic reproduction theory*.[1]

It is important to recognize that phenomena associated with 'religion' are complex and contested (like the term itself). For the purpose of this interdisciplinary experiment, however, I am using the term to indicate an aggregate of features that have in fact been found in every known culture, past and present, namely, *shared imaginative engagement with axiologically relevant supernatural agents*. Where do conceptions of gods come from, and why do groups keep them around? Belief in supernatural revelations and participation in supernatural rituals are the result of the integration of evolved perceptive and affiliative tendencies that I call 'anthropomorphic promiscuity' and 'sociographic prudery'. The coordinate grid in Figure 8.1 provides a conceptual framework for discussing the possible correlations between these types of cognitive and coalitional dispositions – and their contestation.

Why are humans so prone towards *superstition*, that is, to proposing and accepting interpretations of ambiguous (and especially frightening) natural phenomena that are based on false conceptions of causation? Such interpretations are due, in part, to evolved *cognitive* defaults that pull us towards the left side of the horizontal line in Figure 8.1. When we encounter some

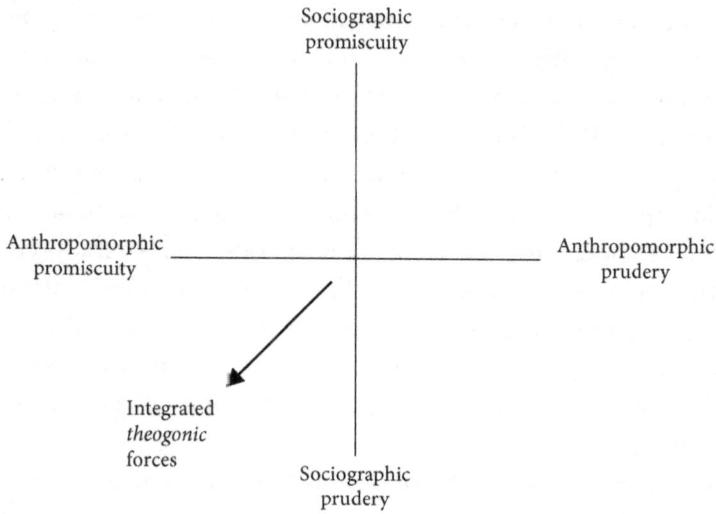

Figure 8.1 Theogonic forces.

pattern or movement we do not understand, our first guess is likely to involve the attribution of characteristics like mentality and animacy. This overactive predilection helps to explain why we so easily see 'faces in the clouds' and worry about hidden forces that may intend us harm. Moreover, we quite often double down on such guesses and keep scanning for human-like agents even when there is no clear evidence of their presence. This tendency to assume that hard-to-detect agents are the cause of hard-to-understand events served our Upper Paleolithic ancestors well; otherwise, we would not be here to write and read about them.

Early hominids who developed hypersensitive cognitive devices that scanned for agency were more likely to survive than those who did not. What made that noise in the tall grass? Was it a human enemy or some other animal? Or was it just the wind? Those who quickly guessed 'intentional force' and acted accordingly were more likely to avoid being eaten (if the animal was a predator) and more likely to find food (if the animal was a prey). Despite almost constant false positives in the short run, this overactive perceptual strategy would have granted survival advantage in the long run. It would have paid off to keep searching for and believing in such hidden agents. Anxiety about the failure to find an actual agent generates other hypotheses; just because we are paranoid does not mean that an animal-spirit or angry ancestor-ghost was not really lurking in the grass before it mysteriously disappeared.

Contemporary humans have inherited this anthropomorphic *promiscuity*. We jump at any opportunity to postulate human-like entities as causal explanations even – or especially – when these interpretations must appeal to counterintuitive disembodied intentional forces, that is, to 'supernatural agents'. Of course, it is also possible to contest this sort of evolved default. Scientists and philosophers, for example, are trained to become anthropomorphically *prudish*. Far more cautious about such appeals, and typically critical of superstition in general, they are more likely to resist ascribing intentionality to unknown causes. If something strange happens in a test tube during an experiment, the chemist will not guess that it was a 'ghost'. If something seems to be missing in a causal (or logical) chain, the (non-religious) philosopher will not insert a 'god'.

Why are humans also so easily prone towards *segregation*, that is, to making and reinforcing inscriptions of the social field that protect their own in-groups from contamination or domination by out-groups? Our evolved *coalitional* defaults pull us towards the bottom of the vertical line in Figure 8.1. This (often vehement and sometimes violent) fortification of boundaries is engendered, in part, by an evolved overactive tendency to embrace and defend conventional modes of segmenting and regulating society. This naturally generated prejudice for one's own collective makes it tempting to just stay at home where the proscriptive and prescriptive norms feel most comfortable. This default tendency is so powerful that we will often engage in costly and painful behaviours in order to follow the rules – and willingly inflict pain on those who do not. It makes sense that such a hypersensitive propensity towards protecting one's own coalition would also have served our early *Homo sapiens* ancestors well.

When it comes to competition among small-scale societies, especially when resources are low or under other stressful conditions, those groups that are most likely to survive are those in which the individual members are able to cooperate and remain committed to the group. Natural selection reinforces the tendency of an individual organism to watch out for itself, but if there are too many cheaters, freeloaders, or defectors in a society, it will quickly fall apart. Research in the biocultural sciences of religion suggests that this problem was solved in some hominid coalitions during the Upper Paleolithic by an intensification of shared belief in and ritual engagement with potentially *punitive* supernatural agents (such as animal-spirits or ancestor-ghosts). Such coalition-favouring 'gods' could catch misbehaviour that regular natural agents might miss and could punish not only the miscreants but their offspring or even the entire group. Belief in invisible or ambiguously apparitional 'watchers' helped to enhance the motivation to follow the rules and stay within the coalition.

Contemporary humans have also inherited this sociographic *prudery*. Most people somewhat automatically follow the authorized social norms of their in-group, or at least put great effort into building up a reputation for doing so. Here too, however, the evolved default can be contested. Those who are *promiscuous* in their sociography are less likely to accept claims about or demands for the segregation of human groups that are based only (or even primarily) on appeals to authorities within their own coalition. They are more likely to be open to intercourse with out-groups about alternate normativities and to the pursuit of new modes of creative social engagement. In-group bias helped (some of) our ancestors survive in small-scale societies in difficult socio-ecological niches. Today, however, this evolved default does not always serve us well – especially those of us who live in large-scale, urban societies characterized by the pressures of globalization and radical pluralism. A growing number of policy-makers and legislators in such contexts refuse to appeal to 'ghosts' or 'gods' in their attempts to inscribe the public sphere.

Anthropomorphic promiscuity and sociographic prudery reinforce one another. Conceptions of gods may be easily born within human minds but it takes a village to raise them. Supernatural agents who are cared for and ritually engaged within a coalition then become easy imaginative targets for the hair-triggered agency detection mechanisms of each new generation. In the environment of our early ancestors the selective advantage went to hominids who developed cognitive capacities that quickly *detected* relevant agents in the natural milieu and whose groups were adequately *protected* from the disruption that could result from too many cheaters in the social milieu. All living human beings share a phylogenetic inheritance shaped by the integration of these god-bearing biases, which explains why we are so easily drawn into the biocultural gravitational field of the lower left quadrant of Figure 8.1.

The explanatory power of the disciplines that contribute to the biocultural study of religion challenges the plausibility of belief in ghosts, gods, and other culturally postulated disembodied intentional forces. Scientists and (non-religious) philosophers may not be able to provide deductive logical arguments that *disprove* the existence of supernatural agents or inductive evidence that *invalidates* claims about their causal relevance, but they can offer powerful abductive and retroductive arguments that render their existence *implausible*. The more reasonable hypothesis is that shared imaginative intercourse with supernatural agents emerged over time as naturally evolved hypersensitive cognitive tendencies led to mistaken perceptions, which in turn slowly became entangled within erroneous collective judgements about the extent of the social field (cf. Shults 2014c).

The (relative) success of science and the (relatively) peaceful cohesion of democratic, pluralistic societies require that those who want to participate in the academic and public spheres learn how to challenge the cognitive and coalitional defaults that promote superstition and segregation. But if the biases that lead to shared imaginative engagement with supernatural agents were so deeply woven into the genetic and memetic structures of human life, why and how did they come to be challenged in the first place? Scientific naturalism and political secularism are expanding in many parts of the world. A growing number of us do not think we need gods to make sense of the natural world or to act sensibly in the social world. Where did such 'atheistic' ideas come from? They were already gestating during the axial age.

3. Monotheistic memories: The birth of (a)theism

During the tenth millennium BCE, shared belief in local animal-spirits or limited ancestor-ghosts was enough to hold together small-scale societies of hunter-gatherers. Shamanic engagement with such finite supernatural agents even sufficed for the egalitarian sedentary collectives that began to form during the Neolithic. Over the millennia, however, in many contexts across the most fertile areas of the globe, human groups grew in size and complexity and claimed ever-larger plots of land for themselves. So did their gods. As coalitions were amalgamated or assimilated by one another, smarter and more powerful supernatural agents were needed – 'high gods' who could monitor the behaviour of more human agents and trump the local spirits or ancestral authorities of the newly merged coalitions. Ever bigger groups required ever bigger and ever more punitive gods in order to ensure that everyone cooperated and stayed committed (cf. Norenzayan 2013).

During the first millennium BCE, within the largest and most complex literate states across east, south, and west Asia, a new sort of god-concept was born in the minds of intellectual and priestly elites: an all-encompassing Supernatural Agency, whose influence was universal and in relation to whom all behaviour was punished (or rewarded). The period from approximately 800 to 200 BCE is commonly called the 'axial age' because it represents a turning point, or axis, in the transformation of civilizational forms in human history. The most common ideas about an ultimate Reality that emerged in east and south Asia during this period did not explicitly (or unambiguously) involve the attribution of intentionality to an infinite Force. Dao and Dharma, for example, were supposed to be morally relevant for any and all groups, but most Chinese and Indian religious scholars seriously questioned whether such Realities should be primarily conceived as person-like and coalition-favouring.

There was far less doubt in the monotheist traditions that emerged in the wake of the west Asian axial age: we are made in the *image* of God and God has a special plan for *our* group. The identity of Jewish – and eventually Christian and then Muslim – coalitions was tied to narratives about the creation of Adam and the call of Abraham to a promised land (paradise lost, and found, in west Asia). Theological debates among these religious in-groups centre around questions about the extent to which (or even whether) Moses, Jesus, or Muhammad mediate divine law-giving and care-giving. Which group has the definitive revelation of – and ritual access to – the one true God who will personally punish (or reward) everyone for all eternity? Monotheism is anthropomorphic promiscuity and sociographic prudery gone wild – superstition and segregation applied to infinity.

As we will see in the next section, Deleuze often noted a special relation between monotheism and what he called the *despotic* machine. When the coding of flows in the 'primitive' territorial socius is overcoded in the despotic socius, then 'the ancestor – the master of the mobile and finite blocks – finds himself dismissed by the deity, the immobile organizer of the bricks and their infinite circuit' (2004a: 217). For Deleuze, the main role of the deity seems to be the inscription of debt into the very existence of the despot's subjects, who now owe their very being to the despot-god. '*There is always a monotheism on the horizon of despotism*: the debt becomes a debt of existence, a debt of the existence of the subjects themselves' (2004a: 215, emphasis added). Even if the priest (or the prophet) connected to the king-despot does not see the disobedient actions or disrespectful attitudes of the people, the inescapable Eye of God will – and no sinner can hide from his judgemental Voice and punitive Hand.

Among the despot's bureaucrats, the monotheistic priest has a special role, that is, administering the face of God and interpreting His intentions. 'A new aspect of deception arises, the deception of the priest: interpretation is carried to infinity and never encounters anything to interpret that is not already itself an interpretation' (2004b: 126–128). The revelation that is allegedly encountered in holy texts and engaged in rituals is ambiguous; it can be (and must be) endlessly interpreted in new ways because ideas about counter-intuitive discarnate forces are not empirically constrained. What does the Torah (Bible, Qur'an) *mean*? What does God *want* us to do *now*? The transcendent God of monotheism, Deleuze notes, 'would remain empty, or at least *absconditus*, if it were not projected on a plane of immanence of creation where it traces the stages of its theophany'. Whether it takes the form of imperial unity or spiritual empire, 'this transcendence that is projected on the plane of immanence paves it or populates it with Figures' (1994: 88–89).

On the one hand, the intellectual and priestly elites of monotheistic coalitions insist that their supernatural Agent has appeared and will continue to appear in the finite world. On the other hand, they also insist that His glorious nature is infinitely transcendent and beyond comprehension – even the despot may misinterpret God (cf. Eisenstadt 1986; Bellah 2011). This tension has always characterized *theology*, which was also born during the axial age. Broadly speaking, theology is the construction and critique of hypotheses about the existential conditions for axiological engagement (cf. Shults 2014b). What is it that makes possible – or actual – the real, finite human experience of valuing and being valued? In their attempts to answer this sort of question, the majority of theological hypotheses within the monotheistic coalitions that eventually came to dominate most of west Asia and Europe (and much of the rest of the globe) followed the theogonic trajectory depicted in Figure 8.1.

Even among theologians (as well as priests and prophets) who were committed to the sacerdotal regulation of religious minds and groups within particular monotheistic in-groups, however, one can also find minority reports that contest the idea of God conceived as a person-like, coalition-favouring, punitive disembodied Entity. We have already alluded to the first reason the intellectual elite in such religious groups might have for resisting finite images of God as, for example, a 'Father' or 'Judge': whether material or semiotic, such images (icons) are all too easily taken by regular religious folk as actual representations of an infinitely glorious and holy divine Reality that ought not to be represented. This is (part of) the motivation behind warnings against idolatry and occasional acts of physical iconoclasm. An infinite God *must not* to be represented for doxological reasons.

However, God *cannot* be represented for logical, psychological, and political reasons. One of the existential requirements for intentionality is being in relation to something not identical to oneself, that is, to an object of intention. This is the case even if one is intentionally relating to one's imagined, future self – intending, for example, to become a better person.

Intentionality presupposes an in-tensional relation to that which one is not, or which one does not yet have. In other words, it requires being-limited, which is the definition of finitude. This is why absolute infinity cannot be intentional: to conceive it as such would be to imagine it as *related* to an object that it was not (such as a finite creation), in which case it would not be *absolutely* unlimited. Moreover, cognitive and coalitional defaults evolved to engage *finite* supernatural agents, and the pressure exerted by the notion of an all-knowing and all-powerful *infinite* despot-God is simply psychologically and politically unbearable (cf. Shults 2014c). People may memorize and repeat orthodox doctrinal formulations about God's omniscience, omnipotence and impassibility but, especially under stress, they immediately fall back into their default tendencies and imagine a finite, temporal god who is interested in their kith and kin (cf. Slone 2004).

The idea of 'God' as an infinite disembodied intentional Force was tentatively born(e) in the minds of theologians who pressed the evolved defaults towards anthropomorphic promiscuity and sociographic prudery as far as they would go – which turned out to be too far. If God is so transcendent that He cannot be represented, then He cannot be conceived (or perceived) as a human-like agent (or anything else). If God eternally foreknows and preordains *everything*, then it is hard to understand the point of praying to or ritually engaging Him. Throughout the centuries, monotheistic theologians have worked hard to defend hypotheses about the conditions for axiological engagement that utilize images (icons) of God as a Person who cares about a Group while simultaneously emphasizing that such images must be broken.

Evolved cognitive defaults for detecting finite agents crumple under the pressure of trying to think an infinite intentional Entity. Evolved coalitional defaults for protecting in-groups implode (or explode) under the stress of trying to live in complex literate states. It is not hard to understand why and how atheism would emerge as an option (albeit rarely, slowly, and tentatively) as monotheism took over within large-scale, pluralistic societies. The abstract, transcendent God described by the priest does not seem to have any relevance for daily life. All these people around me have different views of gods whom they think care about their group. They try to explain the natural world in superstitious ways that make no sense to me. They try to regulate the social world in segregative ways that make it difficult for me and those I love. Perhaps we can make sense of the cosmos and behave sensibly in the socius without bearing God – or any other finite supernatural agents preferred by particular in-groups.

The assemblage of the atheist machine involved the contestation of the evolved theogonic mechanisms, which opened up lines of flight that were previously unimaginable. Although its use within and effect on the mental and social fields of the civilizations that emerged out of the west Asian axial age were initially quite limited, the atheist machine began to unveil the implausibility of the various (contradictory) ideas and the infeasibility of the various (contradictory) ritual strategies for organizing normativity. Even when contesting the relevant cognitive and coalitional biases is not consciously used to clear the ground of religious Icons, it automatically has a theolytic (god-dissolving) effect. The intensification and integration of the forces of anthropomorphic prudery and sociographic promiscuity are part of the actualization of the atheist machinic assemblage (Figure 8.2).

The effects of the atheist machine are obviously destructive but, like all schizoanalytic (rhizomatic, pragmatic, micropolitical) proceedings, its uses are also productive.

Its most palpable productions are naturalism and secularism. There are many varieties of *naturalism*, but most share a resistance to appeals to supernatural agency in theoretical explanations of the natural world, especially in the academic sphere. Individual scholars may continue privately to harbour superstitious beliefs, but most are (at least) methodologically naturalistic in the sense that they exclude god-concepts from their scientific hypotheses. There

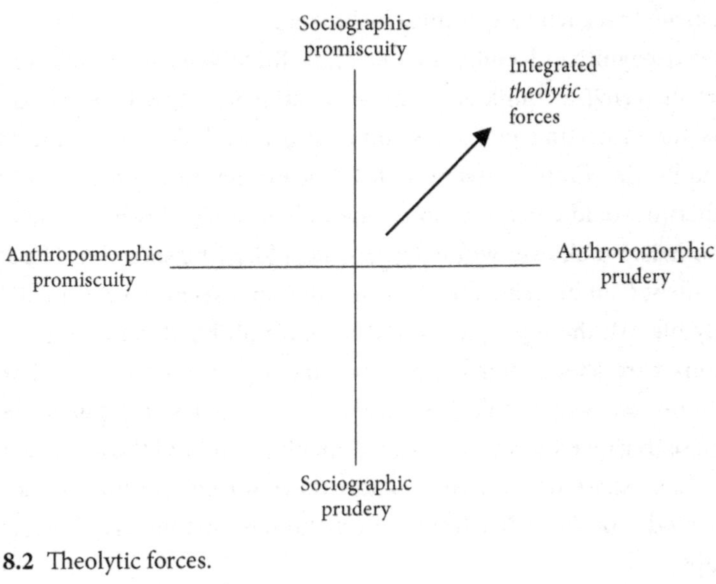

Figure 8.2 Theolytic forces.

are also many varieties of *secularism*, but most share a resistance to appeals to supernatural authority in practical inscriptions of social worlds, especially in the public sphere. Individual civil leaders in complex, democratic contexts might maintain membership in religious in-groups, but a growing number are (at least) methodologically secularist in the sense that they exclude divine-sanctions from their political proposals.

We do not yet know what naturalist-secularist bodies can do. Whatever they *can* do, hypothesizes the atheist, their axiological engagement is not conditioned by human-like, coalition-favouring gods. Atheism follows out the logic and practices that flow from the integration of the theolytic forces, pressing beyond methodological versions of anthropomorphic prudery and sociographic promiscuity and insisting on *metaphysical* naturalism and secularism. The atheist machine cuts away at superstitious beliefs and segregating behaviours based on shared imaginative engagement with supernatural agents, and constructs pragmatic plan(e)s within socio-ecological niches in which survival no longer depends on the detection and protection of the gods of particular in-groups.

I have argued that the naturally evolved theogonic defaults operate 'well beneath' monotheistic ideology, reproducing repressive religious representations that fuel the despotic machine. I now want to make more explicit the relation between the theolytic forces and the other three social-machines described in the *Capitalism and Schizophrenia* project.

4. Scientific models: Deleuzian social-machines in biocultural perspective

It is important to remember that Deleuze does not think of the social-machines as concrete, historical formations of the socius that were (or will be) realized in a particular order. Rather, they are abstract machines that are actualized in diverse ways within all complex social assemblages, precisely in their intensive mutual interactions. The territorial, despotic, and capitalist machines are all social-productions that 'fall back' on desiring-production; each in its own way creates a 'full body', a 'recording surface' that inscribes lack, law, and idealization on the schiz-flows of the Real, which is pure becoming. As we will see, although the war machine can be captured by the State, in itself it is the creative element or productive force of rhizomic lines of flight that escape repressive representations.

The territorial (or primitive) machine is the 'first form of socius, the machine of primitive inscription' (2004a: 155). A socius is produced whenever there is a coding (inscription) of stock (consumption) that falls back upon the flow (production) of desire. This first mode of representation organizes itself at the surface by the coding of filial flows through alliances, thereby creating a 'territory'. The unit of alliance is debt, and alliance, suggests Deleuze, is 'representation' itself. When it falls back on the desiring-production of human bodies, the territorial machine constitutes a debt system involving 'a voice that speaks or intones, a sign marked in bare flesh, an eye that extracts enjoyment from the pain'. An element of transcendence (representation of an ideal) is introduced, but it remains 'quite close to a desiring machine of eye-hand-voice' (2004a: 207). The territorial assemblage is declined on the full body of 'the earth' through the *coding* of lateral alliances and extended filiations.

The despotic (or barbarian) machine, on the other hand, appears with the force of a 'projection that defines paranoia', in which a 'subject leaps outside the intersections of alliance-filiation, installs himself at the limit, at the horizon, in the desert, the subject of a deterritorialized knowledge that links him directly to God and connects him to the people' (2004a: 211). Deleuze describes despotism as the first principle of a paranoiac knowledge that withdraws from life and from the earth, producing a judgement of both. The socius will now be inscribed on a new surface, not the earth, but the full body of 'the despot' (or his god). The voice is no longer one of alliance across filiations, but 'a fictitious voice from on high'. The *overcoding* of the despotic machine (or imperial barbarian formation) is characterized by the mobilization of the categories of *new* alliance and *direct* filiation.

The eyes watching the hands' inscription of bodies are replaced by the Eye and the Hand of the despot, who watches everyone through the eyes of his bureaucrats, officials, and priests, and subordinates graphism to the Voice that 'no longer expresses itself except through the writing signs that it emits (revelation)'. Now, interpretation becomes all important: 'The emperor, the god – what did he mean?' (2004a: 224). Having claimed a direct and transcendent filiation, the despot appropriates all the forces of production. All alliances are now organized around and oriented towards him. Instead of blocks of mobile and finite debt coded by horizontal alliances, the despot extracts taxes for a vertical tribute that feeds a constantly expanding glorious expenditure.

In *A Thousand Plateaus*, this is also spelled out in relation to the 'facialization machine', which effects an overcoding wrought by the signifying despotic Face, irradiating a surveillance that reproduces paranoid faces. The savage system of *cruelty* is replaced by the barbarian system of *terror*. The despotic State, Deleuze insists, is an abstraction that is realized only as an abstraction (2004b: 240). As an abstract machine, it can be conceived as 'the common horizon' to what comes 'before' and what comes 'after', that is, as a complex of syntheses that can overcode the territorial machine's coding of break-flows and, in turn, that can become relativized and incorporated within the capitalist machine's axiomatization of decoded break-flows.

This *decoding* of flows that characterizes the capitalist (or civilized) social-machine has also always been present in human populations, even if only as that which was 'warded off' by primitive and barbarian social inscriptions (and the nomads). This machine has a deterritorializing effect, but it is only 'relative'. It immediately reterritorializes the decoded flows on the 'full body' of Capital. The surplus value of production as well as the qualities of alliances, which had been coded through kinship or overcoded through tribute, are now decoded, rendered quantitative, and relativized in relation to the surplus flux of the market, which registers value on the basis of the potential for earning wages or generating profit. The capitalist machine is fully installed when money begets money, when Capital itself becomes filiative. 'It is no longer the age of cruelty or the age of terror, but the age of *cynicism*, accompanied by a strange *piety*' (2004a: 245, emphasis added).

What about the war (or revolutionary) machine? Despite its name, the primary use (and effect) of this machine is not war. Only when it is appropriated by the State apparatus of capture does war necessarily become its object. The essential aim of the war machine is 'revolutionary movement', escaping the molar organization and conjugation of flows through a becoming-molecular that effects an *absolute* deterritorialization (whether artistic, scientific, or philosophical). Once the capitalist machine has relativized the despotic machine's overcoding of the territorial machine and taken over the socius, every struggle involves the construction of '*revolutionary connections*' in opposition to the '*conjugations of the* [capitalist] *axiomatic*' (2004b: 522). Resisting facialization (and oedipalization), the war machine creates and populates smooth space with 'probe-heads' that draw lines of flight, cutting edges of deterritorialization that become positive and absolute, 'forming strange new becomings, new polyvocalities' (2004b: 211).

How can the conceptual framework of theogonic reproduction theory, derived from biocultural scientific models of the origin and evolution of religion, shed light on the repressive (and liberating) functions of the Deleuzian social-machines? In this context, I limit myself to a quick summary of the fuller answer to this question provided in Chapter 5 of my *Iconoclastic Theology* (2014b). In the next subsection I will apply the heuristic model to two case studies: Neolithic Çatalhöyük and Modern Istanbul. My intuitions about the way in which evolved cognitive and coalitional defaults operate 'well beneath' social-machinic ideologies are depicted in Figure 8.3.

Let us begin with the 'primitive' territorial machine. Archaeological evidence (and ethnographic analogy) suggests that the hominids that flourished in the Upper Paleolithic were extremely anthropomorphically promiscuous. They somewhat automatically postulated ambiguously embodied intentionality behind everything – rivers, trees, crystals, the weather, and the earth itself. Apparently early hominids were also relatively sociographically promiscuous. In the wide open spaces of Africa and the Levant, interaction with other in-groups would have been rarer. It seems that *Homo sapiens* got along surprisingly well even with Neanderthals in some places, at least until around 35,000 BCE. The integration of these two tendencies can still be found today in some New Age groups, and in idealized science fiction portrayals of tree-hugging indigenous people like the Na'vi in the movie *Avatar*.

That movie also provides us with an example of a coalition that is prudish in both its anthropomorphism and its sociography. The RDA mining corporation is only interested in profiting from the 'unobtainium' under the surface of the Na'vi's home planet Pandora. Formed by an extreme actualization of the

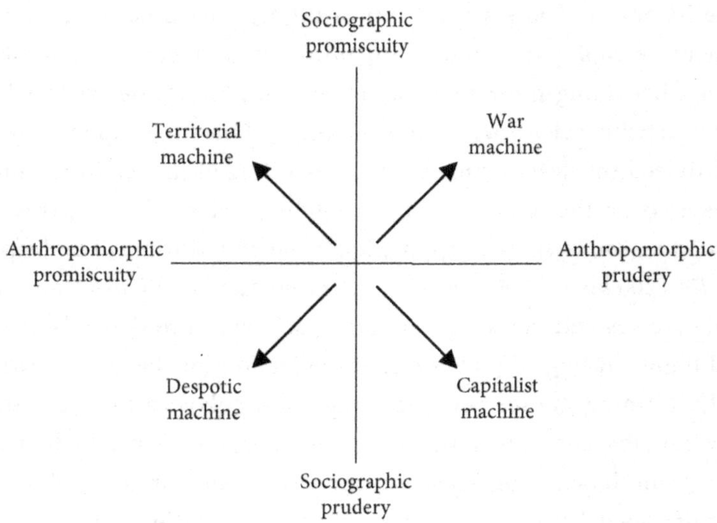

Figure 8.3 Social machines.

'civilized' capitalist machine, the leaders of RDA do not detect human-like agency even in the human-like Na'vi, whom they refer to as 'blue monkeys'. It might initially seem like Capitalism promotes sociographic promiscuity since it decodes the qualitative alliances that code human affiliations and encourages the multiplication of images. In fact, however, its inscriptive prudery is absolute: the capitalist machine forces *all* surplus value to fall back on the 'full body' of Capital, converting all codes to abstract quantities (Money). It spreads a universal anxiety: everyone must accumulate surplus value for their own group.

The anxiety spread by the 'barbarian' despotic machine, on the other hand, is of a different sort: everyone must follow the laws of our group's god. As we have seen, monotheism is sociographically prudish. The one true God has revealed the norms by which all human groups are to be regulated and judged. There is no point in arguing with or trying to trick an infinite, unchanging despot-God, whose prescriptions and proscriptions are absolute. Unlike the capitalist machine, however, the despotic machine is excessively promiscuous in its anthropomorphism. First and foremost, it promotes the detection of a Supernatural Agent who is allegedly everywhere at all times. However, it also promotes paranoia about His bureaucrats (whether Spirit-filled embodied priests or disembodied spirits like angels, demons, or saints) who are also watching and waiting to enforce divine judgements.

The nomads who invent the 'revolutionary' war machine, on the other hand, want to 'have done' with the judgement of God (Deleuze 1997: 126). The monotheistic machine exists only by overcoding territories and resisting the axiomatizations of the immanent capitalist field that relativize its preferred religious Figure. The territorial and capitalist machines promote tendencies that partially challenge the despotic mode of theogonic reproduction (Figure 8.3). Their inscriptions inevitably throw wrenches into the monotheistic machine. The war machine, however, fractures the repressive 'representations' of all three of the other modes of social-production. It has no time (or place) for the segmentarity of Oedipus, much less for the sedentary arborescence of the transcendent Icons of monotheism. In this sense, it is always consuming, registering and producing an *atheist machine*.

The war machine is anthropomorphically prudish and sociographically promiscuous. It escapes the facialization machine and draws positive and absolute lines of deterritorialization, populating a smooth space with 'probe-heads … that dismantle the strata in their wake, break through the walls of significance, pour out of the holes of subjectivity' (2004b: 210). The nomads refuse the segmentation of sedentary collectives whose striation of the socius finds its centre of gravity in the State. The *nomos* of the war machine is a movement and composition of people that cannot be captured in the apparatus of the 'law'. Its becoming is a celerity that constantly invents tools and weapons that can be used on the move in the encounter with and the production of new modes of social assemblage.

All of these abstract social-machines, argues Deleuze, are operative in every human population – although in each concrete context they are more or less successful in their coding, capturing, axiomatizing, or escaping in relation to one other. I have tried to show how they are also shaped by underlying cognitive and coalitional tendencies, which are distributed and contested in various ways across human populations. I now briefly explore some of the ways in which this conceptual integration of machines, memories, and models might illuminate some of the factors at work in two of the most interesting social assemblages in the geographic region we now call Turkey.

5. Case studies: Neolithic Çatalhöyük and modern Istanbul

Centrally located on the Konya plain in south central Turkey, Çatalhöyük is one of the most well-known archaeological sites in the world. The domestication of plants and animals had occurred well before the founding of this Neolithic 'town', but it has a special significance because of its unusually large size (up to 5,000 people on about thirty-four acres) and its unbroken temporal extension (continuous settlement from 7,400 to 6,000 BCE). The material culture and artistic symbolism of Çatalhöyük is also more complex than earlier sites in the region such as Göbekli Tepe and Aşıklı Höyük. Since 2006 I have been collaborating with a team of interdisciplinary scholars who descend on Çatalhöyük every summer in order to reflect 'at the trowel's edge' (cf. Hodder 2006) on the role of religion in the transformation of civilizational forms during the Neolithic.

Elsewhere I have discussed some of the evidence for anthropomorphic promiscuity and sociographic prudery at Çatalhöyük (Shults 2014a). A wide variety of artefacts indicate that shared imaginative engagement with supernatural agents was pervasive within the community. Feasting deposits, wall art, pottery symbolism, the installation of wild auroch buchrania, and the hiding of other animal and human skeletal remains within the houses and under the foundations, all suggest ritual interaction with imagined disembodied agents. The cognitive tendency to detect human-like intentionality in inanimate objects is also implied by the way in which the inhabitants of Çatalhöyük buried (some of) their dead within their houses, usually immediately under the sleeping area, occasionally unearthing their bones and engaging them in a variety of ways. Ethnographic analogy (cf. Coe et al. 2012) suggests that the discovery of hundreds of figurines at the site is a sign that the young were socialized to imaginatively engage animal-spirits and ancestor-ghosts.

Even more relevant for the purposes of this chapter, however, is the apparent shift in *sociographic* strategies over the centuries at Çatalhöyük. Based on an extensive review of the archaeological evidence, Whitehouse and Hodder (2010) argued that there was a slow shift of ritual modes during the life of the settlement. Initially it was characterized by the dominance of the 'imagistic' mode, in which rituals tend to be highly emotionally arousing but relatively infrequent – this is typical of small-scale, non-hierarchical societies. In the later levels of the site, however, the consistency of symbolic patterns, the use of moulds, and the reduction of wild animal parts (*inter alia*) suggest the emergence of a more 'doctrinal' mode, which is characterized by more frequent, less emotionally arousing rituals – this is typical of larger, more hierarchical societies.

This hypothesis was expanded in light of more recent data and analysis in Whitehouse et al. (2014), where the authors argue that religious routinization was a major factor in the emergence of more complex social forms at Çatalhöyük. One of the primary functions of religion in hunter-gatherer societies was holding small groups together, but 'gradually, as agriculture intensified, this ancient function faded and religion became a means of reproducing much larger (if more diffuse) group identities'. The vitality of religious life would have shifted from 'esoteric mystery cult to something more ideologically uniform, in some ways less awe-inspiring and more controlling' (2014: 134). In other words, it appears that the 'doctrinal' ritual mode slowly began to replace the 'imagistic' mode, with a phase shift around the year 6500 BCE. Several factors would have played a role in this shift but cross-cultural multiple regression analysis indicates that agricultural intensity is the most significant predictor of this sort of change in civilizational form (Atkinson and Whitehouse 2010).

Although not directly based on evidence from Çatalhöyük, a recent computer simulation analysis based on wider empirical data from the Neolithic suggests that at least two other conditions were in place that would likely have contributed to the shift from egalitarianism to a more 'despotic social organization': (1) the generation of surplus resources generated by agricultural leaders, which would have led to demographic expansion of their groups and the reduction of the viability of acephalous niches in the region, and (2) subsequent limitation of outside options for followers as a result of high dispersal costs (Powers and Lehman 2014: 8). This does not mean that 'despotism' or 'monotheism', in the sense they emerged millennia later in the bronze and iron ages, were already present in the Neolithic.

Rather, I am suggesting that what Deleuze calls the abstract machine of despotism was increasingly installed in some places during this revolutionary period in human history. At the very least, Çatalhöyük represents one example of an apparatus of capture in which the coding of various terrestrial machines (hunter-gatherers) was slowly overcoded as the socius on the Neolithic Konya plain became more stratified, arboreal, and hierarchical. Anthropomorphic promiscuity continued to run wild, but as the population grew and religious routinization intensified at the settlement, its members became increasingly sociographically prudish. Over time the default slowly shifted from the upper right to the lower left quadrant of Figure 8.4.

It would be several millennia before despotic monotheism would be fully installed and take over the social fields of west Asia. Such an installation occurred only after the emergence of a class of intellectual and priestly elites who tried detecting the biggest God they could conceive (an infinite intentional disembodied Force) and ended up protecting the cohesion of empires by inscribing the most terrifying social segmentarity imaginable (the negative disjunction between eternal pleasure and eternal pain).

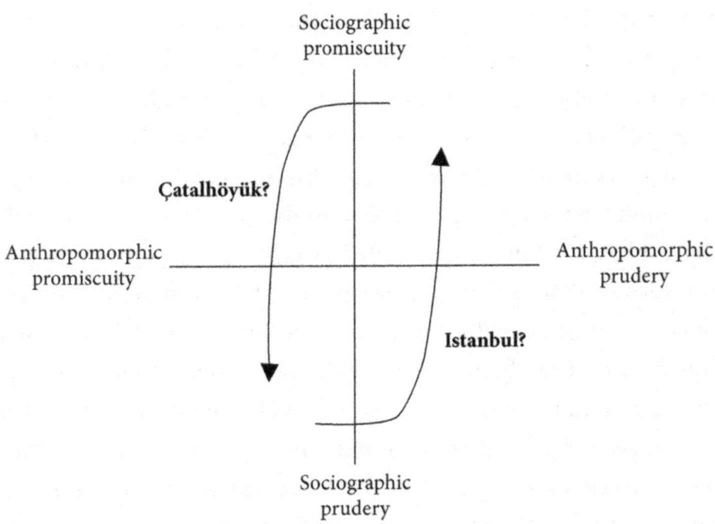

Figure 8.4 Shifts in social machines.

Leaping ahead a few thousand years I turn now to a brief exploration of the uses and effects of the other social-machines on the complex metropolitan settlement(s) we now call Istanbul. The upward arrow in Figure 8.4 suggests a way of thinking about the overcoding and decoding of this geographical space over the last few centuries. Istanbul has had its share of despots, including leaders of the Byzantine empire (e.g. Constantine I in the fourth century CE) and the Ottoman empire (e.g. Mehmed II in the fifteenth century CE). The city has been the origin and goal of more than its fair share of religious crusades, and the effects of centuries of theological debates and holy wars are still evident in its architectural ruins and reconstructions.

The most significant events shaping the social texture of *modern* Istanbul were the establishment of the Republic of Turkey in the early 1920s and the consequent reforms instituted by Mustafa Kemal Attaturk and the 'Kemalists'. For our purposes, the most important of these reforms were policies that supported naturalist interpretations of reality and secularist inscriptions of society. Several universities were founded during the first half of the twentieth century, and Turkish scientists of all sorts have contributed to the development of anthropomorphically prudish hypotheses and theories in a wide variety of disciplines. As in so many other modern societies in which the *ancien regime* was held together by a dominant monotheism, methodologically *naturalistic* scientific research came into conflict with traditional religious education in Turkey. The difference between 'empirical sciences' and 'religious sciences' was not new; such a distinction had already been made by al-Farabi in the tenth century.

The tension between these types of 'science', however, intensified throughout the twentieth century. Akşit and Akşit (2010) have traced the way in which shifts in the conceptions of science, religion and society have been linked to the transformation of the cultural, economic and political structures of Turkey. From the 1930s to the 1960s, modern rationalist modes of thinking were promoted by Kemalists and consolidated in Turkish universities. Eventually the word *bilim*, derived from the Turkish word 'to know', came to be used for 'science', and distinguished from the older (Arabic-based) Ottoman word *ilim*, which also means 'knowledge', but more often connotes *religious* knowledge. As in most Western societies, the universities in Turkey were also shaped by the move away from positivism and towards more postmodern, pluralistic conceptions of science later in the century.

Given our interest here in social-machinic assemblages, it is important to note the concomitant shift towards *secularism* in modern Turkey, which required more sociographically promiscuous modes of inscribing the social field. Scholars (and politicians) continue to argue about the real nature, and the deeper causes, of the tension between religion and secularism in Turkey. Some suggest that it is not primarily a battle between opponents and proponents of religious freedom, but a struggle 'between two rival middle classes' (Başkan 2010), or even between 'two totalizing Islams' (Pinar 2013). It seems clear, however, that what Ahmet Kuru (2009) calls the relatively 'aggressive' secularism favoured by the early Kemalists (as compared to the more 'passive secularism' in the United States and France) led to a sense of alienation and oppression among conservative Muslims, who still make up the majority of the population in Turkey. Perhaps the most visible example of the resulting conflict, which also evoked some of the most vocal protests, was the 'headscarf controversy' (cf. Arat 2010; Warhola and Bezci 2010).

How we can conceptualize the uses and effects of the capitalist and war machines on the Turkish socius? I want to suggest that 'well beneath' the ideological debates in modern Turkey we can discover the tension between the theogonic and theolytic mechanisms depicted in Figure 8.4, which in turn fuel the operation of the Deleuzian social-machines. Several scholars have pointed to the importance of Turkey as a potential model for political change in the wake of the 'Arab spring' (e.g. Erdem 2012; Ünver 2013). Such analyses and prognostications are important and necessary, but my argument is that unless we *also* unveil and work towards weakening the forces of anthropomorphic promiscuity and sociographic prudery, they will continue to undermine efforts for reform and reinforce the sort of superstition and segregation that helps despotic regimes to thrive.

As we have seen, the axiomatic of capitalism relativizes the coding (and overcoding) of the territorial and despotic machines. Its quantification of surplus value, which always falls back on the full body of Capital, tends to dissolve the absolute, qualitative claims of monotheism. The current government of Turkey, led by the AKP (Justice and Development Party), is more religiously conservative than the Kemalists. According to Howard Eissenstat, however, even the Gulenists within the AKP, who disapprove of Prime Minister Erdogan's antagonistic style, share with him 'a long-term vision of a Turkey that embraces both modern *capitalism* and Islam .... (and) assume that devout Islamic faith and *secular* modern institutions can – and indeed must – coexist ... (and) that Turkey should take a leading role in world affairs and serve as a bridge between civilizations' (2013: 25, emphases added). But can subjects in a modern socius really serve both God and Mammon?

But why should we serve either? The (creative, nomadic, revolutionary) war machine resists the repressive representations of the other social-machines, refusing to fall back on the full body of the Despot or Capital. The 'six arrows' at the foundation of the modern Republic of Turkey were secularism (*laiklik*), republicanism (*cumhuriyetçilik*), statism (*develtçilik*), nationalism (*milliyetçilik*), populism (*halkçilik*), and reformism or, as it is sometimes translated, revolutionism (*devrimçilik*). What is the relation between this last 'arrow' and the others? There are certainly many residents of Istanbul who want to follow what Deleuze called the 'revolutionary path'. It should be obvious enough that Deleuze was not (nor am I) calling for a return to an idealized, historical period in which we all give up our actual houses and begin literally roaming around like nomads.

The real question is whether or not we can learn to contest the evolved defaults of anthropomorphic promiscuity and sociographic prudery, mechanisms that served (some of) our ancestors well in the Upper Paleolithic and the Neolithic, but which do not seem to be serving us well today as we try to adapt within pluralistic, globalizing socio-ecological niches. Superstitious renderings of the cosmos and segregative striations of the socius that appeal to the gods (or God) of a particular in-group are no longer contributing to our survival. Where does this leave the citizens of Istanbul – and the rest of us? How can we use the atheistic, schizoanalytic machine; what creative effects will it have? We do not yet know what Turkish bodies can do. But we are coming to a better understanding of the underlying theogonic and theolytic forces that can block or facilitate their revolutionary lines of flight.

6. Becoming-atheist

Deleuze has helped clear the ground for revolutionary experimentation by disclosing the repressive power of social-machinic representations. I have tried to show how *theogonic* machines, which integrate and intensify superstitious and segregative tendencies, make this process of clearing far more complicated than it initially appears. The repressive representations they (re)produce are reinforced by naturally evolved biases that all too easily lead to the detection of gods and the protection of in-groups. This is why we also need to pay closer attention to the uses and effects of *theolytic* machines. How can we produce atheistic registrations and consumptions on the field of immanence as we clear the ground of the religious Figures of transcendence that make us anxious and distract us from creating new connections? As Deleuze consistently emphasized, the criteria for answering such questions can only be discovered in the actual, problematic process of schizoanalysis.

Developments in the biocultural sciences provide us with conceptual tools that can supplement the insights that arise in the debates among defenders and detractors of psychoanalysis. They help us unveil the secrets of theism, especially the cognitive incoherence and coalitional irrelevance of representations of an infinite personal God. Such prodding exerts a pressure that intensifies the secretion of atheism. But this is not enough; the forces of theogonic reproduction have led to adaptive defences that continue to hold subjects within religious coalitions. For example, theologians committed to monotheistic in-groups can insist that these 'mysteries' are part of what is adorable about the divine nature or part of what is hidden in the divine plan. Appealing to concealed secrets, secrets that are appealing in part because of their concealment, keeps the secretion in check. This is one of the reasons that theology should not be left to theists.

It is important to keep talking about where the god-conceptions within in-groups come from in the first place because unveiling theogonic mechanisms automatically weakens them; they function well only when they are hidden. I have argued elsewhere (2014c) that having 'the talk' about *religious* reproduction should involve more than simply explaining how 'it' works. It is equally important to work out the physical, emotional, and social consequences of 'doing it'. This is just as true for religious education as it is for sex education. We need a theological version of 'the birds and the bees' that deals with the dynamics by which supernatural agents are reproduced in human minds and the consequences of nurturing them in human coalitions. Part of the problem is that we are socialized not to ask where gods come from, and we learn early that it is not polite to ask folks why they keep them around.

When it comes to having the talk about where babies come from and what it takes to care for them, we know that waiting too long can have devastating effects. Of course, it can be equally devastating if the conversation makes people feel attacked, afraid, or ashamed. The activities that lead to sexual and religious reproduction can feel terrific to our bodies, but baring our souls about them can feel terribly vulnerable. When discussing such intimate issues, it is important to be sensitive – but it is also important to be direct. We do not know where such conversations will lead. We cannot know ahead of time what effects the atheist machine will have; the secretion of productive atheism will not solve all our problems and will surely create some new ones. However, insofar as it clears the ground of arborescent religious Icons that reinforce mythical and superstitious interpretations of nature and divide us through supernatural segregations of society, at least it gets us moving.

We do not yet know all that godless bodies can do, but we do know they can move on the surface, liberate lines of flight, construct rhizomes, feel the movement of the pack, and unleash the creative forces of art, science, and philosophy. For obvious reasons, such movements threaten groups whose molarity depends on centralized imaginative engagement with supernatural agents. Like the State apparatus, despotic religious societies treat their secrets with gravity, but inevitably – it is the nature of secrets – something oozes out, something is perceived. The war machine treats secrets with celerity, molecularizing their content and linearizing their form (Deleuze and Guattari 2004b: 320). This is why the atheist machine feels so dangerous to the monotheistic machine, which uses its massive arsenal to crush or domesticate it. But we nomads have no reason to fear: we have weapons of mass secretion that work just by bringing them into the open.

Note

1 See especially Shults (2014c). Some of the material in the current chapter is adapted from this book, and overlaps with fuller arguments developed in Shults (2014a, 2014b, 2014d). For other integrative presentations of some of the most salient empirical data and theoretical developments by leading scientists in the fields that make up the 'biocultural' study of religion, see, for example, Boyer (2002, 2011), Atran (2002, 2010), and Lewis-Williams (2010). For extensive bibliographies and reviews of relevant literature, see the *Institute for the Bio-Cultural Study of Religion* website: http://www.ibcsr.org/.

Bibliography

Akşit, Bahattin and Elif Ekin Akşit (2010) 'Shifting Conceptions of Science, Religion, Society and State in Turkey', *Middle East Critique* 19:1, pp. 71–87.

Arat, Yeşim (2010) 'Religion, Politics and Gender Equality in Turkey: Implications of a Democratic Paradox?', *Third World Quarterly* 31:6, pp. 869–884.

Arnason, Johann P., S. N. Eisenstadt, and Bjorn Wittrock (eds.) (2005) *Axial Civilizations and World History*. Leiden: Brill.

Atkinson, Quentin D. and Harvey Whitehouse (2010) 'The Cultural Morphospace of Ritual Form: Examining Modes of Religiosity Cross-Culturally', *Evolution and Human Behavior* 32:1, pp. 50–62.

Atran, Scott (2002) *In Gods We Trust: The Evolutionary Landscape of Religion*. Oxford: Oxford University Press.

Atran, Scott (2010) *Talking to the Enemy: Faith, Brotherhood and the (Un)Making of Terrorists*. New York: HarperCollins.

Başkan, Filiz (2010) 'Religious versus Secular Groups in the Age of Globalization in Turkey', *Totalitarian Movements and Political Religions* 11:2, pp. 167–183.

Bellah, Robert (2011) *Religion in Human Evolution: From the Paleolithic to the Axial Age*. Cambridge, MA: Harvard University Press.

Boyer, Pascal (2002) *Religion Explained: The Human Instincts that Fashion Gods, Spirits and Ancestors*. London: Vintage.

Boyer, Pascal (2011) *The Fracture of an illusion: Science and the Dissolution of Religion*. Gottingen: Vandenhoeck & Ruprecht.

Coe, Katherine, Christine S. Van Pool and Craig T. Palmer (2012) 'Figurines, Religion, and Tradition in Human Evolution', in Patrick McNamara and Wesley Wildman (eds.), *Science and the World's Religions, Volume 1: Origins and Destinies*. Santa Barbara, CA: Praeger, pp. 91–116.

Deleuze, Gilles (1983) *Nietzsche and Philosophy*, trans. Hugh Tomlinson. New York: Columbia University Press.

Deleuze, Gilles (1984) *Kant's Critical Philosophy*, trans. Hugh Tomlinson and Barbara Habberjam. Minneapolis: University of Minnesota.

Deleuze, Gilles (1990a) *Expressionism in Philosophy: Spinoza*, trans. Martin Joughin. New York: Zone Books.

Deleuze, Gilles (1990b) *The Logic of Sense*, trans. Mark Lester with Charles Stivale. New York: Columbia University Press.

Deleuze, Gilles (1991) *Empiricism and Subjectivity*, trans. Constantin V. Boundas. New York: Columbia University Press.

Deleuze, Gilles (1994) *Difference and Repetition*, trans. Paul Patton. New York: Columbia University Press.

Deleuze, Gilles (1995) *Negotiations*, trans. Martin Joughin. New York: Columbia University Press.

Deleuze, Gilles (1997) *Essays Critical and Clinical*, trans. Daniel W. Smith and Michael A. Greco. Minneapolis: University of Minnesota Press.

Deleuze, Gilles (2007) *Two Regimes of Madness: Texts and Interviews 1975–1995*, trans. Ames Hodges and Mike Taormina. Los Angeles, CA: Semiotext(e).

Deleuze, Gilles and Félix Guattari (1994) *What Is Philosophy*? trans. Hugh Tomlinson and Graham Burchell. London: Verso.

Deleuze, Gilles and Félix Guattari (2004a) *Anti-Oedipus*, trans. Robert Hurley, Mark Seem, and Helen R.Lane. London: Continuum.

Deleuze, Gilles and Félix Guattari (2004b) *A Thousand Plateaus*, trans. Brian Massumi. London: Continuum.

Eisenstadt, S.N. (1986) 'The Axial Age Breakthroughs: Their Characteristics and Origins', in S.N. Eisenstadt (ed.), *The Origins and Diversity of Axial Age Civilizations*. Albany: State University of New York Press, pp. 1–28.

Eissenstat, Howard (2013) 'Unrest in Istanbul: Turkey's Season of Struggle', *Christian Century* (September 18), 130:5, pp. 22–25.

Erdem, Burcu Kaya (2012) 'Adjustment of the Secular Islamist Role Model (Turkey) to the "Arab Spring": The Relationship between the Arab Uprisings and Turkey in the Turkish and World Press', *Islam and Christian-Muslim Relations* 23:4, pp. 435–452.

Hodder, Ian (2006) *Çatalhöyük - The Leopard's Tale: Revealing the Mysteries of Turkey's Ancient 'Town'*. London: Thames & Hudson.

Kuru, Ahmet T. (2009) *Secularism and State Policies toward Religion: The United States, France and Turkey*. Cambridge: Cambridge University Press.

Lewis-Williams, David (2010) *Conceiving God: The Cognitive Origin and Evolution of Religion*. London: Thames & Hudson.

Norenzayan, Ara (2013) *Big Gods: How Religion Transformed Cooperation and Conflict*. Princeton: Princeton University Press.

Pinar, Candas (2013) 'Religion-State Relations in Turkey since the AKP: A Changing Landscape? Evidence from Parliamentary Debates on the Alevi Matter', *Journal of Muslim Minority Affairs* 33:4, pp. 507–520.

Powers, Simon T. and Laurent Lehman (6 August 2014) 'An Evolutionary Model Explaining the Neolithic Transition from Egalitarianism to Leadership and Despotism', *Proceeding of the Royal Society: Biological Sciences* 281, pp. 1–9.

Shults, F. LeRon (2014a) 'Excavating Theogonies: Anthropomorphic Promiscuity and Sociographic Prudery in the Neolithic and Now', in Ian Hodder (ed.), *Religion at Work in a Neolithic Society: Vital Matters*. Cambridge: Cambridge University Press, pp. 58–85.

Shults, F. LeRon (2014b) *Iconoclastic Theology: Gilles Deleuze and the Secretion of Atheism*. Edinburgh: Edinburgh University Press.

Shults, F. LeRon (2014c) *Theology after the Birth of God: Atheist Conceptions in Cognition and Culture*. New York: Palgrave-Macmillan.

Shults, F. LeRon (2014d) 'Theology after Pandora: The Real Scandal of the Evangelical Mind' (and Culture)', in Derek J. Tidball, Brian S. Harris, and Jason S. Sexton (eds.), *Revisioning the Triune Center: Essays in Honor of Stanley J. Grenz*. Eugene, OR: Cascade Books, pp. 361–381.

Slone, D. Jason (2004) *Theological Incorrectness: Why Religious People Believe What They Shouldn't*. Oxford: Oxford University Press.

Ünver, H. Akin (2013) 'The Forgotten Secular Turkish Model', *Middle East Quarterly* 20:1, pp. 57–64.

Warhola, James W. and Egemen B. Bezci (2010) 'Religion and State in Contemporary Turkey: Recent Developments in *Laiklik*', *Journal of Church and State* 52:3, pp. 427–453.

Whitehouse, Harvey, Camilla Mazzucato, Ian Hodder, and Quentin D. Atkinson (2014) 'Modes of Religiosity and the Evolution of Social Complexity at Çatalhöyük', in Hodder Ian (ed.), *Religion at Work in a Neolithic Society*. Cambridge: Cambridge University Press, pp. 134–155.

Whitehouse, Harvey, and Ian Hodder (2010) 'Modes of Religiosity at Çatalhöyük', in Hodder Ian (ed.), *Religion in the Emergence of Civilization: Çatalhöyük as a Case Study*. Cambridge: Cambridge University Press, pp. 122–145.

Index